The Case for Bureaucracy

Charles T. Goodsell
Virginia Polytechnic Institute and State University

The Case for Bureaucracy

A Public Administration Polemic

Fourth Edition

CQ Press
A Division of Congressional Quarterly Inc.
Washington, D.C.

CQ Press
1255 22nd Street, N.W., Suite 400
Washington, D.C. 20037

Phone, 202-729-1900
Toll-free, 1-866-4CQ-PRESS (1-866-427-7737)

www.cqpress.com

♾ The paper used in this publication exceeds the requirements of the American National Standard for Information Sciences—Permanence of Paper for Printed Library Materials, ANSI Z39.48-1992.

Printed and bound in the United States of America
07 5 4 3 2

Library of Congress Cataloging-in-Publication Data

Goodsell, Charles T.
The case for bureaucracy : a public administration polemic / Charles T. Goodsell.—4th ed.
p. cm.
Includes bibliographical references and index.
ISBN 1-56802-907-1 (alk. paper)
1. Bureaucracy—United States. I. Title.
JK421.G64 2004
302.3′5′0973—dc22 2003025823

To the New Generation of Grandsons:

Christian Andrew Fechtmeyer
Maximilian Thomas Fechtmeyer
Dylan Patrick Lloyd
Brody Christopher Lloyd

Contents

Tables and Figures

Tables

Figures

Preface

This book is a polemic. I consider it a gentle polemic in that I avoid ad hominem attacks and support my position with evidence. But it is, nonetheless, a polemic, or "controversial argument."

The book comes from a belief that has burned in my mind for a quarter century: the quality of public service in the United States is vastly underrated. Our government's administrative agencies and those who work in them are commonly portrayed as inefficient, incompetent, and wasteful—and often uncivil and devious as well. This is simply not true.

Of course, not all bureaucracy in America works well. Our government agencies are riddled with examples of incompetence, negligence, inflexibility, and many other flaws. So, too, our government bureaucrats include men and women who should not be in their positions for reasons of sloth, bad manners, poor judgment, and other faults. My point, however, is that the flaws and the faults are far fewer on a proportionate basis than is generally thought. And they are more than outweighed in frequency and importance by instances of dedicated service on behalf of public missions important to all citizens. Most governments of the world would be pleased to possess a public bureaucracy of the quality of our own.

I make this case for bureaucracy not to defend the wrongly maligned—although that motivation might be justified—but to reaffirm the value to all of us, as citizens, of our relatively effective and honest governmental administration. To put the point succinctly, we can take heart in the quality of service of which our democracy is capable. Recognition of this great asset may help to mitigate, at least somewhat, the distrust and cynicism we often feel about our government. Perhaps it can even offer us a basis for drawing together somewhat more closely as a political community. Even if these ideals prove impossible, however, I hope the book will strengthen the resolve of our current public servants to carry on their important work with good cheer, despite all the frustrations. Also, I hope it may encourage many citizens, young and old, to entertain the possibility of entering public service as a calling that can add meaning to their lives.

The book was conceived in 1978 and first published in 1983. Second and third editions appeared in 1985 and 1994, respectively. This fourth edition reiterates the basic argument of its predecessors and follows essentially the same format. Its text, however, has been almost totally rewritten to update and sharpen the case for bureaucracy. Much new material has been introduced to account for the passage of a turbulent decade since the previous edition. New consideration is given to the growing body of positive literature on bureaucracy, the quiet policy successes of American government, the complications of dispersing public action outside government, individual stories of bureaucratic work, attempts to remake bureaucracy in the image of business, the importance of citizen engagement to bureaucracy's work, contributions by bureaucracy to the political system beyond implementation of law, and, of course, the implications of the new century's war on terrorism.

I wish to thank publicly several individuals whose actions over the years were indispensable to the creation of this book. The first is Edward Artinian, who founded Chatham House Publishers in 1979. When I first met Ed in November of that year, he immediately expressed interest in the idea that became this book. He also named it. Until Ed's untimely death in 1997, he was the book's publisher and its tireless promoter. The second individual is Robert Gormley, who for several years kept pushing me to write a fourth edition. I resisted his campaign for a long time, but he finally had his way. Bringing *The Case for Bureaucracy* into the new century was a big job—and without Bob's encouragement, it never would have been done. A third person to whom I am indebted is Katharine Miller, who gave the manuscript and its author much devoted attention in the lengthy period prior to the sale of Chatham House to CQ Press in late 2003. The director of the CQ Press College Division, Brenda Carter, and her able staff have been highly professional and more than gracious in producing the final book, and for that I am most grateful.

My wish is that readers will find the book provocative. I care less about whether you agree or disagree with me than that you arrive at a view of your own, perhaps even one that is likewise polemical. If you would like to share it with me, I sit ready at goodsell@vt.edu.

Chapter 1 Bureaucracy Despised, Disparaged, and Defended

To make the case for bureaucracy. What a ridiculous idea! The author must be a Lucifer incarnate or just plain mad. Only the devil himself would make a case for evil. Only a lunatic would come to the defense of the indefensible.

I hope, dear reader, that you will eventually lay aside any such initial suspicions about your author's character or sanity. Several pages may have to be turned before you do so.

Clearly, I have a large task ahead to convince you to accept my case for bureaucracy. We have all heard about police raids that are brutal, welfare departments that are heartless, defense contracts that waste billions, and public schools that graduate illiterates. Also, we have all personally encountered individual government employees who are arrogant, rude, lazy, condescending, apathetic, and incapable of writing in clear English. How, then, can any self-respecting person write a book on *behalf* of bureaucracy?

Before launching into the rational and logical side of my argument, let me begin by indicating exactly where I am "coming from" emotionally. As the reader, you deserve to know. I do this by relating a few personal experiences with bureaucracy. Perhaps you have had similar things happen to you. As you will see, they are quite ordinary and simple events.

Being a good citizen who likes to stay clear of the law, I take care to pay my income taxes on time. In Virginia the state income tax is paid to the Commissioner of the Revenue of your county. One tax season, after sending in my return, I got a call from a woman at the commissioner's office who said I had misinterpreted the tax form instructions and had paid too much. Even though the tax deadline had by this time passed, she told me to drive over to the county seat that afternoon and come to her office. Upon arriving at the courthouse, I found her behind a well-worn wooden counter. On the spot, she rewrote the form in front of me, had me re-sign it, tore up the old check, and waited until I wrote a new one—at a considerably lower figure.

Once I was driving across my university campus, trying to get somewhere quickly. At a congested area across from the gym, I encountered several cars double-parked, blocking my lane. Despite a double yellow line in the center of the street, I carefully passed all of them. Just as I pulled clear of the last car, I noticed that it was marked "police." Instantly its motor sprang to life and roof lights flashed. I gulped, pulled over at the next driveway, and resignedly got out my driver's license. When the officer came up to the window, he said with a big grin, "Now *that* was a dumb thing to do, wasn't it?" Embarrassed, I readily agreed. He then went back to his cruiser, checked me out on the computer, and returned to give me my license back with the comment, "Now you won't do that again, will you?" Again, I agreed.

In preparing this fourth edition of *The Case for Bureaucracy*, I needed some updated census data for one of the tables. I called my university library to see if the document in question was available. The librarian said no, but provided a Web page address at the Census Bureau. Upon reaching the page, I located the report but saw that it was too long to download. Noticing an 800 contact number on the page, I dialed the number. After two rings, a friendly voice answered, asking what document was needed and requesting my address, so that a copy could be put in the mail right away. I asked how much it would cost. The voice replied, "Let's not look that up, because if I charge you it will take much longer to get the report in the mail." It arrived three days later.

On another occasion, my wife and I landed at Dulles Airport after a trip to Great Britain. The United Kingdom had been badly hit that year by foot-and-mouth disease, and as we prepared to go through Customs we were warned that we must state whether we had visited a farm while overseas. Since we had in fact spent three nights at a farm bed-and-breakfast in Dorset and had tramped all over the barnyard, I debated whether to admit the truth. Others had told us that if we did so we could experience long delays and perhaps be forced to clean our outer clothing. I decided to risk telling the truth to the Customs official, who sent us to a Department of Agriculture inspector nearby. The inspector asked in a friendly way whether the shoes we were currently wearing had trod about the farm. We said yes, whereupon he told us to turn around and lift up our feet one at a time. After looking carefully at the underside of each, he merely said, "They look all right," and sent us on.

For me, these simple experiences say something important. Despite the negative images of bureaucrats to which we are subject from every quarter, when we interact with them in our daily lives, their actual conduct often is much different from what we have been led to expect. Whether tax officials, police officers, Census employees, or agricultural inspectors, it is possible to encounter bureaucrats who work hard, show concern for our interests, do not flaunt their authority, exhibit courtesy and good humor, and go the extra mile to help out. Yet these very same people are not well paid in their jobs. Their daily work is often tedious, difficult, or even dangerous. In our private-enterprise culture, they are subject to kidding if not taunts for "doing government work." In my mind and heart, these bureaucrats and their bureaucracies are worth a closer look than we usually give them.

These thoughts are not learned propositions. They are personal feelings. It is from them that this case for bureaucracy springs. If that be madness, you have been forewarned.

A Brief for Bureaucracy

Lawyers prepare *briefs* to conduct their cases. My brief for bureaucracy, most simply put, is that governmental administration in America may be regarded as generally competent and effective if we look at it in a balanced way and in relation to what is possible. Whereas public bureaucracy in the United States, at all levels of government, inevitably involves individual instances of waste, incompetence, abuse of power, and breakdown, it does, *on the whole and in comparison to most countries and even the business sector in this country, perform surprisingly well.*

I say "surprisingly" because we Americans are taught throughout our lives, from hearth and home on through school and career, that our government is a sea of waste, a swamp of incompetence, a mountain of unchecked power, an endless plain of mediocrity. Our media and politicians tell us that public bureaucracy is bloated in size, inefficient compared to business, a stifling place to work, indifferent to ordinary citizens, the problem rather than the solution. *Bureaucrats*—with the word uttered in contempt—are alleged in all quarters to be lazy, incompetent, devious, and even dangerous.

We encounter this attitude everywhere we look. T-shirts mock bureaucrats. Bumper stickers ridicule them. Movies stereotype them. Parlor games parody them. A nationally televised presidential campaign ad subliminally flashes the word *BUREAUCRATS*, highlighting the last four letters. A full-page newspaper ad placed by a tobacco company features the heavily jowled face of a smugly grinning man. The caption below asks, "Who should be responsible for your children, a bureaucrat or you?"[1]

Government as a whole and bureaucracy by implication are condemned even inside government. The web site of a prominent congressman displayed a "Waste-O-Meter" that tallied the ongoing flow of uncovered waste that supposedly exists in government. The Commonwealth of Virginia issued a "GOVT SUX" vanity license plate. The county executive of Montgomery County, Maryland, bans the word *government* from official letterheads because of its negative connotations. A right-wing religious broadcaster suggested that the Department of State be blown up by a nuclear device.[2]

Bureaucrat-bashing is not confined to political broadsides or to the popular media. Many books and tracts have been devoted to the cause. Just a few examples: *The Federal Rathole, Fat City, Burning Money, Alice in Blunderland, The Government Racket, B.S.: The Bureaucratic Syndrome, America by the Throat*, and *Why Government Fails or What's Really Wrong with the Bureaucracy.*[3]

Also, academic instruction in our colleges and universities is not immune to a grossly negative portrayal of America's administrative institutions. Examining the image of public administration presented in eighteen introductory college texts in American government, Beverly Cigler and Heidi Neiswender found that the books overwhelmingly stressed bureaucracy's size and permanence, its unintelligible language and political power, and its uncontrollability by the president. Not one of the texts made any reference at all to the profession of public administration or the call to public service.[4]

While perpetuating this deeply embedded mistrust of public administration may be a good way to fuel our spirit of individualism, love of liberty, and readiness to revolt against injustice, it leads to a drastically misleading picture of our public employees and government agencies. Even worse, instead of addressing the many problems that *do* exist in bureaucracy, this attitude can exacerbate them by encouraging the kinds of political rhetoric and public policy that demoralize agencies, adversely affecting their performance and encouraging the best staff members to leave. Furthermore, it promotes a set of negative assumptions about government employment that keeps the brightest of our young people from considering a public service career.

The thesis of this book, then, is that a wide gap exists between bureaucracy's reputation and its record. Despite endless rantings to the contrary, American bureaucracy *does* work—in fact, it works quite well. It is something like your ten-year-old car, an immensely complex mechanism made up of tens of thousands of parts, which is by no means perfect or totally reliable. But it starts more often than it stalls, and it completes the vast majority of trips you take. In fact, the old thing is usually working so well that you do not even think of the possibility that you may get stuck somewhere. The first time you are stuck, however, you take notice, and if this happens more than once, you, too, start to rant.

It is the same with government agencies, especially big ones. They are imperfect, vastly complex, and usually reliable, and they come to our attention only when they break down. One of the most visible, and certainly one of the largest and most complex, is the U.S. Postal Service, which collects and delivers 650 million items to 130 million addresses six times a week, with 93 percent of them arriving on time. Rarely is *any* piece lost. Still, we take this service for granted—and without knowing a thing about the immense administrative, processing, and transportation systems needed to make it work. We complain when one letter is a few days late, allowing that one late letter, not the thousands of on-time deliveries we have received, to shape our image of the whole.

One way to keep the quality of American bureaucracy in perspective is to realize that it is far better than that found in many other parts of the world. We may not sense this if we have not traveled or lived abroad. To the billions of people who reside in the poor nations of the world, the routine hallmarks of government bureaucracy are inordinate delays, long lines, undependable service, officious indifference, immense waste, and, not infrequently, corruption. The principal aim of bureaucrats in many countries is not to help the public at all but to get through the day with minimal work. The aim of the bureaucracy as a whole is not to increase the quality of national life but to support the current regime and give employment to friends and relatives.

Most people on this planet would be thrilled to receive even a small part of their mail safely and on time, let alone most of it.

But wait a minute, you might say. We are talking about *American* bureaucracy here, and we need an *American* standard of comparison. How does government bureaucracy in the United States measure up to what is really efficient in America, private business? It clearly does not, will be your instant reply. Business *must* be efficient, because it has to outperform competitors, control costs, adopt new technologies, and satisfy customers—so that it can make profits and survive. Government agencies, by contrast, are legal monopolies, supported by annual appropriations from revenues collected by compulsory taxes and staffed by bureaucrats who cannot be fired. How could they *possibly* be efficient, adopt change, or please citizens?

Yet, as we see later in this book, this seeming irrefutable argument is undermined by facts that do not confirm its assumptions. Many comparative studies have been made to assess private and public organizations doing comparable work, and their overall conclusion is essentially that in terms of operational efficiency, performance, productivity, and service, the differences between the two realms are greatly exaggerated or even minimal. The mantra that business works and government fails—no matter how frequently repeated in legislative chambers, luncheon club speeches, economics textbooks, and the local bar—must be reexamined.

We observed earlier that the Cigler-Neiswender study concluded that American government textbooks stress bureaucracy's size, power, and uncontrollability. Our brief must address these matters, for they raise the possibility that bureaucracy is an enemy of democracy. We deal with this question at length later, but let us make two preliminary points here. First, the singular term *bureaucracy* refers not to one aggregate mega-institution but to thousands of separate organizations. These departments, bureaus, agencies, commissions, and countless other kinds of bodies do not act in concert or in conspiracy. In fact, they often have little to do with one another and in some ways are rivals. Moreover, as we later see, huge size is not necessarily characteristic of bureaucracy—in fact, small size is more common.

Second, our bureaucracies, just like our citizens, operate within the context of regular elections, representative government, and a system of constitutional law that provides for divided and limited governmental power and guaranteed rights. They are continuously monitored and investigated by auditors, judges, budget examiners, performance evaluators, legislative committees, public watchdog groups, clientele associations, citizen bodies, and media organizations eager for a good scandal. While public agencies clearly can and must possess political clout in varying degrees in order to do their jobs, they are channeled and checked in more ways than one might think. In fact, sometimes the checks are nearly disabling.

We conclude this brief by explicitly defining the word *bureaucracy.* Some uncertainty arose on this point in response to earlier editions of this book, so let me be clear about how I define the term. When using the word *bureaucracy* I am referring, quite simply, to the institutions of public administration in America. By this I mean the organizations and their unit offices whose employees are paid from public funds, at all levels of government in the United States. This includes the ubiquitous county welfare office, the departments of transportation (DOTs) in every state, the Environmental Protection Agency headquartered in Washington, D.C., the Centers for Disease Control and Prevention in Atlanta, the thousands of police departments and public schools scattered across the nation, and—don't forget—the several branches of the U.S. armed forces.

The descriptive category, then, is vast. It embraces thousands of institutions and millions of people. It incorporates an incredible variety of activities, from investigating child abuse to filling potholes to combating AIDS to negotiating international treaties and conducting wars. The very enormity of the category speaks eloquently of the critical importance of our subject. The vast range of organizations included cries out for thoughtful assessment of individual bureaucracies rather than characterization by stereotype.

Many readers will be aware of the sociological model of bureaucracy posited by Max Weber early in the past century. To Weber, a bureaucracy was an organization with specified functional attributes: large size; a graded hierarchy; formal rules; specialized tasks; written files; and employees who are salaried, technically trained, career-appointed, and assigned stated duties requiring expert knowledge. Weber regarded his model as an ideal type, useful for description and analysis.[5]

Many academic theorists and researchers contend that by possessing these characteristics, an organization tends automatically to exhibit certain patterns of behavior. These include rigidity, proceduralism, resistance to change, oppressive control of employees, dehumanized treatment of clients, indifference to citizen input, use of incomprehensible jargon, and tendencies toward empire building and concentration of power. These ascribed traits are, obviously, all pejorative. They also happen to spring, for the most part, from predisposed beliefs about large organizations rather than from empirical study. When academic writers on bureaucracy reflect negatively on the consequences of the "Weberian model," they are often being not neutral social scientists at all but ideological critics of hierarchical organization—a position shared by many intellectuals. As if by a kind of original sin embedded in its organizational form, bureaucracy is seen as automatically and perpetually condemned to incompetence and antidemocratic excess.

Returning to my own use of the word, I do not deny that much if not most of American public administration is made up of organizations that answer to many if not all of Weber's basic structural characteristics. Yes, steps are often taken to flatten chains of command, create flexible roles and teams, empower employees and citizens, and stress service to citizens. Still, most public-sector organizations and jurisdictions continue to feature differentiated levels of office, bounded areas of authority, internal rules, electronic or paper files, career or at least long-term employees, and professional experts of one kind or another. So, to that extent, most administrative components of U.S. government are still essentially "bureaucracies" in the Weberian sense—whatever that may mean in terms of resultant behavior. (They are not, however, necessarily very big, as we discover later.)

Let me make myself abundantly clear. I do not deny that selected attempts to deemphasize these structural characteristics in our public administration institutions would be helpful in many instances. I do not, however, accept the deterministic thought implicit in theories of bureaucracy that automatically equate *any* substantial presence of Weber's characteristics with incompetence or rigidity, dehumanized or oppressive conduct, or imperialistic behavior. Hence I am not, obviously, using the term *bureaucracy* in the typical pejorative sense. To put the matter another way, my debating opponents and I disagree not over whether American public administration is essentially bureaucratic, but over whether that means it is inevitably pathological.[6]

A Bit of Bureaucratic History

The balance of this introductory chapter is devoted, first, to reflections on selected aspects of the history of public bureaucracy in America. Following this, statements by other scholars and commentators on bureaucracy are examined. These assessments, we find, fall into two distinct camps: those many who denounce bureaucracy and those several who praise it.

The first modern republics in the world were the thirteen original American states, established in the eighteenth century. Our republican national government was founded a few years later. These republics sprang from the principle of popular sovereignty rather than from the prevailing notion of divine right of kings. Their bureaucracies evolved not from the king's household as in Europe, but from the practical need of the people's representatives to achieve aims in the common weal—such as regulating commerce, fostering agriculture, raising armies, and providing for orphans and the insane. Administrative bodies were needed to carry out these purposes. They too were created not by divine authority, but simply because of the need of the people to care for themselves as collective communities.

These republics were formed by newly written constitutions, also an eighteenth-century American invention. Some critics of bureaucracy like to point out that the words *bureaucracy* and *administration* are not found in the U.S. Constitution. This does not mean that public administration was unanticipated by the founding fathers, however. Most of these fifty-five men had been government officials or legislators in their own states prior to 1787, and they realized full well that if government were to act, it needed to have institutions of action—that is, bureaucracy.[7]

The young bureaucracies of the time were not sophisticated organizations. The establishment of government departments with hierarchical authority, specialized subunits, trained employees, and complex duties began for the most part after the Civil War. These institutions were created not because someone went to Germany and met Max Weber but because the young nation had to attend to such matters as professionalizing the army and diplomatic corps, collecting sufficient taxes through customs duties, distributing western lands and making it possible to reach them, and—in the growing cities and towns—building streets, water systems, sewer systems, post offices, police departments, and fire brigades. Toward the close of the nineteenth century, another step was taken when the Progressive movement spawned the formation of a self-conscious field of public administration. This too was the outcome of practical concerns, such as the desire to improve government by saving money, reducing corruption, and laying the basis for prosperous business enterprise.

Centralized, in-house bureaucracy experienced its heyday in America in the middle third of the twentieth century. Once more it was seen not as inherently good but as necessary to higher ends. Examples were combating the Great Depression in the 1930s, fighting World War II in the 1940s, launching the Interstate Highway System in the 1950s, and, in the 1960s, seeking to achieve civil rights, an end to poverty, safer consumers, and a protected environment. It was in this midcentury period that what we think of as the "administrative state" came into being, with its procedures of administrative law, powers of rulemaking and adjudication, systems of executive management and financial control, and arrangements for civil service recruitment, classification, and compensation. At the time, the best agencies and leaders of American bureaucracy were widely thought of as equal to, and perhaps better than, any in the world.

Then, in the late sixties, the tide of bureaucratic history seemed to turn, and a period of general disillusionment with government set in. The causes of the epochal change are multiple and intertwined. The long-drawn-out Vietnam tragedy probably started the disenchantment; then along came the Watergate scandal, the energy shortages, the Iran-*contra* disclosures, and the savings-and-loan debacle. As a result, government no longer seemed competent or trustworthy. Its legitimacy was further tainted by cynicism-producing practices in political campaigns, ethical lapses by politicians, gridlock between the branches of government, and a drumbeat of antigovernment negativism in the media. The University of Michigan's trust-in-government surveys, at the 70–80 percent range in the late fifties and early sixties, declined quite steadily to around 25 percent by 1980. They temporarily rose above 40 percent during the Reagan years, hovered around 30 during the first Bush presidency, and then dropped to almost 20 in Clinton's first term.[8]

Starting in the 1970s the bureaucracy, always the handy scapegoat for public problems, fell itself under attack. Candidates for public office, including the presidency, routinely campaigned on specious claims that vast amounts of fraud, waste, and abuse existed in government. Numerous investigations were launched to correct the situation, and various study commissions and laws were instituted to "reform" what was characterized as a grossly incompetent and out-of-date administrative establishment. Ways were also sought to counter or bypass normal channels of administrative authority, such as more layers of political appointees, independent inspectors general, and protected whistle-blowers. Meanwhile, in the media, legislators, editorial writers, and business leaders "bashed" bureaucrats in every conceivable way, and scorn was heaped on government workers in Sunday supplements, cartoons, paperweights, call-in radio programs, and a multitude of other instruments of the popular culture.

Specific events aggravated the attacks from time to time. The FBI sniper shootings at Ruby Ridge, Idaho, in 1992 and the fire associated with the siege of the Branch Davidian compound at Waco, Texas, in 1993 provoked accusations of ruthlessness and incompetence against federal law enforcement agencies. Spokesmen for the National Rifle Association mounted pernicious attacks on federal authority, leading to an angry resignation from the organization by the first President Bush, a lifelong member. In western states, fringe groups such as antigovernment militiamen and sagebrush-rebellion activists made the daily life of federal land management personnel literally dangerous. Perversely, this atmosphere of recrimination seemed to result in condemnation more of its victims than of its perpetrators.

Against this background, it is remarkable that in the mid-nineties the tides of bureaucratic history seemed again to reverse themselves. At least to some extent, antigovernment rhetoric in the media and on the part of politicians began to subside. On the morning of 19 April 1995, Timothy McVeigh parked a Ryder truck loaded with two tons of explosives in front of the Alfred P. Murrah Federal Building in Oklahoma City. Shortly after 570 bureaucrats had arrived for work, and a few moments after many federal workers had placed their children in a daycare center on the first floor, the explosion killed 168 people, including 19 children, and injured more than 500. The nation was confronted with its first major terrorist incident inside the country; the image of a savagely defaced government building filled television screens for days. When McVeigh was later captured, he made it clear that profound hatred of the federal government had been the motivation for his action.

Then, later in that same year, President Clinton and the Republican-controlled House of Representatives became locked in political combat over budgetary appropriations. The president refused to give in to attempts to make an issue out of budget deficits and vetoed several bills. In November, when temporary continuance resolutions necessary to fund the government ran out, a large part of the federal government was closed for six days. Brief funding interruptions of this kind had occurred before, so no one was much worried. But then, in December, a second appropriations deadlock closed an extensive segment of the national government for approximately three weeks. During this time the nation was suddenly confronted with the hard reality that, for the foreseeable future, unemployment checks had stopped, Medicare payments had been ended, applications for passports were not being processed, cost-of-living statistics were not being collected, and contractor payments in the billions were not being made. Thus, in a single year, domestic terrorism was for the first time killing American public servants, and the fiscal means for carrying out many of their duties had dried up. The unrecognized value of government in general and bureaucracy in particular was being brought to the public's attention to an unprecedented degree.

In the years immediately following 1995, more terrorism broke out, both at home and abroad. In 1996 bombs were placed in the truck of a mine inspector in Vacaville, California, at the Walker Plaza Federal Building in Laredo, Texas, and at the Richard Bolling Federal Building in Kansas City. In the same year, the Khobar Towers military complex in Saudi Arabia was bombed. In 1998 the American embassies in Kenya and Tanzania were both blown up, within five minutes of one another. In 2000 the U.S.S. *Cole* was rammed by terrorists while refueling in Yemen, killing seventeen sailors and nearly sinking the ship.

Then came September 11th. Four civilian airliners were hijacked, intent on destroying Americans and their architectural symbols. In the beautiful sunshine of that morning, the two towers of the World Trade Center in New York City were hit and, incredibly, crumbled to the ground. A short time later, the presumably impregnable Pentagon, on the shores of the Potomac in Washington, was rammed and deeply damaged. The fourth hijacked plane, meant to destroy the U.S. Capitol or the White House, was caused by crew and passengers to drive under full power into the earth in rural Pennsylvania in order to avoid another catastrophe.

All told, over 3,000 people perished on that day. The heroic actions and sacrifices of firefighters and police officers in New York City and Pentagon personnel in Washington, D.C., caught the imagination of the nation. Bureaucrats were now not just essential—they could be the source of admiration and inspiration. As we now know, this terrible and unforgettable day opened a new era of American history. Subsequently, American military forces invaded Afghanistan and drove out the regime that had supported the terrorists responsible. Less than two years later, U.S. and British troops invaded Iraq, taking control of the country in three weeks with minimal casualties. In the aftermath of both actions, public servants in and out of the military risked their lives to pacify and rehabilitate the two countries. Regardless of the political wisdom of these actions, the skill and bravery of the men and women sent into harm's way impressed observers around the world.

Looking back at this history, perhaps we will conclude that a "thirty years war" of rhetoric against American government in the period between 1965 and 1995 had finally subsided. In any case, the bureaucrat-bashing of that earlier time became muted if not silenced. Editorial diatribes against government agencies shifted from general claims of waste and abuse to narrower accusations, such as too much eavesdropping under the Patriot Act or failure to predict the terrorist attacks or the weapons threat posed by Saddam Hussein. Whereas three out of four government-themed television entertainment programs in 1992–1998 had depicted a faulty public sector, in 1999–2001 nearly 75 percent portrayed government as working well. Academic castigation of bureaucracy moved from broadsides about inefficiency and oppression to specific proposals that agencies be made over in the business image. Critical comments centered not on the failures of individual bureaucrats but on their Weberian rather than network forms of organization. Meanwhile, trust-in-government polls began to rise in 1996, reaching new plateaus in the 50–60 percent range. Just after 9/11, they spiked to 78 percent, and afterwards did not return to pre-1996 lows.[9]

What happened? Perhaps America has come of age in a sense. Citizens now have reason to take seriously the role of government agencies in their lives. It has become clear that these institutions are more an asset to the society than a liability. We have them not because we must but because they are indispensable to a secure and civilized life. Indeed, when they stop working, many of our society's wheels immediately stop turning. When bureaucrats and soldiers die in the line of duty, we grieve—if for no other reason that that they are fellow citizens. When terrorism strikes at home and abroad, we count on public servants both in mufti and in uniform to take action. If nothing else, it is evident that in this new century much is at stake for Americans, who now seem to realize that bureaucracy will be needed to face the future.

The Academics Debate Bureaucracy: The Opponents

We examine now what the professors, scholars, and intellectuals have said about bureaucracy. We begin with literature that tend to be critical and later look at those that take a favorable view.

The literature opposed to bureaucracy issues from several disciplinary base camps and attacks it from a number of angles and viewpoints. We survey this extensive material under three topics of criticism: (1) poor performance, (2) excessive power, and (3) oppression of the individual.

Robert Behn, leader of an economics-oriented school of thought in public management, puts the charge of bad performance succinctly: American government at this point in history, he contends, is "plagued less by the problem of corruption than by the problem of performance." The quality of its work must improve greatly, he says, in order "to convince the citizens that government performance is not an oxymoron."[10]

Gerald Caiden, who writes extensively on administrative reform, states his opinion on the need for drastic improvement in the following, more prolix manner:

> The call to American public administration to jettison its outmoded thinking and to reshape its future by improving its performance, its image, its reputation and its modus operandi is the culmination of decades of public dissatisfaction, professional discontent, and intellectual criticism. It echoes universal unhappiness with the administrative state and its failure to keep abreast with the times. Institutions and organizations inherited and developed over the past two centuries seem unprepared and even unfit for the century ahead. Urgent action is needed now if prospects are to improve. The longer reforms are delayed, the worse the situation will become. Something has to be done now to prepare for a future that will be clearly different from the present. Someone has to introduce better ways of doing things or least improve on current practices that fall below public expectations. The time for action is ripe. Frustrated people are willing to consider anything that sounds halfway promising. If their leaders hesitate, the public will take the initiative, shake up complacent establishments, and shunt aside obstacles to progress.[11]

We begin our summary of explanations of *why* bureaucracy is assumed to perform poorly by turning to the market-oriented economists, who are hostile to government bureaucracy on several grounds. By definition almost, they are opposed to government intervention in the private marketplace as a detriment to economic efficiency. This orientation leads them to oppose much of what government does in the first place. Hence they tend to be unfriendly to the institutions of bureaucracy. More basically, they distrust public ownership, government monopolies, and incentive systems based on motivations other than profit maximization. Also, they regard much of government taxation and spending as dampening private capital formation and hence constituting a drag on productivity.[12]

The "public choice" economists, whose conservative views are not shared by all economists, contend that the basic problem with a public bureaucracy is that instead of responding to a proper market, it is dependent on a single "sponsor" or appropriations source. Because heads of bureaus, it is assumed, crave higher and higher salaries and more and more perks and power, they are not profit maximizers but budget maximizers, who automatically demand more funds regardless of need. As such, they inflate costs and generate false demand through "spending advocacy." The consequence is unlimited budgetary expansion and an inefficient allocation of resources within the public sector. This, then, is a major cause of budget deficits. It also explains some environmental degradation, they contend, because treasury-raiding bureaucrats build useless public works projects regardless of their environmental impact.[13]

The next disciplinary camp we visit is sociology. One of the favorite ideas of sociologists is that bureaucracies are destined to work against themselves, that is, to be "dysfunctional." Because of the inherent attributes of organizations following the Weberian model, it is said, bureaucracies inevitably acquire countereffective, "pathological" behavioral patterns. One of the most important of these is obsessive conformity to rules, which creates a phenomenon called "goal displacement," or placing the procedures required ahead of the ends being sought. Another diagnosis is persistent conflict between superiors and subordinates, which results in petty game-playing and eventual organizational breakdown. Still another perceived dysfunctionality is communication blocks that arise in the hierarchical chain of command. Bureaucracy is also perceived as inherently rigid and incapable of innovation.[14]

These worrisome shortcomings affect not only the bureaucracies' own worlds but those of others as well. Some sociologists see bureaucratic values as penetrating all private and public institutions in the society, to their detriment. A "bureaucratization of the world" is depicted as crushing individualism, blocking personal growth, and poisoning human relationships. Bureaucracy's structural characteristics also contribute to crime, world poverty, and hunger, it is said, because of its tight association with elite interests.[15]

A second context in which bureaucracy is criticized is its relationship with political power. One of the earliest critiques of bureaucracy from the political-power standpoint was made by Max Weber himself. Although a tendency exists in the textbooks to portray Weber as a friend and proponent of bureaucracy, in fact, as a liberal activist in his contemporary Prussia he regarded it as a threat to parliamentary democracy. Once bureaucracy is established, Weber contended, it becomes almost impossible to destroy. Moreover, it serves as "a power instrument of the first order—for the one who controls the bureaucratic apparatus." But Weber doubted that even "the one who controls" can truly do so, for bureaucracy is indispensable as an institutional apparatus and in addition is highly technical and secretive in nature. The elected politician, theoretically bureaucracy's master, is in danger of becoming a hapless dilettante before its superior power.[16]

Contemporary students of Weber, as well as subsequent Germanic scholars, carried this argument further, equating bureaucracy with authoritarian or even totalitarian government. One historian considered bureaucracy to be a form of "oriental despotism" created by the technical imperatives of great works projects associated with the use of water. Other writers analyzed it in terms of having reached its fullest and therefore most revealing expression in Nazi Germany and Stalinist Russia. A more recent commentary in this Teutonic tradition blames governmental and corporate bureaucracy for smothering human creativity and individualism, substituting therefor an authoritarian frame of mind. Pointing to the overwhelming forces of big bureaucracy, Wolfgang Kraus asks whether we have actually become "an army in mufti," fighting not for freedom but for a lack of freedom. Michael Ledeen insists that the only acceptable response to government's poisonous control is an outburst of destruction:

> Government must be slashed down to size, its gluttonous tentacles torn out of the body of society, its insidious poisons purged from the lifeblood of enterprise

> and education, its mindless bureaucrats blown away from their telephones and fax machines, its presses stopped, its linen washed, its babies and bathwater thrown out together in a great tidal wave of purifying destruction.[17]

Another theme in political analysis of bureaucracy is that, even if not necessarily totalitarian, bureaucracy possesses an elitist bias and distorts the democratic political process in pro-establishment ways. This tradition, which began with German political sociologist Robert Michels and continues on up through contemporary political science, portrays bureaucracies as inherently oligarchic and conservative organizations. Bureaucrats are seen as unrepresentative of the masses, automatically favorable to the ruling regime, and invariably allied with the most powerful interests in the society. As a consequence, both are said to be against meaningful change, bent on maintaining stability and order, and determined to keep all real power in traditional hands. Furthermore, bureaucrats engage covertly in the formation and manipulation of public policy, despite an official ideology that separates politics from administration. They are seen as taking independent policy initiatives, abusing the discretion granted them by statute, forming alliances with interest groups and legislative committees, and co-opting other centers of power—in order to steer the ship of state in the desired conservative directions.[18]

Hence democracy and representative government are regarded as undermined if not sabotaged by bureaucracy. The political science community in particular is concerned with this issue. More enamored of legislatures, presidents, political campaigns, and electoral behavior, it often regards bureaucracy as a threat to the prerogatives of the appropriately "political" branches of government. As noted earlier, Cigler and Neiswender found that American government texts often stress this theme. One polemicist goes so far as to call bureaucracy an "anti-gravity force," since it pulls people apart more than it brings them together. Government agencies, he says, "will go on aggregating power unto themselves until there is no longer any effective, essential political power left among the people being served." Another polemicist sums up the situation by declaring that "the problem, simply put, is not socialism versus capitalism but bureaucracy versus democracy."[19]

Marx, no doubt, would have had problems with this last statement. Yet in some of his writings he, too, saw bureaucracy as out of control. His reasoning was that bureaucracy is the most important instrument available to the capitalist ruling class in maintaining its domination. To accomplish this feat, bureaucracy becomes a "closed corporation," hidden from view by secrecy, mystery, and deified authority. In his often obtuse way, Marx wrote, "The spirit of bureaucracy is thoroughly Jesuitical and theological. The bureaucrats are the state's Jesuits and theologians. Bureaucracy is the priest's republic."[20]

An allied theme concerning bureaucracy's political power has to do with its expansive growth, which is said to result from various forces related to career advancement and societal support. Since all members of an organization benefit from personnel and budgetary enlargement, it is deduced that this will inevitably happen. External factors—such as the need of the capitalist welfare state to ameliorate economic crisis, train a labor workforce, buy support from alienated groups, and pacify angry masses—also have a growth-perpetuating effect. The picture one gets of bureaucracy is that of an imperialist superpower that inexorably builds its empire larger and larger.[21]

Strange as it seems, other antibureaucracy scholarly voices simultaneously reach the opposite conclusion. The need for small, flexible, and egalitarian work groups means that we are now "beyond bureaucracy" and in the process of rapidly departing from its constraints. Bureaucracy as a "sociobiological form" is in the process of becoming extinct in the evolutionary process, it is said, and hence slated to disappear. To those terrified by an uncontrolled bureaucracy, the prospect of its demise must be reassuring.[22]

The third and final broad theme of academic condemnation of bureaucracy deals not with performance or power but oppression. Bureaucracy is said to treat human beings callously at the minimum and, at the maximum, crushingly.

One major segment of bureaucracy's victims consists of its own employees. The principle of hierarchy is seen as instituting an intolerable pattern of inequality, subordination, and dependence on the working members of the organization. Authoritative direction and mechanistic rules are said to insult individuality. People are reduced to passive agents or even inmates of the system, which denies them the opportunity to give meaningful consent to cooperative action or to participate actively in the making of policy or the improvement of the organization. Bureaucrats are said to be "ants crawling along the chain links of the governing structure. They are the megalops of government."[23]

Furthermore, the specialization of work in bureaucracy creates narrow, humdrum routines that are nearly impossible to bear day after day. The functionary becomes so integrated into structured bureaucratic life that he or she is no longer an autonomous, separate human being who is psychologically capable of individual self-fulfillment. Bureaucracy, according to this view, serves only the individual's needs for security and economic gain, not the need for self-actualization. Employees are required to behave in immature ways and are called on to abandon spontaneity and authenticity. They are forced to make decisions in a fear-ridden atmosphere where failure to achieve according to the organization's dictates ruins careers and breaks personalities. When other forms of coercion fall short, bureaucracy is capable of blackballing, blacklisting, or committing psychological or physical violence against its members.[24]

A second general grouping of victims is made up of bureaucracy's clients. Against these human beings bureaucracy commits several crimes, a leading one being treatment of the person as a mere "case." An individual enmeshed in the organization's processes as a welfare applicant or citizen in some other supplicant capacity no longer possesses uniqueness or personal emotions to be respected. Bureaucrats treat the individual as an impersonal object within the context of rules, such as those defining eligibility for benefits or banned behavior. Rather than considering the "whole person," the official limits attention to the narrow and abstract slice of the client that is of programmatic relevance. Hence bureaucratic behavior toward clients is characterized by remoteness and manipulation. The client is neither a respected citizen nor a valued customer, but a "territorial underdog" to be controlled and restricted. In extreme cases, Heiner Flohr warns, bureaucracy could even be harmful to your health.[25]

Other forms of client mistreatment stem from internal needs and drives of the "bureaucratic personality" (sometimes referred to as "bureaucratic mentality"). This concept is based on the notion that the bureaucrat, occupying a low-level position within a power-conscious hierarchy, also is oppressed. To compensate for this circumstance, he or she lashes out officiously at the citizen, who is deemed an even lower personage. Rules are interpreted without regard for genuine human needs. The client is addressed not straightforwardly in a spirit of goodwill, but in authoritarian and incomprehensible language that is delivered in a flat, passionless tone of voice and with a studied formality of demeanor. To avoid responsibility for handling borderline cases or unusual circumstances, the bureaucrat refers all nonstandard matters to superiors or to another office. The consequence is put-offs and put-downs. Delay, red tape, arrogance, and evasiveness abound.[26]

Still another form of client abuse is repression of the disadvantaged—including the poor, racial minorities, and individuals classified as "difficult" cases. Bureaucracies are viewed as essentially middle-class institutions that are incapable of dealing with the underclass on its own terms. Poor, urban, and "feisty" African Americans and Hispanics are seen as not understanding the culture or the language of bureaucracy. Hence a "war of cultures" is waged across reception counters and in agency waiting rooms and caseworker offices. Another tendency is to ignore clients who are difficult to deal with, possibly dangerous, or unlikely to contribute to success rates.[27]

Bureaucrats working at the "street level" of service delivery are particularly targeted for suspicion. Their breadth of operational discretion is said to provide ample opportunity for the exercise of race and class prejudices. In order to cope with overwork and uncertainty, bureaucrats construct and enlarge spheres of working autonomy by manipulating information and selectively enforcing the rules. Degradation rituals are staged to raise the costs of being a client. These are so offensive that clients may choose to stop seeking help or not request it in the first place. The consequence, it is said, are services characterized by low participation rates, poor delivery quality, and high client alienation, particularly in the inner city.[28]

Finally, in addition to these overt ways in which bureaucracy oppresses, the organization is allegedly capable of occupying a position so deep in our thinking that its social control is hidden from conscious view. Critical theorists, postmodernists, deconstructionists, and some feminists contend that, regardless of what citizens—whether clients or employees—say about bureaucracy, they have in effect been brainwashed. The paradigm of rational authority, positivist science, materialist capitalism, and masculine power is imposed on them in such a manner that they cannot conceive of alternatives. Victims suffer a "pathology of consciousness" or dwell in a "psychic prison" that keeps them from recognizing their mental bondage. Reduced to a condition of helplessness, which is reinforced by the general worldview imposed by the capitalist economy and an inequitable society, women and men cannot realize their potential, are unable to communicate competently, are distracted from self-reflection, and are subject to manipulation by powerful interests of which they are not aware. Public bureaucracy's specific contribution to this unrecognized suppression is to control the definition of problems, divert attention to questions of technique, and perpetuate overall values of social control.[29]

A particularly arresting statement in this vein is *Unmasking Administrative Evil* by Guy Adams and Danny Balfour, who argue that public administration, because of its commitment to modernist technical rationality in the absence of contextual understanding and reflexive moral thinking, can become the perpetrator of absolute evil without the bureaucrats realizing it. The examples given are the Holocaust, the employment of Wernher von Braun in the American space program, and the failure of response to the O-ring problem in the space shuttle *Challenger* disaster. Inasmuch as Adams and Balfour regard administrative evil as a functional phenomenon rather than an intentional act, they blame the administrative system for these wrongs, not Hitler or U.S. policymakers. Looking at administrative evil from a postmodernist perspective, Gerson Moreno-Riano draws on the German philosopher Eric Voegelin to contend that its true source or "etiology" is modernist disinterest in consciousness, freedom, and human dignity.[30]

Bureaucracy's reputation in the halls of academe, then, is quite bad—at least in the minds of many. It is castigated by economists, sociologists, psychologists, political scientists, and even many scholars of public administration and public policy. Bureaucrats are portrayed as poor performers as well as budget maximizers; ants and megalops as well as empire builders; and merciless oppressors of their own kind as well as their clients. It is as a bureaucratic personality that they think, as an authoritarian army in mufti that they march, and as a Jesuitical priesthood that they mystify. Bureaucracy, institutionally, is said to sap the economy, endanger democracy, suppress the individual, and be capable of embodying evil. It is denounced on the right by market champions and public-choice theorists and on the left by Marxists, critical theorists, and postmodernists. One side of the political spectrum finds bureaucracy a convenient target because it represents taxes, regulation, and big government; the other sees it as representing elitism, injustice to the underprivileged, and social control.

The contention that the worst of bureaucracy's alleged evil consequences stem from its hidden power over our minds raises an intriguing question: If that power is truly hidden, how do the critics know about it? But perhaps more than one unconscious reality lurks in our minds. Ithiel de Sola Pool once commented that intellectuals find it "somehow more sophisticated and moral to criticize institutions than to justify them." Charles Perrow has suggested that social scientists castigate bureaucracy because they themselves dislike organizational constraints. For many of them, he writes, "rules are a nuisance; the emphasis upon rules in organizations is bad enough, but the existence of a hierarchical ordering of offices and authority is a barely tolerable evil." Christopher Hood, too, speculates that many critics of bureaucracy may be speaking from a personal bias. He equates "anti-bureaucracy utopianism" with impatience at any kind of administration. Another possibility is that bureaucracy is a symbol for a whole range of disdained, petit bourgeois attributes, from banality and regimentation to predictability and attention to detail. In that case, it is bad by definition. In the words of Stephen Miller, "bureaucracy has come to stand for all that is wrong with the modern world."[31]

The Academics Debate Bureaucracy: The Supporters

Although the academic literature supporting bureaucracy is far less voluminous than that on the "contra" side, it is not insignificant. Indeed it has been growing in recent years.

The first case for bureaucracy to be made in print (as far as I know) appeared in *Scribner's Magazine* in the spring of 1933. This was the opening moment of the New Deal, it is worth noting; Franklin Roosevelt was inaugurated on March 4 of that year. Written by the Progressive historian and prophet of public administration Charles Beard and his son, William, this article bore precisely the same title as this book—a discovery I did not make until well after I had adopted it. The situation they described in 1933 does not seem much different from the one we see seven decades later: "Among the latest deliriums is that of waging war on the bureaucracy, now full of noise and promise. Some of our very best people are doing it, usually without discrimination, for discrimination takes the edge off of propaganda."[32]

Another article that bears the identical title, also run across only after I had written my first edition, was published by Harlan Cleveland, another famous figure in American public administration, in the *New York Times Magazine* in the fall of 1963. It offered "a brief dissent from some of the prevalent notions about bureaucracy—plus some outrageously tolerate thoughts about large government bureaucracies," such as the State Department, where he served. Cleveland denounced several "canards" against bureaucracy, for example, that it exists in the public sector only; that business is necessarily more efficient; and that public organizations automatically stifle initiative and protect the status quo.[33]

Several themes can be identified in pro-bureaucracy writings. One is what the Beards were probably worried about, the damage done to the public service and government agencies by incessant attacks on them. In the early 1980s Werner Dannhauser urged us to realize that "nothing will be gained and a great deal can be lost by magnifying the bureaucracy problem out of all proportion." Herbert Kaufman characterized the fear of bureaucracy as a "raging pandemic," and Zahid Shariff lamented that "public administration is clearly the whipping boy." At the very time I was writing my first edition, two friends, Brinton Milward and Hal Rainey, were penning, without our realizing the coincidence, a stimulating essay entitled "Don't Blame the Bureaucracy!"[34]

In a more recent article, Dean Yarwood, another friend, demands outright that we "Stop Bashing the Bureaucracy." "Much of the antibureaucratic rhetoric of the day," comments William Richardson more mildly, "if taken literally, requires a suspension of belief, and some of the people who use it to mold and mobilize public opinion are fairly described as demagogic." Henry Mintzberg, an organization theorist and consultant, issued the following warning to the *Harvard Business Review*'s executive-suite readers:

> Societies get the public services they expect. If people believe that government is bumbling and bureaucratic, then that is what it will be. If, in contrast, they recognize public service for the noble calling it is, then they will end up with strong government. And no nation today can afford anything but strong government. Isn't it time that all the knee-jerking condemnation of government in the United States stopped?[35]

Others specifically point out how attacking bureaucracy and demeaning public servants tends to drive good people out of government and make it more difficult to attract the best of young talent. Bernard Rosen points to a "hemorrhaging of excellence from the federal service." Bruce Adams warns that negative rhetoric, because of its adverse effects on recruitment, becomes a self-fulfilling prophecy. Larry Lane and James Wolf state that presidential campaign attacks on the bureaucracy have contributed to a "tangible sense of federal institutional breakdown and declining morale." To them, "America has squandered one of its most critical resources—a fine civil service." Indeed, the downsizing and buyouts of the 1990s, together with the anticipated retirement of half the remaining workforce in the 2000s, have amplified the national government's "human capital crisis."[36]

A second theme in the pro-bureaucracy literature echoes Harlan Cleveland's "outrageously tolerate thoughts" about government departments. A number of books say that bureaucracy's critics exaggerate the problems and do not acknowledge that government is capable of working quite well. George Downs and Patrick Larkey note that comparisons between the efficiency of business and government are often invidious, and they conclude that government often performs better than the public thinks, and business worse. Mark Holzer and Kathe Callahan assert, "By no means is the public sector 'dead in the water.'" Kenneth Meier and John Bohte, having analyzed student failures in the Texas public schools (i.e., absentees, hold-backs, and drop-outs), found that the frequency of such failures had no statistical relation to proportion of bureaucrats per 100 students. Steven Kelman, in what he calls "a hopeful view of American government," says that the policy process of this country performs better than its reputation and thereby deserves the people's participation. Christopher Leman, analyzing the direct performance of tasks by government bureaucracies as opposed to indirect means such as grants and loans, points out that distrust of government may lead to reliance on third parties when in-house action by public agencies could get the job done better. Lewis Mainzer goes so far as to state that the quality of the American public service "is no mean achievement."

> Compared with governmental bureaucracies elsewhere or in other times, it achieves an impressive record combining competence, dignity, and responsibility. The variety in quality and style of American public administration is incredible, the worst is admittedly bad, but a fair amount is quite decent and the best is impressively good. In a world so bungled, whatever worth has been achieved merits a restrained word of praise.[37]

Even within the public choice school of economists, some dissent is appearing in the unanimous verdict that bureaucracy must be inefficient. At a conference organized by economists André Blais and Stéphane Dion to consider the supposed bureaucratic practice of budget maximizing, many papers pointed to the lack of empirical support for the thesis. In another examination of the topic, Patrick Dunleavy argues that rational bureaucrats have few incentives to engage in budget maximizing and several reasons not to. Hugh Stretton and Lionel Orchard go further, insisting that theories of rational self-interest "select only one of the many motives at work" in government and do not realize that efficient markets depend on the presence of law, culture, and morality, all of which are sustained for noneconomic reasons.[38]

Also undergoing reassessment are some of political science's pet theories about bureaucracy. Theorist David Beetham argues that the concentration of information and organizational capacity in bureaucracy can make it a potentially antidemocratic force, but that this does not necessarily occur—and even when it does, the pressures come not from the administrative system itself but from the tasks bureaucracy is required to accomplish (such as those mandated in the USA Patriot Act of 2001). Eva Etzioni-Halévy weighs the dilemmas of bureaucracy and democracy from a comparative standpoint, concluding that while bureaucrats around the world help politicians make policy, they also counter their power and serve as a bulwark against corruption. Dan Wood and Richard Waterman determine, after extensive empirical study of policy shifts in Washington in the wake of electoral change, that contrary to principal-agent theory and the iron-triangle model, *both* the president and Congress are able to exert control over administrative agencies.[39]

In addition to urging us to stop attacking bureaucracy and start realizing that it may not be as bad as we thought, a third theme in the supportive literature is more aggressive. It asserts outright that government and its administration make crucial, indispensable contributions to the society. "There is much to celebrate in terms of the public's achievements through the use of democratic governance," states Max Neiman, " . . . operating through its government institutions." "Bureaucracy is the cod liver oil of social institutions," Barry Bozeman writes. "It smells bad and leaves a nasty aftertaste, but sometimes it is just what you need." To Gary Wills, government is "a necessary evil" that protects liberties as well as endangering them. H.T. Wilson observes that bureaucracy mediates contending interests in the political system; without it powerful forces favoring capital would always win out. Gyorgy Gajduschek asserts that one of bureaucracy's important contributions to society is uncertainty reduction, a feature identified by Weber but ignored by his interpreters. Larry Preston argues that bureaucracies—both public and private—support individual freedom by giving us the ability to make choices, learn, create, and achieve higher purposes. In a striking reappraisal of Weber's model, Paul du Gay contends that the notion of ethos of office permits the democratic state to act forcefully, morally, and accountably, contrary to managerial or entrepreneurial concepts of administration. My former professor Carl J. Friedrich, to whom bureaucracy is "the core of modern government," used to say that the success of democracy itself depends on a successful bureaucracy, for without it no elected government can succeed.[40]

Has bureaucracy in fact allowed democratic government to achieve its aims? Some writers back in the Reagan era made that claim, even though it was highly unfashionable at the time to do so. Comparing the America of 1960 with the America of 1980, John Schwarz found substantial improvement in conditions of poverty, health, housing, and environmental protection; he concluded that the image of generalized public sector failure in this period was a gross illusion. When Paul Peterson and associates studied the condition of intergovernmental programs in health, education, and housing around 1980, they uncovered not the bureaucratic bungling and red tape they had expected but a process of shared responsibility and cooperative accommodation among administrators at all levels of government. On examining the operation of the Social Security program at the end of the Reagan administration, Merton and Joan Bernstein concluded that the system had fewer daunting problems than was commonly supposed and was far more secure than most believed.[41]

Parallel studies have been conducted more recently as well. Benjamin Page and James Simmons, asking what government really does to correct poverty and inequality, find that Social Security programs significantly help the poor, that the national income tax lessens after-tax inequality, and that the public schools do more than most realize to give minorities a chance to advance. Jonathan Crane and associates describe nine successful social programs of government, including the nutrition and education program known as Women, Infants, and Children (WIC). An evaluation study found that when WIC-benefited babies and non-WIC babies are compared (with mothers of both covered by Medicaid), the initial birth weight of the first group is greater by an average of 51 to 117 grams. In a comprehensive study of national goal achievement, former Harvard University president Derek Bok tracked seventy-two indicators of economic, social, and safety well-being over time. Comparing the 1960s to the 1990s, he discovered improvement in fifty indicators, with no appreciable change in five. In the remaining seventeen measures a decline occurred, but Bok believes government was not in a position to prevent most of them.[42]

A fourth and final theme on the "pro" side of the debate supports bureaucracy not at the institutional level but at the individual level. Several books and articles have been written on the work of individual public administrators. Probably the first was Theodore Taylor's 1984 *Federal Public Policy*, which presents the personal stories of ten federal senior civil servants, which, Taylor holds, it is impossible to read "without being emotionally moved and mentally exhilarated." Shortly thereafter two additional works in this vein appeared. One was Howard Rosen's *Servants of the People*, which noted that most of the Nobel prizes in medicine and physiology over the previous twenty-five years had been awarded to scientists employed by or supported by the federal government. The other was Jameson Doig and Erwin Hargrove's *Leadership and Innovation*, which explores how administrators such as Gifford Pinchot, David Lilienthal, Hyman Rickover, Austin Tobin, and James Webb possessed remarkable skills both to manipulate symbols and build coalitions in behalf of public innovation.[43]

In the 1990s other scholars continued this kind of analysis. Christopher Bellavita analyzed the work of ten relatively unknown federal bureaucrats within the classic framework of "hero" and found the fit quite good, down to such steps as the call to adventure, the ordeal, and the ultimate transformation. Terry Cooper and Dale Wright conducted a biographic analysis of public servants, using the notion of "exemplary" leadership and examining the work of George Marshall, George Hartzog, and C. Everett Koop, among others. Still another organizing concept is "unsung hero," adopted by Norma Riccucci to examine the achievements of six professionals of the Senior Civil Service in such areas as cleaning up the savings-and-loan mess, helping to negotiate the end to apartheid, and bringing the U.S. government into active engagement with the AIDS crisis. Robin Bittick comments specifically on unsung heroes of the war on terrorism, discovering an unfortunate tendency to "dispose" of them emotionally after the emergency is over by harshly judging their conduct with 20/20 hindsight.[44]

Let me conclude this opening chapter on a personal but relevant note. One weekend in January 1982, my colleagues and I at Virginia Tech's Center for Public Administration and Policy met at the Federal Executive Institute in Charlottesville to compare our larger thoughts about public administration. Much to our surprise, this diverse group had much in common. A coauthored statement, the "Blacksburg Manifesto," which emerged from that meeting, then caused considerable stir in the field. In brief, the paper took the position that the American administrative state is deeply legitimate as a positive force in the society. Grounded in the American Constitution and a public-values approach to the public interest, our administrative agencies are a crucial institutional force in sustaining public norms and brokering policy amid the separation of powers. Rather than going into more detail here, I urge the reader to examine the two main volumes that stemmed from this project, *Refounding Public Administration* and *Refounding Democratic Public Administration*; they now form a significant part of the corpus of public administration literature that is supportive of government agencies. Now that I am an emeritus member of this faculty, it is an appropriate time for me to express publicly how much a privilege it was to join in dialogue with my colleagues over the years.[45]

Chapter 2 What Citizens Experience from Bureaucracy

Having reviewed the academy's *theories* about bureaucracy, let us now find out about ordinary citizens' *experiences* with it. Initially, we do this by means of citizen surveys. Later, we examine statistics on performance and accomplishment.

Surveying the Surveys

Bureaucratic transactions in a nation the size of the United States number in the millions every day and in the trillions every year. Since no human institution can be perfect, the issue in this vast quantity of interaction is not the absolute absence of inadequate transactions but their *proportionate* occurrence. The positive way to phrase the matter is to inquire into percentages of citizen encounters with bureaucracy that meet certain levels of satisfaction or desirable outcomes.

Much opinion survey research has been conducted that bears on citizen experience with bureaucracy. This work varies considerably in scope, methodology, and original purpose. Probably the earliest citizen survey on the subject was conducted by Leonard D. White, a principal founder of the field of public administration, who in 1929 published the results of a survey of 4000 residents of Chicago. One question he asked was: *"Do people generally think more highly of employment in the city hall than of employment with private corporations?"*—to which 58 percent replied in favor of private corporations. To another of White's queries—*"Have your own dealings with public employees and officials been satisfactory?"*—the response was 69 percent "yes" or equivalent.

White was struck by the difference between these two reactions. He speculated that the bad image of machine politics in Chicago accounted for the lesser reputation of City Hall employment, even though the machine's bureaucrats delivered services satisfactorily a majority of the time. Offering a summation of his results that should not have been forgotten for all these decades, White concluded "the great bulk of city officials and employees are more sinned against than sinning."[1]

Today, many students of government are, in effect, following White's lead by asking residents of communities their opinion of municipal services. In a telephone survey published in 1995, citizens of Phoenix were asked, among other questions, *"Would you say that you are very satisfied, somewhat satisfied, somewhat dissatisfied, or very dissatisfied with the overall performance of the city in providing services to Phoenix residents?"* The responses to the categories were, respectively, 15, 64, 16, and 5 percent—with those in the two positive categories totaling 79 percent.[2]

A "quality of life" survey conducted in 2003 for the State of Virginia involved telephone calls to randomly selected numbers across the state. The survey's questions included some on the quality of services received at the local level of government. Table 2-1 shows ratings given to several local public institutions, including local government as a whole. As can be seen, the combined ratings for "excellent" and "good" range from a high of 91 percent for fire departments to a low of 70 percent for public schools. The fact that local government as a whole receives a lower rating than its component institutions—about 59 percent—illustrates a phenomenon that recurs again and again in citizen surveys. Respondents tend to rate personal experiences with specific bureaucratic organizations higher than more general references to government as a whole.[3]

Local governments themselves utilize citizen surveys as a tool for monitoring their operations. Over the years, these surveys have accumulated as a body of information for others to examine. Thomas Miller and Michelle Miller analyzed the results of surveys conducted by 261 local governments located in forty states and serving a combined population of over 40 million. To allow aggregated evaluation of these data, which came from 3,000 questions asked of 215,000 citizens, they converted the average response distributions to a common measure, expressed as "percent to max" (PTM). This statistic constitutes the degree to which the responses collectively attained the highest possible point on whatever scales were used, expressed as a percentage.

Globally, Miller and Miller calculate the average adjusted PTM as 67.2 percent. This means that the average question's response was more than two-thirds of the way toward a perfect rating. The highest quartile of questions averaged 79 PTM and the lowest 56. The authors conclude that this finding "is particularly important for the administrator who hesitates to conduct a citizen survey for fear that citizens will vent their spleen on bureaucrats in city hall." They also note that this pattern parallels the positive evaluations by cit-

Table 2-1 Virginia Survey of Local Public Services (in percentages)

Ratings	Fire department	EMS service	Law enforcement	Public schools	Public library	Parks, recreation	Local government
Excellent	58.8	55.1	41.1	27.4	40.4	36.7	10.1
Good	32.7	33.0	41.6	42.6	42.6	44.6	49.2
Excellent + good combined	**91.5**	**88.1**	**82.7**	**70.0**	**83.0**	**81.3**	**59.3**
Fair	3.8	6.3	11.5	16.6	9.1	11.7	29.3
Poor	0.8	1.7	4.2	5.3	1.7	5.1	8.7
Don't know, won't say	3.9	3.9	1.7	8.0	6.1	1.9	2.8

SOURCE: Susan M. Willis-Walton and Alan E. Bayer, *Quality of Life in Virginia: 2003* (Blacksburg: Center for Survey Research, Virginia Polytechnic Institute and State University, 2003), D9–D10.

izens reported in earlier editions of this book. The average PTMs found by the two Millers for each of eight categories of community services are as follows:

Service category	PTM
Cultural and arts programs	76.7
Public safety	75.1
Parks and recreation	71.5
Public utilities	69.5
Support services	67.8
Public works and transportation	72.8
Health and human services	62.6
Planning and growth management	55.4[4]

Theodore Poister and Gary Henry conducted telephone surveys of citizen opinion regarding both public and private institutions in Georgia. In one subsample, respondents were asked to rate the quality of service experienced from these institutions on the scale of very good/good/fair/poor/very poor, without reference to whether they had interacted with the institutions personally. A second subsample was asked to rate the services only if they had recently experienced them. The outcome is shown in table 2-2, expressed in the uniform PTM units developed by Miller and Miller. As can be seen, the highest ratings exceed 80 percent, and those below 60 percent are rare. In almost all program areas, both public and private, respondents evaluate recently experienced services more favorably than was reflected in past impressions or those received from others. Another observation is that no general pattern of superiority is observable in service ratings of business over government. For recent consumers, ratings for the two sectors were essentially the same, an average of just under 74 percent. For general respondents, government averaged slightly better, 69.0 versus 67.5 percent. Poister and Henry comment, "Given the conventional wisdom about the poor quality of services provided by government and the general superiority of the private sector in delivering services, the private services included in this survey might have been expected to receive consistently higher ratings than the public services. But this was clearly not the case."[5]

Many surveys have also been conducted on citizen experiences with the federal government. The U.S. Postal Service, which received ratings in the 70s in the Georgia study—even though private carriers (UPS and FedEx) reached the 80s—has been the subject of numerous opinion polls over the years. In 1983, 1984, and 1985 the Roper organization asked a sample of citizens their opinions regarding twelve federal agencies. Each time, the Postal

Table 2-2 Georgia Survey of Public and Private Services (in PTM units)

	General respondents	Recent customers
Public		
Fire department	80.0	82.8
U.S. Postal Service	72.8	76.1
Public health clinics	70.5	74.4
Municipal trash collection	70.2	75.5
Police	70.1	71.3
Parks and recreation	66.1	77.1
Public transportation	65.1	76.6
Public schools	63.5	68.2
Street maintenance	63.0	59.2
All public	69.0	73.5
Private		
Private mail carriers	81.2	84.5
Grocery stores	75.1	77.1
Banks, savings & loans	71.2	81.7
Private doctor's offices	70.7	80.6
Fast-food restaurants	68.9	68.5
Movie theaters	67.3	75.5
Auto garages	61.2	71.7
Cable TV providers	58.2	66.2
Taxicabs	54.2	59.6
All Private	67.5	73.9

SOURCE: Theodore H. Poister and Gary T. Henry, "Citizen Ratings of Public and Private Service Quality: A Comparative Perspective," *Public Administration Review* 54, no. 2 (March/April 1994): 158.

NOTE: PTM (percent to max) units reflect degree to which collective responses attain to highest possible point on whatever measurement scales are used (see p. 25).

Service came out on top. In a 1987 Roper poll, the Postal Service was included in a comparative rating survey along with eleven categories of private institutions, the professions, and business. Its rating of 73 was topped only by supermarkets at 79. In 1999 the Associated Press sponsored a Postal Service survey in which almost three-fourths of respondents evaluated the Postal Service as doing an excellent or good job, compared to just over 60 percent five years earlier.[6]

For some years the Postal Service has sponsored its own satisfaction evaluation studies. One survey, a quarterly instrument known as the Customer Satisfaction Measurement (CSM), is administered by the Gallup organization. A summary question in the CSM asks respondents in residential households to rate the "overall performance" of the Postal Service on a scale of excellent/very good/good/fair/poor. The results for fiscal years 1999 and 2000 are shown in table 2-3. As can be seen, the ratings are quite steady over quarters. The percentages for the "excellent" and "very good" categories typically combine to the low 70s, while a summation of "excellent," "very good," and "good" tends to be in the low 90s.[7]

In 2000 the Pew Research Center published the results of a survey of service performance by five federal agencies: the Internal Revenue Service (IRS),

Table 2-3 Postal Service Customer Satisfaction Measurement (in percentages)

	Fiscal Year 1999				Fiscal Year 2000			
	1st quarter	2d quarter	3d quarter	4th quarter	1st quarter	2d quarter	3d quarter	4th quarter
Excellent	30	29	29	30	29	30	29	29
Very good	42	41	42	42	41	41	42	41
Excellent + Very good combined	**71**	**71**	**70**	**71**	**71**	**71**	**70**	**71**
Good	21	22	22	21	22	21	22	21
Excellent + Very good + Good combined	**93**	**92**	**92**	**93**	**92**	**92**	**92**	**92**
Fair	6	6	6	6	6	6	6	6

SOURCE: CSM data obtained by e-mail from Christopher Lind, U.S. Postal Service, 6 February 2001.

the Social Security Administration (SSA), the Environmental Protection Agency (EPA), the Federal Aviation Administration (FAA), and the Food and Drug Administration (FDA). The poll was unusual in that it surveyed not only ordinary citizens—for example, the recipients of Social Security and the payers of the federal income tax—but several kinds of professional and business users, such as medical professionals, business payroll officers, airplane pilots, and professional tax preparers. The respondents were asked about the extent to which they had a favorable view of the agency and of the government as a whole. Also, they were asked about the extent to which they agreed that the agency does not work too slowly, does not issue overly complex regulations, and deals with people in a courteous manner. The results are shown in table 2-4.[8]

We note that respondents in the Pew study, as in the Virginia survey, are more favorable in their views of the concrete than of the abstract—ratings are uniformly higher for the named agencies than for the government in generic terms. Another point is that the manner of bureaucrats is more favorably seen than is the substance of their actions—respondents find the bureaucrats courteous even while being impatient over the pace and complexity of their work. This distinction is noteworthy in that while an employee's personal conduct is immediately observable and open to user evaluation, a fair assessment of the factors underlying decisions and timing requires behind-the-scenes knowledge. On a mean basis, these ratings are somewhat counterintuitive; the relatively positive ratings for the FDA on speed and the IRS on complexity and courtesy might surprise many. No consistent patterns are observable between citizens and professionals.

A relatively new source for comparing the public and private sectors is the American Customer Satisfaction Index (ACSI), which is produced jointly by the University of Michigan Business School, the American Society for Quality, and the CFI Group. Developed initially for Sears, Roebuck and Co., since

Table 2-4 Users' Ratings of Five Federal Agencies (in percentages)

Agency/user group	Favorable view of agency	Favorable view of government	Agency performance: Not too slow	Agency performance: Not too complex	Agency performance: Shows courtesy
Food and Drug Administration					
Business regulatory officers	84	43	21	18	72
Medical professionals	84	45	22	23	61
Advocates	88	44	18	22	68
Chronically ill	82	58	24	19	59
Social Security Administration					
Recipients	82	44	43	32	83
Payroll taxpayers	57	47	23	19	64
Business payroll officers	77	32	45	49	77
Federal Aviation Administration					
Passengers	80	46	27	28	61
Pilots	65	25	25	21	81
Air traffic controllers	61	41	15	26	94
Business regulatory officers	71	39	21	26	88
Environmental Protection Agency					
Public	68	48	24	20	56
Business regulatory officers	52	35	24	12	61
Environmental advocates	84	68	14	30	80
Internal Revenue Service					
Taxpayers	43	42	42	21	57
Business tax officers	40	36	22	20	70
Professional tax preparers	60	41	22	18	88

SOURCE: Pew Research Center survey, *Washington Post*, 13 April 2000.

1994 it has been used on a nationwide basis to measure the degree of customer satisfaction with the quality of goods and services available to households in the private economy. It does so by means of random telephone surveys in which questions are asked on the quality expected with specific goods and services, the quality actually experienced with those goods or services, and information related to complaints and plans to continue purchasing the items. From this information, using a complex statistical model, index scores are developed for individual firms, separate industries and sectors, and the national economy as a whole. The score is on a scale of 0 to 100, with 100 indicating perfect satisfaction.

Although since 1994 ACSI scores were calculated for the Internal Revenue Service, in 1999 an index for the federal government as a whole was launched. To incorporate government into the methodology, the statistical model was modified to exclude price and repurchase variables, since they are seldom pertinent in the public sector. At the same time an outcomes measure was added. Initially, thirty-one "customer service" areas were identified; the list was later expanded to fifty-three. By 2002, thirty-nine user groups served by twenty-four agencies were being contacted, embracing 90 percent of the government's public customers. Table 2-5 shows satisfaction scores over four years by sector, attribute, and activity.[9]

With respect to sector scores, we see that the aggregate index scores for the private sector and the national economy (which combines the private and public sectors) have been quite stable over the four years, varying modestly but remaining in the low 70s. However, the federal government's score improved substantially in 2001, rising from the high 60s to the low 70s. Indeed, in the year 2001, the federal score actually exceeded that of the private sector. (For some reason the latter figure was withheld from publication in 2002.) The larger point is that, despite antigovernment rhetoric to the contrary, the federal government achieves essentially the same degree of satisfaction for its services as corporate America does for its products. Moreover, the general level of satisfaction attained is almost precisely where we would anticipate it to be from other surveys of citizen evaluation of government.

ACSI index numbers have also been produced for the federal sector with respect to confidence in government, the degree of courtesy and professionalism shown by bureaucrats, and the timeliness of their services. Confidence rose substantially over the period—a change commensurate with our hypothesis that the "thirty years war" against government subsided after 1995. The other attribute ratings are quite stable, with courtesy and professionalism substantially higher than timeliness. This differential is in keeping with the Pew survey findings reviewed earlier.

On ratings of selected activities, Social Security came out the highest, followed by veterans' medical centers, Medicare, and tax filings, in that order. We note that the SSA-IRS difference also parallels what was found in the Pew

Table 2-5 American Customer Satisfaction Index Scores (on scale of 0–100)

	1999	2000	2001	2002
Aggregates by sector				
National economy	72.1	72.9	72.0	73.1
Private sector	71.9	71.2	70.5	N/A
Federal government	68.6	68.6	71.3	70.2
Overall federal ratings				
Confidence	67	72	77	73
Courtesy	83	82	84	82
Professionalism	81	80	81	80
Timeliness	73	71	73	73
Selected federal activities				
Social Security retirement	82	84	82	83
VA outpatient services	79	78	79	79
Medicare coverage	71	74	79	76
IRS tax filings	51	56	60	62

SOURCE: Mary-Jo Hall, "The American Customer Satisfaction Index," *Public Manager* 31, no.1 (spring 2002): 23–26, 30 and the University of Michigan Business School Web site.

study. While scores for the SSA and VA are relatively constant, considerable improvement over time is reflected for both Medicare and the IRS. In the latter case, gains persisted over all four years. According to Claes Fornell, director of the ACSI, this rate of improvement has not been matched by any organization, whether private or public, in the history of the index. The fact that the Internal Revenue Service is an enforcement organization rather than a service agency makes such a feat even more remarkable.

Reflections on the Surveys

Let us now ponder the meaning of this survey of surveys regarding citizen-bureaucracy interaction. One finding that comes through loud and clear is that citizen assessments of specific, personal experiences with administrative agencies tend to be positive. This does not mean, of course, that these experiences are never bad—only that *most* are good.

As noted, the poll in Phoenix found that 79 percent of respondents stated that they are "very satisfied" or "somewhat satisfied" with local government services. In the Virginia quality-of-life survey, public safety, parks, and library services were rated "excellent" or "good" by 81 to 91 percent, and schools by 68 percent. In Miller and Miller's aggregate analysis of 3,000 survey questions asked by 261 local governments, the overall PTM was 67.2. In the Georgia study, the aggregate PTM for public services was 69 for general respondents and 73.5 for recent users. Among surveyed customers of the U.S. Postal Service, 71 percent rate the service "excellent" or "very good," and the level of positive responses rises to 92 percent if one includes just plain "good" as well. In the Pew study, 82 percent of Social Security beneficiaries had a favorable view of the agency, and in 2002 the ACSI index for the federal government was 70.

Scholars of survey research debate the meaning of such findings. Some dismiss them as gross exaggerations of the public's assessment of government, for several reasons, including biased phrasing of questions and social pressures to give upbeat responses. Another argument is that lay citizens do not have enough knowledge of bureaucracy to evaluate it accurately. Still another objection is that citizens approach government agencies with such low expectations that, when they encounter barely adequate service, they are surprised by its quality.

Survey biases can certainly exist, and in fact they may be unavoidable. For example, the simple decision to list multiple-choice responses in the order of positive to negative options may "lead" unsophisticated respondents. Still, ways of encouraging all options are possible, such as the question asked in the Virginia study: *"As you know, people have different feelings about the quality of organizations and services in their communities. Using the categories 'excellent,' 'good,' 'fair,' and 'poor,' how would you rate the quality of. . . ."* [10]

Also, we should remember that bureaucracies are not uniformly well rated. Where a positive instrument bias exists, it can be overridden if people are sufficiently unhappy. In the Miller and Miller aggregate analysis, for example, public safety received a PTM of 75, while city planning received 55. In the Georgia study, the PTM for the fire department was 80 while for street maintenance it was 63. In the Pew survey, many ratings were above 75 percent while many others were below 25 percent. In fact, some clearly negative bias was introduced in the wording of the Pew questions, such as whether the agency works too slowly or has rules that are too complicated.

Concerning the matter of having sufficient knowledge to assess a bureaucracy, certainly lay citizens do not have in-depth information about the program from which they are seeking service. As mentioned, they may be able to gauge levels of personal courtesy but not the program's inner workings. And courtesy evaluations can be high, as we saw in the Pew study. Another relevant point is that many of bureaucracy's users are not ordinary citizens but knowledgeable professionals and businesspeople who employ its services frequently. That too is accounted for in the Pew study, and its results yielded high ratings in most categories.

In the literature on polling methods, the accuracy issue is sometimes approached by comparing citizen perception scores with objective program information. One school of thought asserts there is little correlation between the two, because citizens experience at an individual level while program statistics are aggregative. Others disagree, arguing that when appropriate program information is compared, the validity of citizen observations can be shown to be quite high. In a study of police response, Stephen Percy found, for example, that when citizens were interviewed several days after calling the police, their recollections of how long it had taken the officer to get to their homes or businesses were remarkably similar to the times actually recorded.[11]

Still other commentators on this matter argue that since all indicators of program quality are socially constructed, none is "true" in an objective sense. While this may be, it can be argued that citizen evaluations, subjective or not, are nonetheless inherently important in a democracy—indeed, for government programs that serve the public, they may be what really counts. Blanche Blank and associates contend that since government's goals are inevitably multiple and conflicting, citizen surveys, in fact, offer the most manageable calculus for measuring overall goal attainment by government.[12]

As for the low-expectations argument against the validity of favorable citizen reactions to bureaucracy, it is possible to factor prior expectations into the survey process. This was explicitly done in the American Customer Satisfaction Index—and, as we saw, the overall index rating for the federal government is quite positive. Another point is that in many program areas citizens are indeed experienced in interacting with bureaucracies, because they do so continuously over time—as in mailing letters, putting out the trash, and receiving Social Security checks and Medicare reimbursements.

Two more comments on the surveys are needed. One is to reiterate our finding that when citizens are queried about specific, concrete experiences with administrative agencies, their attitudes are much more favorable than when they are asked about government in general. In the early White study, recollections of personal dealings with the city administration were superior to the reputation of Chicago's city hall. In the Virginia quality-of-life study, ratings for specific local government programs were higher than those for local government as a whole. In the Georgia survey, PTMs for citizens who had recently experienced a program were higher than those who had been selected randomly for interview. In the Pew study of federal agencies, views of the agencies themselves were higher than those for the government in general. The main point here is that the contradiction can be explained. Citizens' views of government as an abstraction are influenced by the cultural myth that government fails. Citizens' views of their individual bureaucratic experiences are, by contrast, controlled by direct experience—which tells them that government usually works.

A final reflection on the surveys also flies in the face of conventional wisdom in America. This is the radical idea that performance in the private sector is not necessarily superior to that in government. We noted that the principal finding of the Georgia study is that PTMs for publicly-provided and privately-rendered services are not much different, either individually or in the aggregate. Moreover, a main point to be taken from the ACSI data is that calculations of consumer satisfaction with the federal government are very close to those encountered in the private economy. In fact, for the most recent year for which data are available, the government's score actually exceeded that of the private sector slightly. We return to this subject shortly, when we examine some private-public comparisons of productivity, and in chapter 3 the topic is taken up again when the extensive literature comparing the two sectors' efficiency is reviewed.

Direct Performance Measures

We now turn to some nonsurvey statistical data on how well government works. Measures are available in two program areas for which we have citizen survey data, the Postal Service and Social Security. As Percy did for police response times, we will see whether citizen perceptions parallel how program statistics portray these bureaucracies. We recall that in the Georgia study the Postal Service's PTM was 76.1 for recent customers, and that the Postal Service's own CSM typically posted 92 percent of customers as satisfied to some degree. As for Social Security, in the Pew study 82 percent of recipients had favorable views of the agency, and 83 percent approved of its courtesy.

Every business day, 7 million American residents visit the U.S. Postal Service's 38,000 post offices, stations, and branches. Each year, the system handles in excess of 200 billion pieces of mail, approximately 40 percent of the world's total. With a total revenue of $65 billion per annum and over 800,000 career employees, the Postal Service ranks 26th in *Fortune* magazine's "Global 500," one place ahead of another communications giant, AT&T.[13]

Over the years the Postal Service has hired outside companies to evaluate various aspects of its performance in handling this tremendous volume of business. Timely delivery of the mail is monitored by the auditing firm PricewaterhouseCoopers, using unmarked test mailings in scores of cities across the country. Average percentages of successful on-time delivery of local (mainly intracity) mail were 91 in 1996, 92 in 1997, and 93 in 1998. Percentages for longer hauls tend to be in the 80s.[14]

In another postal study, Chilton Research Service was hired to record what happened, mail-wise, in 5300 households picked randomly across the country. The percentage of mail considered to have arrived late was 1.4 in 1988, 1.2 in 1989, and 1.0 in 1990. In still another study, customer waiting times in post offices were observed. The waiting time was five minutes or less in 83 percent of the 1,440 test observations, a finding that agrees with a study I had done some years earlier.[15]

A test of the accuracy of transactions performed by postal clerks was also carried out, using confederates. Three-fourths of the clerical actions were judged correct, with many of the incorrect decisions the consequence of attempting to err on the side of customer convenience, for example, by accepting undersized letters or poorly wrapped packages. The General Accounting Office also conducted a study of postage error rates, and found that on only 4.6 percent of a sample of 5,925 letters and packages was the wrong postage charged. In over half of these cases, the error was not the clerk's fault but the customer's, for example, in affixing too many stamps to the piece of mail.[16]

Turning now to the Social Security Administration, the Dalbar Financial Services firm of Boston has developed data of interest with respect to the way corporations treat their customers on the telephone. By placing test calls to the organizations and then evaluating the responses, Dalbar evaluated five aspects of the calling experience:

1. *attitude*, or tone of voice and level of professionalism shown by the answering representative;
2. *accommodation*, or the representative's effort to respond to the caller's inquiry or supply more information;
3. *knowledge*, defined as the representative's ability to respond in a clear and confident manner;
4. *ring time*, i.e., the number of seconds that elapse before the call is answered; and
5. *queue time*, the number of seconds that elapse from the time the call is answered until the automated response menu turns off and a real person comes on the line.

Dalbar scored the first three criteria on a scale of 3 for excellent, 2 for average, and 1 for inferior; outcomes for ring and queue time were expressed as average number of seconds.

In 1995 Dalbar issued a report on the outcome of telephone evaluations for nine organizations: the Social Security Administration, AT&T Universal Credit Cards, the Disney Companies, Federal Express, L.L. Bean, Nordstrom, the Saturn Corporation, Southwest Airlines, and Xerox. In a conclusion that probably surprised many, Social Security did very well, even in such company—it was rated first among the nine on accommodation, knowledge, and ring time, and second for attitude, just behind Southwest Airlines. The agency's combined score was 2.38, the highest in the group, with ring time a mere 3.94 seconds. The one fly in the ointment was queue time—it was a disastrous 482.2 seconds (about eight minutes), putting Social Security at the bottom rank in that category.[17]

Another surprise comes from a study on federal regulation released by the Office of Management and Budget in 2003. In its annual report on regulatory costs and benefits to state and local governments and business, OMB stated that for the 1992–2002 decade, monetized health and social benefits of 107 rules and unfunded mandates outweighed their costs by three to five times (see table 2-6).[18] This finding astonished both conservative and liberal interest groups, in that a similar report the previous year had showed the two about the same. OMB explained that it had previously left out the beneficial effect of sulfur dioxide limits designed to curb acid rain that were contained in the 1990 amendments to the Clean Air Act. Also, it had mistakenly added $20 billion in costs generated by ambient air quality standards for ozone and particulate matter. While technically these data measure the performance of rules and not of organizations, agencies administered them and hence deserve some of the credit.

We look now to program statistics for two mammoth eligibility programs, food stamps and unemployment insurance. How are their needy clients treated?

The federally financed, state-administered food stamp program is the largest single feeding enterprise in the world. It affects 25 to 30 million

Table 2-6 Estimated Annual Benefits and Costs of Major Federal Rules, 1992–2002 (in millions of dollars)

Agency	Benefits	Costs
Environmental Protection Agency	120,753–193,163	23,359–26,604
Health and Human Services	9,129–11,710	3,165–3,334
Department of Transportation	6,144–9,456	4,220–6,718
Department of Agriculture	3,094–6,176	1,643–1,672
Department of Energy	4,700–4,768	2,472
Department of Labor	1,804–4,185	1,056
Department of Education	655–813	361–610
Housing and Urban Development	511–625	348
Total	146,812–230,896	36,625–42,813

SOURCE: Office of Management and Budget, "Informing Regulatory Decisions: 2003 Report to Congress on the Costs and Benefits of Federal Regulations and Unfunded Mandates on State, Local, and Tribal Entities," September 2003, Table 2, p. 7, available at www.whitehouse.gov/omb/inforeg/regpol-reports_congress.html.

people a year, at a cost in excess of $15 billion. Millions of eligibility decisions are made every month by food stamp workers. By means of sample audits and state data, error rates are regularly calculated on these actions. On a national weighted basis for the 1999 fiscal year, errors in underissuance of stamps—that is, denying rightful eligibility—constituted 2.85 percent of dollar volume. Overpayments, or granting eligibility when it was incorrect to do so, amounted to 7.01 percent. In other words, mistakes were proportionately low, and they were more often in favor of clients than against them.[19]

Unemployment insurance is another state-run, federally directed program, which in 1999 dispensed more than $19 billion in cash payments to the unemployed, taken from taxes levied on employers. The cost of administering the program was 4 cents per dollar of unemployment taxes received and 7 cents per dollar of benefit payments made. Error sampling indicates that, for 1999, underpayments to the unemployed, on a national dollar-volume basis, amounted to .9 percent, while overpayments were ten times as much, 9.2 percent. We notice once again the discrepancy between overgenerosity and wrongful denial of benefits. It is also noteworthy that when the source of overpayment errors is analyzed, state employment bureaucracies were responsible for only 20 percent in dollar volume, with the rest caused by claimants and businesses or a combination of the two. A final performance statistic relates to timeliness: 87 percent of first-time payments to in-state applicants and 70 percent to out-of-state applicants were mailed within three weeks.[20]

We examine finally a direct performance measure that concerns not just individual bureaucracies but the federal government as a whole. A Federal Productivity Index (FPI) was maintained by the Bureau of Labor Statistics (BLS) for more than a quarter-century. It was begun in 1967 and terminated in 1994 because of budget cuts. Hence its numbers are of value not for present-day relevance, but for the patterns of change they show over several decades.

The index was conceived as a measure of output-per-employee-year and was calculated by counting the number of full-time employees needed to carry out specified tasks. At its maturity, the FPI covered some sixty agencies, 2,500 program outputs, and 69 percent of the federal civilian workforce. Examples of types of measured output were numbers of transactions completed, numbers of loans approved, and numbers of inspections conducted. In addition to an overall annual federal productivity statistic, individual indexes were calculated for twenty-four functions of the government.[21]

Table 2-7 shows the index figures for the total government over the entire series at five-year intervals. Fiscal year 1967 is the baseline for the index. When measured output rises faster than full-time-equivalent (FTE) employment, productivity defined as output-per-employee-year goes up. As can be seen, over all five-year periods, federal productivity did increase. This was the combined result of improvements in the factors of technology, capital investment, capital utilization, office design, workforce skills, managerial capability, and statutes and regulations. The four top program areas in terms of

Table 2-7 Federal Productivity Indexes, 1967–1994

Fiscal year	Output	Employment	Output per employee year
1967	100.0	100.0	100.0
1972	109.1	102.5	106.3
1977	115.8	100.1	115.5
1982	126.0	100.4	125.5
1987	140.6	107.6	130.5
1992	144.6	109.7	131.6
1994	147.1	109.4	134.3

SOURCE: Donald Fisk and Darlene Forte, "The Federal Productivity Measure Program: Final Results," *Monthly Labor Review* 120 (May 1997): 19–28.

productivity increases over the history of the measure were finance and accounting, library services, regulatory rulemaking, and social services.

As can be seen, over the 1967–1994 period, federal productivity advanced beyond the 100 baseline by 34.3 percent. The average annual growth rate was 1.1 percent. Between 1967 and 1982 the rate was considerably faster, at 1.5 percent, but after 1982 it slowed to .6 percent. The methodology of this index differs in many ways from how productivity is calculated for the national economy, but it is interesting to note that in 1967–1982 nonfarm business productivity grew annually by 1.4 percent, a bit less than government productivity, while in 1982–1994 it advanced twice as fast, at 1.3 percent.

The BLS also developed partial productivity indexes for selected state and local government functions, launched at different points in time. Of the eleven indexes calculated, three are shown in table 2-8. They are of particular interest because they offer comparisons with indexes for the private sector in provision of the same services.[22]

Table 2-8 Public and Private Productivity Indexes, 1967–1992

	Electric power utilities		Natural gas utilities		Alcoholic beverage sales	
Year	State-local government	Investor-cooperative	Local government	Investor-owned	State government	Private sector
1967	100.0	100.0				
1972	137.7	131.5			100.0	100.0
1974			100.0	100.0		
1977	159.0	153.7	93.2	98.1	115.3	99.3
1982	154.8	137.3	90.9	87.3	121.6	107.2
1987	153.8	154.3	78.5	70.6	119.2	106.3
1992	166.2	176.4	75.1	66.9	119.8	120.1
Average annual rate of change	+2.1	+2.3	−1.6	−2.2	+0.09	+0.09

SOURCE: U.S. Department of Labor, Bureau of Labor Statistics, *Measuring State and Local Government Labor Productivity: Examples from Eleven Services,* Bulletin 2495 (June 1998): 43, 49, 87.

NOTE: Baseline date for natural gas utilities is 1974; otherwise, data are presented in five-year intervals.

Again the public-private differences are enlightening. We see that state and local electric utilities tended to advance faster in productivity growth than did investor-owned or cooperatively-owned utilities up into the 1980s, when they were surpassed by their private counterparts. Overall for the 1967–1992 period, they ended up some 10 points behind the private utilities, showing an average gain for the whole period of 2.1 percent, slightly below the private sector's 2.3. With respect to natural gas, substantial productivity declines are shown over time for both sectors, but government's rate of decline was substantially less than that of investor-owned utilities. As for alcoholic beverage sales, public-sector productivity grew faster than the private sector in the 1970s and 1980s, but the private liquor business drew even in the 1990s.

In conclusion, we find that many direct measures of performance cast quite a favorable light on bureaucracy, as was the case with citizen satisfaction surveys. The Postal Service and Social Security Administration, well-regarded by citizens, seem to deserve these evaluations in performance terms. A high proportion of the mail is delivered on time; postal clerks are usually accurate in their decisions and typically do not make customers wait long. In most areas of phone conduct, the SSA outdoes many well-known and prestigious corporations; Social Security phone representatives rate high on courtesy and responsiveness although their overloaded phone systems create lengthy holds. Eligibility workers in the food stamp and unemployment insurance programs make correct determinations more than 90 percent of the time, and when errors do occur, far more are in favor of claimants than against them. The initial processing of unemployment claims is efficient to the degree that most first checks are mailed in three weeks. With respect to its overall productivity over a quarter-century, the federal government has posted impressive and steady gains, averaging 1.1 percent growth per year, not greatly different from that of the private sector. Productivity increases—particularly in finance, accounting, and social services—have no doubt saved taxpayers many dollars. When productivity gains of government and private utilities and beverage outlets are compared, the two sectors are exceedingly close.

Accomplishments of America

We conclude our discussion of what citizens experience from bureaucracy by noting some of the achievements that have been made in recent years with respect to economic, social, and environmental conditions in the country. Others' writings on this point were mentioned in the pro-bureaucracy literature covered in chapter 1. These achievements are not accomplished by bureaucracy alone, however, but by the United States as a whole. The reason I put it this way is that while the work of bureaucracy can be crucial to social progress, individual improvements are often influenced by other institutions and forces active in the society as well. Needless to say, policy intervention to improve conditions in any society is a complex and unpredictable business.

Plans to meet goals or solve problems by even the best bureaucracies are at best educated guesses. In fact, few policy problems are ever completely "solved" in a final sense.

To prepare successive editions of *The Case for Bureaucracy* over the decades, I have been in the habit of clipping from the newspapers on a daily basis. Beginning with the mid-1990s, I began to notice, with increasing frequency, articles that report statistics showing significant and often surprising improvement in various aspects of the quality of American life. Table 2-9 summarizes some of the trends I encountered in my clippings. Notably, the data for these gains (1) cover a wide range of problem areas, (2) run counter to cynical thinking that government action can lead to no good, and (3) all take place within a narrow span of years, in the late twentieth and early twenty-first centuries.[23]

Throughout this information we see significant, if incremental improvement. This is so in the quality of the air we breathe and of the water in which we swim, as well as in the safety of our streets, roads, and places of work. Fewer babies die, people live longer, and smoking and the incidence of some cancers are down. There is less hunger, teen-age pregnancy is diminished, and fewer teens die before their time. Growth in the prison population and in wetlands destruction is lower, and fewer animal and plant species are in danger. For several years the poverty rate declined, although that trend was unfortunately reversed more recently as the result of an uneven economy.

These statistics have real meaning for real people. The lives of millions of Americans have been made markedly better as a result. At the same time, of course, any rate of progress on serious social problems can never be enough, not even where it is greatest. It is regrettable that the rate of improvement is often lower for members of racial and ethnic minorities than for the white population. Moreover, in many areas of social need, little or no headway is being made. Yet, overall, *a substantial spread of notable socioeconomic progress has been made by America*, particularly in the past two or three decades.

As mentioned, bureaucracy is not the only source of this accomplishment. Elected officials are responsible for initiating and funding programs, and much implementation of public policy is carried out not by government at all but by private parties. Yet government agencies are often at the center of it all. It is in bureaucracy that all the necessary elements for collective social action are brought together—legal authority, public resources, professional expertise, institutional knowledge, and a sense of mission in behalf of all citizens. Moreover, bureaucracies are not just passive implementers but social and political advocates for their missions. The Environmental Protection Agency, to a degree that is dependent on the administration in power, presses for compliance with the standards of the Clean Air and Clean Water Acts. The Fish and Wildlife Service urges developers to save habitat for endangered species. Police departments of the nation seek out more tools and resources to fight crime. The National Highway Traffic Safety Administration and the

Table 2-9 Accomplishments of America

Environmental protection:

- Between 1988 and 2001, the poundage of chemical toxins released by industry dropped by 54.5 percent. In 2000–2001 alone, the reduction was 1,052 million pounds.
- Between 1991 and 2000, lead levels in the air declined by 50 percent, carbon monoxide by 41 percent, sulfur dioxide by 37 percent, and nitrogen dioxide by 11 percent. Since 1988, the total poundage of toxic chemicals released by industry has dropped 55 percent.
- By 1995 the incidence of smog had dropped to about one-third of its 1970 level, despite the fact that 85 percent more cars were on the road.
- Whereas in 1972 only a third of all bodies of water in the United States were safe for fishing and swimming, by 1995 almost two-thirds were safe.
- Between 1986 and 1997 the annual loss of wetlands to development was 58,500 acres, or 80 percent less than the rate in the previous decade.
- In 1998 some twenty-nine formerly threatened animals and plants were scheduled for removal from the Fish and Wildlife Service's endangered list, including the bald eagle.

Public safety:

- The number of victims of violent crimes other than murder dropped from 50 per 1,000 residents in 1993 to 23 in 2002. For property crimes, the rate declined from 319 to 159 per 1,000 residents.
- In 2000 the murder rate dropped to its lowest point in thirty-five years. The number of homicides recorded in New York City decreased from 2,262 in 1992 to 756 in 1997.
- In 2000 the total prison population registered its lowest growth rate since 1972. Thirteen states, including New York and Texas, had fewer prisoners than the year before.
- The number of motor vehicle deaths per 100,000 population declined from 26.8 in 1970 to 15.1 in 1999. In 2000 the number of boating deaths hit a forty-year low.
- The number of workers killed on the job dropped by 11 percent between 1997 and 2002. Workplace homicides also declined.

Health and welfare:

- The infant mortality rate declined from 8.9 deaths per 1,000 live births in 1990 to 6.9 in 1999. The mortality rate for infants under 3.3 pounds dropped by 8 percent in 1965–1999.
- Life expectancy for persons born in 2000 is 76.9 years, compared to 68.2 years for those born in 1950. Fewer than 25 percent of adults smoked in 2000, compared to over 45 percent in 1965.
- During the 1990s the incidence of prostate cancer dropped by 5.1 percent and that of colon cancer by .7 percent, although the incidence of breast cancer increased by 1.2 percent.
- The poverty rate declined from 11.8 percent in 1999 to 11.3 percent in 2000, the lowest point since 1974. The recession and unemployment brought the rate back up to 12.1 by 2002.
- The number of families with at least one member hungry during the year dropped from about 4 million in 1995 to about 3 million in 1999.

Child well-being:

- Teen pregnancy dropped from a high of 37 per 1,000 girls in 1990 to 27 per 1,000 in 2000, a twenty-year low. The percentage of teens who declared themselves virgins rose from 46 in 1991 to 54 in 2001.
- The percentage of tenth-graders who had smoked in the previous month dropped from 30.4 percent in 1996 to 21.3 percent in 2001. For eighth-graders, the drop was from 21.0 to 12.2 percent.
- The percentage of children living in extreme poverty declined from 9.9 in 1992 to 6.4 in 1999. In 1999, 54 percent of children were read to daily; in 2000, this was the case for 58 percent.
- The rate of serious, violent crimes involving youths aged 12–17 dropped from 39 per 1,000 in 1990 to 26 per 1,000 in 1999.
- Deaths of teenagers by accident, homicide, and suicide went down by 24 percent between 1990 and 1999.

Occupational Safety and Health Administration advocate highway and workplace safety. The National Institutes of Health and Centers for Disease Control and Prevention promote medical research and good health practices, as do the tens of thousands of public health departments and public schools throughout the United States. Unlike the policy-making activity of elected officials, this work by bureaucrats is undramatic, hidden, ongoing, and persistent. It is through bureaucracy, directly or indirectly, that much of America's collective action takes place. Without it, our nation's widespread accomplishments in recent decades would not have been achieved.[24]

Chapter 3 More Bureaucracy Myths to Delete

This chapter takes on four myths about American bureaucracy. I use the word *myth* for common misconceptions that are accepted uncritically, not legends that tell fundamental truths. The myths to be considered and disproven here include (1) the implicit assumption that all bureaucracies are the same; (2) the suspicion that bureaucracy is a middle-class institution that is biased against minorities and the poor; (3) the notion, previously discussed, that the private sector is more efficient than the public sector; and (4) the idea that bureaucracy is not innovative and fights change.

The Myth of Determinism

A "determinist" view of bureaucracy is one that claims this form of organization will always behave in essentially the same way. The reasoning is that its characteristics—hierarchy, rules, specialization—dictate that result.

In chapter 1 we reviewed many of the theories underlying this determinist point of view. These theories are generally deductive, and they spring from projected, extreme consequences of Weber's model of bureaucracy. As noted at the beginning of this book, my definition of *bureaucracy* does not necessarily equate to this sociological model. Instead, I simply apply that term to all public administration institutions in the United States, whether they adhere to the Weberian model or depart from it.

In any case, we are presented with a viewpoint that is common in academic and popular discourse: all bureaucracies are bad, and they are bad in the same essential ways. This is a mindset that dismisses bureaucracy outright and categorically, regarding it not as a set of highly varied, "real" institutions, but as an abstract, homogeneous evil. But do all bureaucracies in fact exhibit the traits that the anti-bureaucracy theorists of chapter 1 predict? Are they invariably authoritarian, inflexible, preoccupied with rules and channels, and likely to be incomprehensible and degrading to clients?

Let's test the matter empirically, by means of a conscious method: examining how multiple bureaucracies with comparable structures and functions actually behave. If the determinist theories are right, bureaucracies possessing the same structures and performing the same functions should behave roughly the same. The first step in our test is to look at a series of available studies in which, in each case, the investigator examined two examples of the same kind of bureaucracy. You might call them "twin" studies. Each identical twin is definitely Weberian in structure. They should, then, each show the same dark characteristics predetermined by that structure.

Our first "twin" research project is a comparison of two air force wings carried out by James Thompson. Both military units operated under the same regulations, directives, and tables of organization; they reported to the same headquarters and were comparable in equipment, personnel, age, and mission. Yet Thompson found the two units to be extremely different in frequency of internal communication, the arrangement of true power hierarchies, and even whether command-staff or functional control channels were favored. "Despite its many characteristics of 'bureaucracy' in the technical sense of that term," Thompson concluded, "the roles in an Air Force wing are not completely standardized."[1]

Another study, by James Price, examined ways in which new scientific knowledge was absorbed by two wildlife management agencies of the same state, Oregon. The Fish Commission and the Game Commission of that state were agencies of similar size, related jurisdiction, and comparable organization. They even had in common a specific program, fish propagation. In making use of newly discovered knowledge of natural spawning methods, however, the organizations differed sharply. Hatchery workers in the Fish Commission resisted change because of antipathy toward the biologists in their organization. In the Game Commission, by contrast, a close bond existed between hatchery personnel and biologists, and the new knowledge was quickly absorbed.[2]

Still another comparative study, conducted by William Turcotte, involved two state liquor agencies. Both organizations ran statewide wholesale and retail operations; hence, they possessed an identical mission. Yet they contrasted sharply in behavioral terms. Whereas one agency was politicized, loosely run, and characterized by store autonomy, the other employed the latest managerial techniques of integrated control, planning, and accounting. The latter's operating expenses as a percentage of sales were a fraction of the former's, and its profits per employee were almost double.[3]

A final twin organizational study is Tana Pesso's examination of two intake units, comparable in size and structure, of the Massachusetts Department of Public Welfare. After observing them directly for two months, Pesso found that in one office the intake clerks dealt with applicants in an abrupt, impersonal manner, while in the other clients were handled in a helpful and sympathetic way. Whereas in the first office, workers called clients from the waiting room with a shout, in the second they were summoned quietly and politely. Interviews were conducted impersonally and without privacy in the former unit; in the latter they were carried out informally with the door closed. Also, workers in the second office explained more fully the documents that had to be signed and made themselves more easily accessible to telephone calls and subsequent visits from the clients.[4]

To sum up, the paired air force wings, wildlife commissions, state liquor agencies, and welfare intake units operated in radically different ways despite their formal organizational similarities. In the Thompson study, two different power systems were encountered. In the Price study, two entirely different learning capabilities were found. Turcotte discovered a political culture in one ABC store and a managerial culture in the other. Pesso reported demeaning treatment of clients in one welfare office and humane treatment in the other. In short, the notion of one single, homogeneous "bureaucracy" failed the test.

We turn now to a second kind of comparative empirical investigation. Here, the method is not to control for type of structure but for category of functional activity. That is, we examine many organizations in selected behavioral areas where uniform conduct of a "bureaucratic" nature is particularly expected. The studies were done by none other than your author, back in his distant youth. Both comparative examinations are in the area of welfare bureaucracy—a type of which theorists opposed to bureaucracy are particularly suspicious.

The first locus of study is the welfare waiting room. Theorists of bureaucracy and urban service delivery who discuss this physical space tend to depict it as, at best, a dreary antechamber, and at worst, a scene of degradation and mortification. The welfare client is seen as a powerless individual with zero prestige whose entrance to the system is callously manipulated. Welfare officials are expected to flaunt their superior power and status, and they are presented as capable of driving away applicants in order to reduce workload and expenditures. Given these theories, how could one expect more than joyless or even hostile welfare reception areas?[5]

I decided to study the subject by personally visiting twenty-eight welfare office waiting rooms in some fourteen communities across the United States. These offices were located from coast to coast, in both North and South, and in large cities as well as small and medium-size towns. My sample included, in approximately equal proportions, offices for Social Security, AFDC and food stamps, and unemployment compensation.[6]

I entered each waiting room unannounced, as if a first-time client, and sat quietly in a reception chair or waited in line, depending on what seemed appropriate. Without actually engaging in transactions with workers, I observed the scene for some time and inconspicuously took notes. What struck me as the project unfolded were the extreme differences between the various rooms. Instead of being consistently dreary or Kafkaesque, the chambers were highly differentiated along several dimensions. In order to make sense of the differences, I worked out a set of metaphorical categories.

"Dog kennel" rooms were characterized by a labyrinthine layout of rooms and hallways. They imparted a sense of crowdedness and projected a coercive and suppressive atmosphere by means of armed guards and threatening signs. A second type, "pool hall," was distinguished by large, open space, empty drabness, and a disinterested, rather than coercive, atmosphere. Clients were ignored more than threatened. "Business office," a third group, displayed blandness of decor and an air of efficiency, much like a commercial establishment.

Still another type, "bank lobby," was impressive, even sumptuous, in both exterior façade and interior appointments. It displayed color accents in decorator hues—burnt orange was a favorite—and contained mood cues stressing physical security. A final category, "circus tent," was full of color, commotion, and animated conversation. Even some degree of institutional "heart" was evident, such as posters urging courteous conduct and offers of help for various personal problems. In short, not only were the five categories of waiting rooms greatly different from one another, but the last three are hardly what we would expect from theories that anticipate welfare bureaucracy to be authoritarian, passionless, and degrading.

In a second comparative study of bureaucracy, I persuaded three doctoral students to join me in conducting a systematic examination of the texts of forms distributed by various state government agencies. One category of these consisted of the application forms and instructions handed out by state welfare departments for those seeking Aid to Families with Dependent Children (AFDC), a program now abolished because of welfare reform. We wrote to all fifty state welfare departments for copies of their forms. All but six sent them, and we set out to study these on a systematic basis by developing criteria for evaluating their "communication effectiveness" and "tone of voice." The first concept concerned the readability, clarity, and usability of the form, while the second had to do with the presence or absence of ten identified expressions of a negative or positive character, for example warnings against fraud or statements of rights.[7]

The various AFDC forms differed greatly. Some presented material illogically, used legalistic language, were written at a difficult (12th grade) level, and emphasized penalties and prohibitions. Others, however, provided clear instructions, registered low readability index scores, used courteous language, and included references to antidiscrimination and pro-privacy policies. To appreciate the contrasts in tone, note the following opening sentences in the instructions:

- *Notice:* The law provides for a fine of up to $500 or imprisonment up to 6 months for anyone who obtains or attempts to obtain public assistance by deliberately withholding information or giving false information. (Delaware)
- You must fill out this form so that we can determine if you are eligible for assistance or not. (Michigan)
- The following is a statement of facts about your situation. Please read each question carefully and answer each one. (Washington)
- You may have a friend, relative, minister, employer, agency worker, or anyone of your choice help you complete this form. (Kansas)
- If you and the people who live with you have little or no income right now, you may be eligible to receive food stamps within a few days. (New Mexico)
- Under Minnesota's Data Privacy Act, you have the right to know why the information we request is needed and how it will be used. (Minnesota)
- I am in need of money for ___ (number) adults and ___ (number) children. (Maryland)

In all cases the forms had to cover certain minimum matters, such as degree of need, family eligibility, application procedures, and legal and privacy requirements. The interesting point here is how the sentences differed in what values they stressed, in substantive emphasis, and in linguistic style. Once again, multiplicity and contrast prevail in that supposedly predetermined, homogeneous monolith, "bureaucracy."

The Myth of Discrimination

A second myth about bureaucracy is that public administrative agencies are middle-class institutions that must be biased against the poor and minorities. As such, they are suspected of being ready to discriminate against these groups, an assumption attractive for liberals who are sympathetic to the less fortunate but not to bureaucracy. The overworked "street level" bureaucrat, mentioned in chapter 1, is pictured as an individual who categorizes poor people as "difficult cases" that must be given secondary attention when allocating precious resources and prioritizing tasks. A cultural clash between intolerant bureaucrats and hostile clients takes place, resulting in hostile treatment of the less fortunate in general and minority residents of the inner city in particular. This idea's credibility is affirmed by poll results that show service-satisfaction ratings as much as 10 to 20 percent lower among minority citizens and residents of poor neighborhoods than among white residents of higher-income areas.[8]

A large body of research has been done to test the discrimination hypothesis. This was accomplished by comparing the quality of public works and public services provided to rich and poor in a number of American cities. In Oakland, California, research by Frank Levy, Arnold Meltsner, and Aaron Wildavsky found that street improvements were not allocated by whether neighborhoods were rich or poor or even in response to a pork-barrel process. Instead, decisions were made by engineers in accordance with professional standards intended to meet the specific objectives of improved traffic circulation and increased motorist safety. Along similar lines, Kenneth Mladenka found in Chicago that citizen requests for new traffic signals or stop signs were handled not by the criterion of whether the wards concerned were black or white, but according to professional decision rules based on accident rates, traffic volume, and the location of elementary schools. Mladenka found a similar situation with respect to street improvements in Chicago.[9]

Another conclusion of the empirical studies was that the condition of the public works infrastructure in poor neighborhoods was sometimes inferior, a difference usually accounted for by its age. In a study of Houston's streets by George Antunes and John Plumlee, it was discovered that streets in black neighborhoods were not appreciably rougher than those in white areas but were more likely to be dirty and to have open ditches instead of storm sewers. When developers built new neighborhoods, they were required to install modern sewer systems, but these neighborhoods tended to be occupied by whites. Yes, discrimination took place, but it was a consequence of the past conditions, not the intention of present-day administrators. Such "institutional" discrimination was a frequent finding of the studies.[10]

Other studies reported a mix of differential consequences. In Tuscaloosa, Alabama, Philip Coulter found inequity with respect to paved versus unpaved streets, but it did not correspond with predominantly white or black census tracts. Random counts of streetlights did show a significant statistical relationship to minority-occupied census tracts, but the patterns were inconsistent: African Americans had fewer lights per mile of street outside their homes but more lights per capita. In a later Tuscaloosa study, Coulter found somewhat more streetlights near valuable (and usually white-owned) properties, but more fire hydrants near concentrations of wooden buildings (often in black neighborhoods).[11]

Some studies discovered a reverse effect whereby the poor were benefited, albeit not intentionally. In San Antonio, Texas, Robert Lineberry discovered that proximity to fire stations, public libraries, and city parks was greater in low-income parts of the city because these facilities had been built before suburban expansion. Lineberry also found that property tax assessments as a percentage of housing value were actually higher in higher-income neighborhoods, probably because assessments there had been more recently calculated. Water mains were discovered to be of smaller diameter in poor sections of the city, but they had been laid in an earlier era, when engineering standards were lower.[12]

With respect to public services, some differentials could be accounted for by differences in demand levels. Kenneth Mladenka noted in Houston that branch libraries in higher-income neighborhoods contained more books, had more librarians, spent more money, and hired more qualified personnel. This inequity appeared to stem from the practice of allocating library resources among branches according to circulation figures, which were higher in middle-class parts of the city. A similar phenomenon was encountered in Oakland.[13]

In refuse collection, service quality exhibited differences, but, again, demand levels and the physical nature of the neighborhood accounted for most of them. Coulter observed that more litter remained uncollected in black sections of Tuscaloosa—a conclusion arrived at by studying photographs—but responses to complaints about garbage pickup there were deemed better. Mladenka noted that whereas black wards of Chicago had fewer refuse trucks assigned to them, the difference disappeared when level of homeownership was held constant—private haulers collect refuse from large apartment dwellings, which disproportionately house African Americans. In a study of Detroit, Bryan Jones also found more trash trucks operating in better neighborhoods, but those areas generated more trash. Jones noted, too, that environmental enforcement (e.g., cutting weeds in vacant lots and towing away abandoned cars) took place disproportionately in high-income areas of Detroit, from which more complaints were received.[14]

As for public schools, service differentials were bipolar. Mladenka noted that predominantly white schools in Chicago had the most-experienced and best-educated teachers, while minority schools ranked first on teacher-pupil ratios because of special education programs. Levy and associates found an almost identical situation in Oakland, with the result that the distribution of education dollars among income and racial groups formed a U shape, with the richest and poorest areas both benefiting over those in between.[15]

On the sensitive subject of police behavior, Lineberry discovered similarly disproportionate allocations of San Antonio's patrol personnel—exhibiting the same U pattern—among predominantly white areas and predominantly minority districts. A study by David Cingranelli of per capita expenditures for police and fire services in Boston found higher expenditures in black neighborhoods than white, although he argues that the differential was not sufficient to compensate for their higher crime rates and more fires.[16]

In a study of grants to welfare clients in a large metropolitan public assistance agency, Naomi Kroeger found no significant differences by age or education, although African Americans and Hispanics received slightly larger grants than whites. In a study of waiting times in the emergency departments of public hospitals in Cook County, Illinois, Barry Schwartz found that black patients were required to wait more than twice as long as white patients when their cases were not urgent and the department was very busy. For true emergencies and under lower-volume conditions, however, Schwartz found that race made no significant difference.[17]

In sum, the evidence that emerged from the studies did find differences in provision of services to rich and poor, but these differences were not necessarily reflective of intentional discrimination by the bureaucrats. Rather, they were a consequence of historical patterns of racial segregation, current patterns of income segregation, the physical nature of neighborhoods, and varied patterns of service demand. Some discriminatory effects were the result of one of these factors plus compensatory actions for the poor, creating reverse discrimination and bipolar favoritism. On the whole, the bureaucrats followed professional criteria in making decisions based on defensible logic. They operated within constraints established by conditions inherited from the past and demand patterns operating in the present. The result was not perfection according to some ideal. Clearly the bureaucrats were not social reformers—but neither were they elitists or bigots.

The Business-Is-Better Myth

If liberals are fond of believing that bureaucracy discriminates against racial minorities and the poor, conservatives never stop insisting that business invariably performs better than government. Indeed, as Julia Beckett has noted, the "government should run like a business" phrase has attained nothing short of mantra status in our pro-corporate culture and market-oriented world. It is so much a part of conventional wisdom that to question the notion out loud in polite company invites laughter if not ridicule.[18]

This mantra is an outgrowth of two beliefs, taken in combination. One is that bureaucracy is a bad if not terrible performer. The other is that private businesses must be good performers, or they would not stay in business. The economic critique of bureaucracy includes, but is not limited to, allegations of its relative incompetence, inefficiency, unresponsiveness, and inflexibility. These expectations are a natural ally to ideological dislike of big government, high taxes, and regulation of business.

As we saw in chapter 1, conservative theorists produce well-developed arguments for why bureaucracy cannot perform well, centered on what might be called its lack of "market exposure." Few, if any, incentives are said to exist to reduce costs, increase productivity, or make a product or service that people actually want. Public bureaucracy operates on appropriations rather than earned income, but bureaucrats can always invent reasons for needing more. Hence budget maximization rather than economic efficiency is the outcome. Moreover, government is a monopolist without competitors, so it has no reason to be efficient or to satisfy customers. Without the necessity of beating out competitors or pleasing customers and investors, those in charge of bureaucracies need only survive, promote expansion for its own sake, and appease important political constituencies.

This "business is better" assumption is also related to the effects of legalistic authority and political intervention found in the public sector. Government imposes too many external restrictions and accountability channels on its managers and workers, it is said. As a result, bureaucrats have less autonomy, flexibility, and motivation than business entrepreneurs. The lack of clear, consistent, and quantifiable goals means leaders in government have less reason or opportunity to assure high levels of performance. The merit system constitutes a further obstacle to performance by blocking discretion in hiring, firing, and promoting. This both undercuts executive control and reduces the incentives of subordinates. Moreover, the rigidity of bureaucratic rules and the political safety found in "not rocking the boat" supposedly make bureaucracy inherently unresponsive and rigid in comparison with the private business world.

Let us respond to this line of argument by first offering some observations that are relatively axiomatic and yet are needed to clear the air. One is that distinctions between government and business are not always clear-cut. The dichotomy of private versus public enterprise is vivid enough in classroom debates on capitalism and socialism, but in the real world, hybrid organizations and intersectoral ties are commonplace, as illustrated by quasi-governmental organizations and public-private partnerships.

Next, business corporations are themselves organized bureaucratically. Hence comparative public-private statistics distinguish not truly between bureaucracy and nonbureaucracy but between different kinds of bureaucracy. Third, the presupposition that the private sector is disciplined by the market while the public sector escapes such discipline hides important truths. For one thing, perfect competition among firms is explained elegantly in economics texts but is not found in most of the real business world. Furthermore, bureaucracies are exposed to external forces that in some ways simulate competition, such as budget battles and turf rivalries

A final point is that comparisons between the two sectors run into inevitable "apples and oranges" problems. While the aims of business are profits and growth, government meets multiple and often not complementary statutory goals. It also must observe due process as defined by the courts; follow election returns when they show a swerve in direction; seek the participation and involvement of citizens; pursue the ends of justice and equity; symbolize an open, caring regime; and uphold the dignity of the state. That is a tall order.

Yet to compare the two sectors empirically, we must do so on dimensions they have in common, such as seeking to reduce costs and be efficient. A number of studies have been done, many of them generated as part of the broader debate over "privatization" and the proper role of government. We look first at several summaries and meta-analyses of public-private comparisons, and then turn to individual studies of interest.

Robert Spann published an overview covering five activity areas, ranging from airlines to health care. He concluded that "for the majority of activities, private producers can provide the same services at the same, or lower costs, than can public producers." Yet a summary by Robert Millward, which reviewed comparisons conducted in Europe and elsewhere, found "no broad support for private enterprise superiority" with respect to unit costs. His conclusion was that "there seems no general ground for believing managerial efficiency is less in public firms." Another overview, by Thomas Borcherding and associates, listed fifty studies of services in nineteen areas in five countries. Forty of these studies were said to show that private supply is more efficient than public. David Parker, in still another multination survey, discovered "that there is no conclusive evidence of lower efficiency in the public sector, especially when cost of production is used as a measure." J. Norman Baldwin and Quinton Farley reviewed some ninety-three comparative public-private studies conducted in the United States, fifty-seven of which measured efficiency, effectiveness, productivity, and similar outcomes. They concluded, "Private organizations are frequently, but not consistently, more cost-efficient and productive than public organizations."[19]

Thus, initially, the picture as a whole looks very confused. For clarification, we examine some specific studies. The unglamorous function of garbage collection has been the subject of many. The lead authority on this topic is E.S. Savas of Baruch College of the City University of New York, who contends that the most thorough studies of the subject indicate that the budget costs of municipal refuse collection are about 35 percent greater than contract collection, even when outlays for preparing, administering, and monitoring the contract are counted. In addition, he argues, if the contractor pays taxes of 15 percent to the municipality, these receipts can be budgeted for other municipal services. Since this taxation does not occur when the work is done in-house, residents in effect pay 58 percent more for municipal collection than for private collection. Furthermore, he says, if we assume that the contractor is taking profits of 10 percent, this means that the process of garbage pickup is costing the municipality 88 percent more than it is costing the contractor.[20]

Savas regards refuse collection as "the most studied municipal service in the world" and "a settled issue" from the standpoint of privatization's desirability. In support of this statement, he summarizes ten studies conducted between 1975 and 1986 in several parts of the United States and Canada, the United Kingdom, Switzerland, and Japan. Although one of these studies finds no clear pattern of difference, the other nine conclude that in-house collection is 14 to 124 percent more costly. Savas believes that these findings tell us that in the refuse collection field, "government is significantly less productive than contractors: it uses more men to do the same amount of work, allows more paid absences by workers, employs less productive vehicles, and therefore services fewer households per hour."[21]

Some agree with Savas, while others do not. A meta-analysis published in 2000 by Graeme Hodge found that contracting out by government in the areas of refuse collection, cleaning, and maintenance seem to yield cost savings of 6 to 12 percent. Hodge found no such broad evidence for similar savings in other areas of government activity, however. William Pier and associates examined refuse collection in Montana, gathering service and cost data from thirty-four public and twenty-nine private haulers. The investigators found "greater governmental than private efficiency for garbage collection in Montana for all but very small communities." W. Hirsch studied garbage collection in twenty-four St. Louis suburbs where differing arrangements prevail. The conclusion was that private removal cost less than public but that the difference was not statistically significant. Also, apparently, citizen customers do not always perceive a difference between private and public haulage. A national telephone survey published by *Waste Age* indicated that 86 percent of respondents were satisfied with their refuse collection, with differences between private and public systems "too small to matter." A survey of Tucson residents by Julia Marlowe yielded similar results, giving precisely identical customer satisfaction ratings to public and private providers—a mean of 8.7 on a scale of 10.[22]

Another municipal function where economic performance can be compared across sectors is water supply. Many communities and water districts acquire, treat, and distribute their own water, while others purchase it from private suppliers for distribution to customers. Again, we find some disagreement among the studies. Ronald Teeples and David Glyer examined the costs of water produced by sixty-seven public systems and fifty-two private systems in southern California; they concluded that differences in overall efficiency were insignificant. Mark Crain and Asghar Zardkoohi studied data available on eighty-eight public water plants and twenty-four private water utilities located in thirty-eight states. They found that the publicly owned firms incurred significantly higher operating costs. To confuse the situation further, Thomas Bruggink performed a multiple regression analysis on published national waterworks data; his analysis showed that government ownership produced an average downward shift of 24 percent in the operating-costs equation.[23]

A large literature exists on electric power utilities, which, like water systems, are both publicly and privately owned (as seen in the productivity data presented in chapter 2). In a landmark study comparing the two types of utility, Sam Peltzman determined that mean residential electricity prices charged by government utilities serving seventy-four cities were substantially lower than those levied by private utilities serving seventy-one cities. Following up on Peltzman's work, Louis De Alessi concluded that municipal utilities, contrasted to investor-owned power companies, tended to incur higher operating costs, offer a smaller variety of output, and favor corporate as against residential users. At the same time, they charged lower prices, possessed greater capacity, spent more on plant construction, engaged in less profit-maximizing price discrimination, and had more stable management. Scott Atkinson and Robert Halvorsen summarized the results of six studies available on the subject and found that three pronounced the government utilities more efficient than the investor-owned, with a fourth coming to the opposite conclusion, and the remaining two finding no significant differences. As was noted in the previous chapter, productivity growth statistics for power and gas utilities are now fairly similar between the two sectors, although for some years government was ahead of investor-owned plants.[24]

In other areas of municipal activity where cross-sectoral comparisons are possible, Roger Ahlbrandt calculated that the city of Scottsdale, Arizona, saved 47 percent on its fire protection costs by hiring the Rural-Metropolitan Fire Protection Company to serve its population. Randy Ross concluded that public-only arrangements for school busing cost 5 to 6 percent more than private-only or a mix of the two. Michael Krashinsky, studying day-care centers in Ontario, concluded that government-subsidized municipal centers cost significantly more to run than unsubsidized private centers, mainly because of better worker salaries, fewer donated goods, and higher-quality care.[25]

Barbara Stevens examined the productive efficiency of eight municipal activities in the Los Angeles area, provided both in-house and under contract: street-sweeping, building-cleaning, refuse collection, payroll preparation, traffic signal maintenance, asphalt overlay, tree-trimming, and grass-mowing. She found that although quality of service was relatively uniform, costs ranged enormously from city to city, regardless of delivery mechanism. But when in-house and contract cities were compared, costs incurred in the first exceeded those in the second by 37 to 96 percent—except for payroll preparation, for which there was no difference.[26]

Systematic private-public comparisons have also been done for mass transit systems. In a 1984 summary of the literature on the subject conducted for the Urban Mass Transportation Administration, James Perry cited seven studies that found private systems more efficient, six that concluded public systems were more efficient, and seven that showed mixed results or no difference. He concluded that while the evidence regarding efficiency was ambiguous, "the performance edge appears to go to publicly owned firms" with respect to service effectiveness. In an analysis of urban bus transit performance using UMTA-collected data, Perry and Timlynn Babitsky found that privately owned and operated systems were more efficient than other arrangements, although public systems managed by contractors performed no more efficiently than publicly owned and managed companies. In short, the presence of private-sector expertise does not necessarily boost efficiency.[27]

With respect to civil aviation, David Davies compared two domestic airlines in Australia: one public, the other private. He concluded that the private operator was more efficient, in terms of both load carried and revenues earned per employee. P.J. Forsyth and R.D. Hocking then challenged his conclusion, noting that statistics based on distance traveled and tonnage carried per employee showed the two airlines as practically equivalent. In a similar study, Douglas Caves and Laurits Christensen compared the Canadian National and Canadian Pacific railroads, the first of which is a crown corporation and the second privately owned. They found "no evidence of inferior efficiency performance by the government-owned railroad."[28]

Hospital administration is another area amenable to public-private comparisons. In 1976 Cotton Lindsay calculated that per diem patient costs in Veterans Administration hospitals were nearly half those in proprietary hospitals: $49.09 versus $82.87. Yet in a study of 338 inpatient psychiatric departments, Lawrence Hrebiniak and Joseph Alutto calculated higher costs for government than nongovernment hospitals. With respect to nuclear medical services, George Wilson and Joseph Jadlow found that proprietary hospitals operated closer to the efficient production frontier than did nonprofit and government hospitals, but that competition among the private institutions created the perverse effect of excess capacity, since each hospital wanted all the latest equipment.[29]

What do we learn from these empirical studies? The bulk of them fall into two main categories. One group, which delivers the verdict of private-sector superiority, includes the literature overviews by Spann, Borcherding, and Baldwin-Farley, the refuse studies by Savas, the water study by Crain-Zardkoohi, and the municipal studies of fire protection, busing, day-care, and Los Angeles outsourcing. The other main category yields a mixed conclusion, reporting empirical findings that are ambiguous or comparisons between private and public performance that show no significant difference. Included in this group are the overview summaries by Millward and by Parker, the refuse study by Hirsch, the refuse polls by *Waste Age* and Marlowe, the water study by Teeples-Glyer, the electric power studies of De Alessi and Atkinson-Halvorsen, the three transportation studies (mass transit, civil aviation, and railroads), and the Hrebiniak-Alutto and Wilson-Jadlow hospital studies.

In short, there is much evidence that is ambivalent. The assumption that business always does better than government is not upheld. Further doubt was cast on that proposition by chapter 2's findings that Georgia's citizens rate services by the two sectors essentially the same, that the federal government's customer satisfaction index is exceedingly close to that of the national economy as a whole, that federal productivity gains over the years have generally paralleled those of the private sector, and that Social Security answers the phone better than Nordstrom and L.L. Bean. When you add up all these study results, the basis for the mantra that business is always better evaporates.

The Bureaucracy-Is-Backward Myth

The final myth to delete is that bureaucracy inevitably and inherently fights change. Because of its supposed dedication to inertia and the status quo, it fails to innovate unless forced to do so. Hence it tends to be behind-the-times and not "with it," especially in comparison to the lively things going on in the business world. As a consequence, change in bureaucracy must be imposed by external forces, such as headlong movements for reform.

Why is bureaucracy necessarily hidebound and resistant to change? The critics offer many explanations. David Osborne and Peter Plastrik say it is a question of organization culture. The bureaucratic culture is timid and conservative, they say, for several reasons: the need to be defensive against enemies, a fear of alienating those in power, the isolation caused by specialized units, and a monopolistic situation in which no pressures are brought to bear from customers or competitors. The resulting culture's central attributes are blaming others rather than taking responsibility, living in fear of making mistakes, compliantly accepting mediocrity rather than creatively reaching for excellence, and resisting change rather than adapting to it.[30]

In 1965 sociologist Richard LaPiere argued flatly that creative and innovative people are not attracted to employment in bureaucracies. Those who become bureaucrats are security-minded, preferring to obey the rules faithfully and not wishing to take risks. Like Osborne and Plastrick, he believed that the monopolistic nature of bureaucracy prevents it from sensing the need to innovate. Mature bureaucracies, he claimed, are isolated, self-validating systems concerned only with their own maintenance.[31]

More recently, Gerald Caiden, whose emphatic call for bureaucratic reform was quoted in chapter 1, contends that the greatest obstacle for public administrators to overcome is probably organizational complacency and inertia.

Perhaps unaware of the rising productivity statistics we encountered in the last chapter, Caiden declares that bureaucracy tends to be "inert." This is not because bureaucrats are lazy, but because of such bureaupathologies as the following (in alphabetical order):

dedication to the status quo,
delay,
fear of change,
foot-dragging,
imperviousness to suggestion,
inability to learn,
indecision,
inflexibility,
lack of imagination,
obstruction,
procrastination,
rigidity,
stagnation,
stalling, and
vested interests.

These characteristics create "a comfortable, serene, and relaxed atmosphere in which work is performed after a style and everything on the surface looks fine," says Caiden. The outcome is that "the same old patterns and routines are preserved; the shortcomings and deficiencies are perpetuated; mistakes and errors are repeated. When the organization does change, it moves slowly, incrementally, predictably, and then not always in the right direction."[32]

As we did in considering the other myths, let us now look at some empirical research. Having reviewed the published literature on innovation, David Roessner concludes that while we do not know enough to arrive at a firm conclusion, there is "reason to doubt the validity of hypotheses that the public sector is inherently immune to effort to increase innovative behavior there." He notes, for example, that studies of technology diffusion in medicine and refuse collection show that the public sector is not always much different from, let alone slower than, the private sector.[33]

Some case studies of innovation in bureaucracies provide useful insights. In his classic work *The Dynamics of Bureaucracy,* Peter Blau argued that bureaucrats are less resistant to change than factory workers. While chronic resisters in both settings are a minority of personally insecure individuals, the possibility of being fired is more real in the private sector, so change is more threatening there and hence is attempted less often. From his case studies of a state employment agency and federal enforcement agency, Blau concluded that "most officials in the government agencies studied here were favorably disposed toward change."[34]

In another case study, Louis Bragaw examined the U.S. Coast Guard to discover whether that agency had received stimuli for innovation over the course of its history. He particularly wished to determine whether the organization was affected in its performance by factors analogous to pressures of the marketplace. Bragaw discovered that, indeed, several innovations had occurred over the years, such as replacement of early revenue and lighthouse functions, development of the Loran navigation system, and establishment of a marine environmental protection program. He explained this innovative behavior in terms of response to threats that had developed from time to time against the agency, such as absorption attempts by the navy, fiscal starvation following wars, and moves to liquidate or control the agency. Bragaw regarded these threats as a "hidden stimulus" that was somewhat comparable to the effects of economic competition.[35]

In recent years the subject of policy innovation in local government has attracted scholarly attention. Mark Schneider and Paul Teske sent out 1,400 questionnaires to city clerks in suburban communities over 2,500 in population. The clerks were asked if anyone was active in their community whose "policy proposals and political positions represented a dynamic change from existing procedures." In about 30 percent of the communities, the answer was yes. When asked who that person was, 43 percent said the mayors, 26 percent indicated members of the city council, and 23 percent pointed to the city managers or bureau chiefs; the remaining 8 percent named private citizens. Statistically, the two most important variables associated with the presence of such entrepreneurship were the existence of a full-time mayor with staff and a professional city manager. While most of the policy entrepreneurs were elected officials, more than 50 of the 257 identified were bureaucrats, mostly city managers. Their training, networks, and strategic position in the government, Schneider and Teske believe, afforded them opportunities to promote innovation.[36]

An area especially associated with innovation is information technology (IT). Bruce Rocheleau and Liangfu Wu became interested in the question of whether the private or public sector is more "pro" IT. Reasoning that the competitive market would force business to invest more in such technology than did government, they hypothesized that private-sector organizations, compared to those in the public sector, would perceive information technology and IT training as more important and would therefore spend more money on these activities. This expectation was tested by surveying IT managers in 97 municipalities and 137 service-oriented private organizations. While Rocheleau and Wu found that the municipalities did not invest as much in IT personnel and training because they could not afford it, a higher proportion of their managers perceived information systems as important (although not to a statistically significant degree).[37]

Since 1986 the Kennedy School at Harvard has run an Innovations in American Government award program, financed by the Ford Foundation.

This program makes cash awards of $100,000 and $20,000 to state and local governments (and, since 1995, to federal agencies) that have introduced policy or administrative changes that are novel, achieve results, and can be replicated. In 2001 Ford gave the JFK School $50 million to continue the program, a record gift by Ford at the time.[38]

Sandford Borins studied award-submittal documents from the Ford–Kennedy School program to learn about the characteristics of governmental innovation. He examined 217 semifinalist submittals from the 1990–1994 period and 104 from 1995–1998. One thing he sought to find out was who had initiated the innovation. Much to his surprise, the most common source was bureaucrats. At the federal, state, and local levels, middle managers and front-line staff were among the initiators in 72 percent of the federal innovations, 46 percent of the state innovations, and 58 percent of those carried out by local government. This compared to 14, 30, and 36 percent, respectively, of innovations initiated by elected politicians and 24, 25, and 26 percent, respectively, initiated by agency heads. When he first encountered this finding, Borins considered it so unexpected and significant that he subtitled the book he wrote on the subject "How Local Heroes Are Transforming American Government."[39]

Examples of projects initiated by these local heroes were creation of voicemail boxes for homeless people in Seattle, introduction of an automated traffic management system in Los Angeles, and development of a computerized Medicaid patient–record system in Indianapolis. In many instances, the changes were initiated not in reaction to a crisis but in an effort to ward off a crisis. The hallmark of bureaucrat-initiated innovation was to solve internal problems and take advantage of new technology. By contrast, innovations initiated by politicians tended to be crisis-stimulated, while those introduced by agency heads were occasioned by their initial appointment. Another finding by Borins was that the bureaucrats were not a prime source of resistance to change. Indeed, uncooperative attitudes, turf fights, and other forms of bureaucratic resistance occurred in only 18 percent of the cases he reviewed from 1990–1994 and in 17.4 percent from 1995–1998.[40]

Another study of the Ford–Kennedy Innovations in American Government program was restricted to the federal agency winners announced for 1995–1998. In a book edited by John Donahue, fourteen innovative projects are summarized and discussed, including a "fast track" product recall at the Consumer Product Safety Commission, a "no sweat" antisweatshop campaign by the Wage and Hour Division, telephone tax filing at the Internal Revenue Service, self-regulation of worker safety under the Occupational Safety and Health Administration, collaborative forest planning by the Forest Service, and disaster computer modeling at the Federal Emergency Management Agency. Donahue notes that in some instances these projects were stimulated by external pressures, such as budget constraints and the National Performance Review, but the main factor in making them succeed was professional pride on the part of the bureaucrats. "Not one of the innovations celebrated in this volume would have been possible without the purposeful engagement of bureaucrats in the trenches."[41]

In sum, we find that the culture of bureaucracy is not inherently opposed to change. Its structure and environment do not automatically mean that government agencies are inert, inflexible, unable to learn, and reluctant to change. Documented cases exist in which bureaucracy has innovated, often even more so than the private sector. Almost a third of suburban governments report policy innovation taking place in their communities, and the existence of a mayor or city manager is more associated with the presence of such activity than any other factor. With respect to involvement with information technology, local governments have just as much interest in this cutting-edge field as private organizations, even if they cannot afford to invest as much in IT personnel and training. Studies of a prestigious national awards competition for governmental innovation show that imaginative and useful changes are taking place in American governments, and that, significantly, the bureaucrats are their lead initiators and not their main opponents. In fact, in many instances the bureaucrats' professional pride was the key factor in winning the award.

"Contrary to the stereotypes," sums up Christopher Leman, "public agencies have been remarkably innovative." One more myth about bureaucracy is ripe for the delete key.[42]

Chapter 4 Ask the Impossible of Bureaucracy? Easy!

A place where I walk every day in our town is Progress Street. The notion of "progress" has always been integral to the American psyche. The earliest settlers came to our shores to seek a new and better life. Industrialization of the country was based on a faith in the future. Our laboratories yielded one astonishing breakthrough after another, suggesting that practically anything can be wrung from nature if we try hard enough. Until recently, a faith in limitless economic development permeated our culture, now dampened just a bit by concern for the quality of life and the future of the planet.

Beginning in the Progressive era and accelerating in two strong pulsations in the 1930s and 1960s, Americans placed major responsibility for realizing their optimistic expectations in the hands of government. This responsibility was not placed casually or for the record. Holding true to their faith in progress, Americans actually *expected* government to make progress for them, no matter the obstacles, costs, or intractability of the problem. If progress did not occur, something was wrong—government was "dragging its feet," "not able to deliver," or "the problem rather than the solution."

Herein lies the rub for bureaucracy. Elected officials, editorial writers, political activists, and intellectual gurus delineate the "progress" to be made. They do so in their rhetoric, laws, policies, editorials, press releases, books, and weekend television interviews. Then, with expectations raised and goals officially set, the bureaucrats must actually get us there. Doing that is relatively easy in some instances, if money is available, as for building highways and schools. In others, such as stopping drug abuse, eliminating AIDS, ending racism, or removing the threat of terrorism, government—even with the best of intentions—tackles the near-impossible.

If, then, we (1) assume that progress is inevitable; (2) assign responsibility for progress to government; (3) expect insoluble problems to be solved; and (4) hand over the job of solving them to the bureaucrats—what is the consequence? The consequence is that we set bureaucracy up for failure.

Moreover, we make it difficult for bureaucracy to succeed at an operational level as well. We give it inconsistent, contradictory, and hence irreconcilable tasks. We lengthen its organizational linkages by involving multiple layers of government in many of its programs. We extend those linkages further by depending on business firms and nonprofit organizations for the implementation of much public policy. Hence great complexity characterizes bureaucracy both in what it is expected to do and in how it is expected to do it. It may be necessary to redefine what we mean by progress.

No-Win Situations and Red Tape

At one point in his book *Bureaucracy*, James Q. Wilson discusses the Immigration and Naturalization Service (INS). This agency, he points out, has an unusually tough row to hoe. It has been given vague and competing goals, contributing to a weak sense of mission and low state of morale. In Wilson's words, the INS is issued the following contradictory marching orders: It is supposed to "keep out illegal immigrants, but let in necessary agricultural workers"; "carefully screen foreigners seeking to enter the country, but facilitate the entry of foreign tourists"; and "find and expel illegal aliens, but . . . not break up families, impose hardships, violate civil rights, or deprive employers of low-paid workers." Comments Wilson: "No organization can do all of these things well, especially when advocates of each have the power to mount newspaper and congressional investigations of the agency's 'failures.' "[1]

The firestorm of criticism that descended on the INS six months after the September 11th terrorist attacks clearly substantiates Wilson's analysis. The contradictions involved in trying to make it easy for "customers" to enter the country while at the same time making it impossible for criminals to do so were exquisitely illustrated when the agency's aging computer system suddenly sent to the Huffman Aviation flying school visa approval notices for two of the hijackers. They were now dead, making the matter of no practical importance, but that did not keep members of Congress from describing the INS as "completely and totally dysfunctional." The fact that Congress had for years refused to appropriate sufficient funds to update that computer system was forgotten in the uproar.[2]

Yet even though outcomes this dramatic are rare, bureaucracies often have contradictory goals imposed on them. Corrections personnel are supposed to confine convicts securely and cheaply in close quarters yet rehabilitate them into good citizens. FDA regulators are told they must keep all dangerous drugs off the market yet not hold up approval of new drugs. Police officers are called on to be tough enough to engage in physical violence at any moment yet friendly enough to walk smilingly around the neighborhood, in the manner of social workers. Whether working at cross-purposes makes sense or not, bureaucracies must accept such situations as a fact of life.

Another contradiction encountered by bureaucracy goes beyond the ambivalent mission. It arises from our competing expectations of government itself. Facing double and sometimes treble standards, bureaucracies are, as the old saying goes, damned if they do and damned if they don't. For example, they are called on to provide the best service possible to citizens yet save money. They are told to procure goods and services at the lowest price yet be responsible for their high quality. They are supposed to safeguard the information in their possession and yet be open to the press. They are expected to be flexible in enforcing rules yet always accountable to the law. Please note: It's not that some of these requirements are "good" and some are "bad." *All* are "good." It is, however, impossible to meet them all fully, simultaneously.

Thus, in the legal-political world in which they operate, bureaucracies lie snugly fixed between a rock and a hard place. This is true in yet another way. Typically, the various programs run by these organizations serve not just one but multiple constituencies. These may even consist of rival groups, such as the timber companies, mining interests, recreation groups, hunters, and environmentalists that are dealt with simultaneously by natural resource agencies. Bureaucracies also typically face more than one external review agency, for example, auditors, legislative committees, budget offices, investigative bodies, and program evaluation units. These watchdogs act not merely in behalf of their own ostensible mission, but in response to all manner of external political forces and power centers, such as executive staff, clientele organizations, employee associations, party factions in the legislature, activists of every stripe, and lobbyists with insider connections. Still another watchdog is the press, ready at a moment's notice to submit a Freedom of Information request and find scandal in the results.

These diverse and contradictory forces lay the basis for criticism no matter what the bureaucracy does. Public schools are attacked for not producing high standardized test scores and also for not retaining creative young teachers who hate teaching to the test. Environmental protection agencies are told to clean up the air, water, and landfills, to keep out of the way of business, and also to subject every regulation to an economic impact statement. When the Border Patrol builds rescue beacons for border-crossers in the Arizona desert, immigrant welfare activists cry "militarization of the border" while anti-immigration advocates say it only signals intruders to try again.

In the budgetary cutbacks of recent years, the competing demands made on bureaucracy create their own no-win situations. Year after year, agencies are told to cut the fat out of their budgets. After a while, the knife is no longer slicing through fat, but hitting bone and marrow: employees must be laid off and programs or levels of service abandoned. Consequently, the quality of program delivery falls below acceptable levels. But the moment the first horror story arising from lack of funds pops up on the evening news, incensed demands are made to account for how this could possibly happen.

Just such a case occurred in the Child and Family Services Agency of the District of Columbia in 2000. The media and residents of Washington were shocked when a twenty-three-month-old girl, Brianna Blackmond, who had been removed from her neglectful mother and placed in foster care, was killed in her house two weeks after being sent back home. The judge who allowed this to happen was later barred from the bench as unfit for service. The child's caseworker knew of the danger but failed to notify the judge in time. She was at that point carrying a caseload of twenty-seven children, which was more than double the legal limit of eleven but necessary because of funding shortfalls.[3]

Another chronic no-win situation is when bureaucrats are placed in the middle of pitched battles—no matter what they do, the losing side cries for their scalp. A notable instance from recent years involved Élian Gonzalez, a Cuban boy who had been rescued at sea while attempting to reach U.S. shores; unfortunately, his mother had perished in the attempt. When Élian's father expressed a wish to take the boy back to Cuba, the six-year-old's Miami relatives and the Cuban exile community in Florida insisted that he stay in America. INS Director Doris Meissner, with Attorney General Janet Reno's concurrence, decided to turn the boy over to his father. Enforcing that decision would be tricky, however, since crowds kept permanent watch on the house where Élian was staying, with five private bodyguards stationed inside.

In the predawn hours of 22 April 2000, under the code name Operation Reunion, 110 INS agents, twenty U.S. marshals, and two medical professionals from the Public Health Service made a carefully planned strike. Within three minutes Élian was in their custody, with no major injuries occurring at the scene or on the street. An AP photographer happened to be on the spot, however, and the next day newspapers everywhere published a picture showing a helmeted and goggled agent gripping an MP-5 submachine gun while opening the door. This image led to charges of an unconscionable use of force against unarmed civilians. The exile community called a general strike and a congressman termed the INS agents "jack-booted thugs." Although much opinion around the country saluted the action, the "dysfunctional" INS itself received little credit.[4]

One of the charges most frequently leveled against bureaucracy is that it creates "red tape"—one of the most enduring pejorative metaphors in the English language. Historically, the expression refers to narrow ribbons used to tie up packets and folders of government documents. Originating in eleventh-century England to bind and seal official documents with wax, by the nineteenth century red tape was woven of twill, brick red in color, and 7/16th of an inch wide when flat. Clerks in Washington used it to bind government documents in trifolded packets until the 1890s, and even today archivists are still at work untying the tapes.

In a meaning popularized by the nineteenth-century Englishmen Sidney Smith, Thomas Carlyle, and Herbert Spencer, the term *red tape* has come to refer to all government with which one is disgusted. It is a classic condensation symbol in that it incorporates a vast array of subjectively held feelings and expresses them succinctly in a way all can relate to on an emotional plane. The very vagueness of the term's meaning enhances its symbolic value: the mental image of endless lengths of ribbon lends itself nicely to any conceivable kind of government excess, as in the cartoonist's rendering of Uncle Sam bound in yards of red-colored tape.

Since the bureaucracy is by popular definition the main repository of government excess, the "*b*" word and *red tape* are easily muttered in the same breath. When a businessperson, social activist, or ordinary citizen does not get what he or she wants from government, the matter is automatically characterized as bureaucracy ensnarled in red tape. Although sociologist Alvin Gouldner argued that perceivers of red tape tend to be resentful conservatives, my experience is that persons of all political persuasion find the concept useful in one situation or another. Let us consider more fully some of the specific situations in which the symbol is called into play.[5]

One common trigger is frustration over what are regarded as stupid obstacles to action. When official roadblocks are thrown up to block or delay the transaction of an urgent item of personal business, we are likely to regard it as an imposition if not an insult. Yet the bureaucratic outsider, by definition, cannot know what is required within that office, in that case, on that day, to carry out that item of business. In his wonderful classic *Big Democracy*, Paul Appleby quoted a manager of his acquaintance as describing red tape as "that part of my business you don't know anything about."[6]

The saga of the gravestone of one Benjamin Franklin Ward, a private in the Georgia Volunteers who was fatally wounded at the Civil War's first Battle of Manassas, is illustrative. A red sandstone marker bearing Ward's name was found in a garage in modern-day Manassas, Virginia, and subsequently turned over to the National Park Service. Later Ward's descendants, including a retired history professor, believed they had discovered Benjamin's place of burial near the battlefield. Aware that the stone had been turned over to the government, they requested it from the office of Manassas National Battlefield Park, where it was stored in a closet. To the family's disappointment, the park superintendent said he could not turn the stone over since it had been officially accepted and cataloged as an historic artifact under federal law, which meant he was legally obligated to protect it as government property. The incensed relatives thereupon went to their U.S. senator for a private relief bill in Congress. A news article on the incident was headlined, "Headstone's Return to Confederate Grave Mired in Red Tape."[7]

A related meaning of *red tape* is invoked when government paperwork is considered to be excessive. In his book on the subject, Herbert Kaufman points out that the filling out of information forms and reports for bureaucratic agencies is at the core of this connotation. If the forms are to be filled out for our own interests—for example, applying for a government grant or a lease to drill for oil on public lands—we regard the time and trouble as well spent. If, however, completing the paperwork does not serve our interests and, to the contrary, taxes our time, patience, or pocketbooks, we denounce the reports as irrelevant, needless, and burdensome.[8]

A final stimulant to the cry "red tape!" has to do with the categorization of clients and the application of rules. Critics of bureaucracy are dismayed that agency personnel treat individual clients, each with individual problems, as mere "cases." The idea of processing a real person as a unit in an abstract category is anathema to many Americans. Further, if strict rules are handed down on what persons in a category can and cannot do or get, images of the totalitarian state come to mind. Yet, without such categories and rules, people could not be treated equally. If welfare agencies handed out money based not on established criteria but on personal friendships with their clients, their operations would degenerate into a nightmare of favoritism and bickering. If police officers arrested suspects in accord with their own racial attitudes or their current mood rather than with department policies, no one would be safe against abusive state action. To put the matter at the personal level, if you were admitted as a graduate student after being required to take the hated Graduate Record Exam (GRE), but then found that other students did not have to submit a GRE score, you wouldn't cry "red tape!" but "unfair!" If, when signing up for classes, you were urged to take a nonelective course from a domineering unpopular professor "for political reasons" but then found a provision in the catalog permitting a substitute class for persons in your particular program, you wouldn't feel controlled but liberated. Michael Hill asks, "Is it better to be confronted by polite and sympathetic officials with a great deal of power over one, or by rude and rigid ones who have no alternative but to provide a statutorily prescribed service if you qualify for it?"[9]

Not all comments on red tape focus on the term's multifaceted and ambiguous symbolic meanings. Barry Bozeman has developed a specific, measurable definition for the term: rules that remain in force and entail a burden but do not carry out their original purpose. Such rules are of two types, those "born bad"—that is, they are undesirable from the start—and those that "go bad," or wear out with time. While the first type should not have been created in the first place, the second pose a subtler danger in that their irrelevance emerges gradually as conditions or policies change. The aim in this situation must be to erase them from the rulebook as soon as this is realized.

Do governments impose more red tape, so defined, than private organizations do? Bozeman reviews the research on the subject and concludes that yes, they probably do. However, the reason is not that the rules systems of government are inherently worse but that public organizations have more controls placed on them from the outside environment to which they have to be accountable. Examples are due process procedures, ethics laws, accounting and auditing requirements, procurement rules, civil service regulations, and Freedom of Information laws. These controls stem from our Constitution, our separation of powers, and our value systems. Bozeman suggests that this greater accountability of public authority is perhaps worth it, as part of the organizational "overhead investment" needed to live in a constitutional republic.[10]

To sum up, bureaucracy is in a no-win situation because it responds not to a single rational calculus or even to net market demand. Instead, it responds—and must respond—to the political process. Since that process involves the pursuit of competing values and claims, inevitably some desires go unfulfilled and some claimants go unsatisfied. The resulting frustrations are multiple and disparate, irritating us to no end when our personal goals are blocked. The cause of the blockage is often seen as a bureaucracy bound in red tape. But the encirclement of Uncle Sam by this nineteenth-century ribbon is not, necessarily, a sign of inefficiency or abject failure. Much of it is in the very nature of government's predicament of doing many things for many reasons for many people.

When Many Governments Act

Another difficulty for bureaucracy is that the implementation of programs in American public administration often involves many different governments. Implementation would be simpler if only a single organization and its field offices were in charge. Christopher Hood notes that, theoretically, the first condition of "perfect administration" is that the administrative system be "unitary, like a huge army with a single line of authority." Lewis Gunn, trying to answer the question, "Why is implementation so difficult?" observes that one way to make it easier would be to have "a single implementation agency which need not depend upon other agencies for success." Malcolm Goggin and associates hypothesize, "The greater the number of organizational units involved in the implementation process, the greater the likelihood of delay and modification during implementation."[11]

The first academic study to stress this point was Jeffrey Pressman and Aaron Wildavsky's classic, *Implementation*, which appeared in 1973. Illustrated by Rube Goldberg cartoons, its subtitle is *How Great Expectations in Washington Are Dashed in Oakland; Or, Why It's Amazing that Federal Programs Work at All—This Being a Saga of the Economic Development Administration as Told by Two Sympathetic Observers Who Seek to Build Morals on a Foundation of Ruined Hopes.*[12] The "hopes" alluded to were for new port and airport buildings for Oakland, California, plus an industrial park and road. A grant had been awarded for the projects by the Economic Development Administration in Washington, and all local parties had agreed *in principle* to their construction. These hopes were "ruined," however, in that after six years only the marine terminal had been built.

The reason for the breakdown was the complexity of coordinating the several agencies and politicians involved. Each actor was capable of slowing down the project or even bringing it to a halt. In a detailed retrospective analysis of decision points, Pressman and Wildavsky found that completion of the project required joint approval on some seventy matters of detail. They calculated that even with an 80-percent probability of agreement on each one, the mathematical chances of achieving all necessary clearances were approximately a million to one (probably a tongue-in-cheek calculation, but the chances were small anyway). The authors found irony in the fact that while it is bureaucracy that is criticized for procedures that require numerous advance clearances, it is much harder to achieve the needed integration when implementation is taken out of the single organization and spread among several.

If it were ever alive at all, the ideal of simplicity in administrative implementation in the United States is dead today. The reality of American public administration is that implementation is very often divided among many parties—both other governments and private organizations, sometimes numbering in the hundreds if not thousands. The reason is that for many decades a principal hallmark of American public administration has been the devolution of implementation responsibilities. Thus if Goggin's hypothesis is correct, bureaucracy starts out every workday facing tremendous odds. The carrying out of law and policy is unbelievably complex under these circumstances. To the extent that U.S. bureaucracy succeeds, it is due not just to competent work *inside* individual organizations but to competent *interaction* among them.

The fact that devolution includes both multiple governments and private organizations makes for a twofold complexity. Figure 4-1 portrays this duality as a Greek cross. The vertical upright represents the multiplicity of governments in our intergovernmental system of federalism; the horizontal crossbar signifies the private sector organizations that participate in implementation.

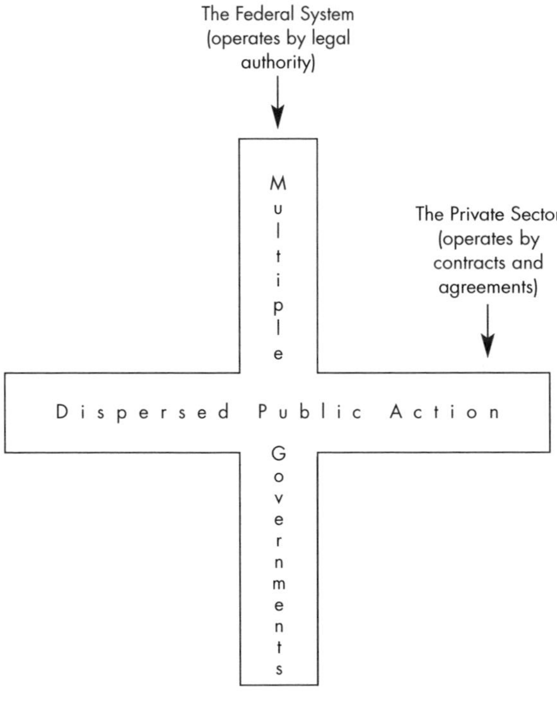

Figure 4-1 The Greek Cross of Implementation Complexity

(This representation is inspired by H.K. Colebatch's fine book *Policy*, although he conceived it somewhat differently, describing the vertical dimension as authoritative decision making, the horizontal as structured interaction.)[13]

The figure emphasizes the two great "axes" of administrative devolution in American bureaucracy. The vertical dimension is created by the American constitutional doctrine of federalism, which incorporates the national government, fifty state governments, approximately 80,000 local governments, and 588 federally-recognized Indian tribes. These thousands of governments interact with each other principally, but not exclusively, through various grant-in-aid mechanisms that are established and administered under legal authority. For its part, the horizontal dimension is composed of private-sector organizations that participate in implementation, primarily for-profit businesses and nonprofit service or community groups. This axis is labeled "dispersed public action" because it is not public administration in the traditional sense but co-joined public-private activity dispersed into the civil society.[14] Although this aspect of devolution also operates under law, the main mechanisms of action are contracts for the performance of specific tasks and grants for agreed-upon purposes. The engagement of each axis or both together is common: a study of 137 new or amended federal programs passed by Congress in 1965–1966 and 1993–1994 showed that well over half required intergovernmental coordination or the participation of private groups, or both.[15]

In this section we deal with the complications created for bureaucracy by devolution among multiple governments. In the next section of this chapter, devolution to the private sector is examined.

The key point with respect to multiple governments is that the bureaucracies of the national, state, local, and tribal governments carry out many of their duties in concert with or in conflict with other bureaucracies. It is worth keeping in mind that when elements of the public sector intermesh, complications arise that are not present among private organizations. The national, state, and tribal governments are sovereign legal entities. Moreover, ambitious political leaders, powerful elected bodies, billions of dollars, the interests of vocal constituencies, and the rulings of federal and state courts are involved. Intergovernmental public administration takes place on a complicated and tumultuous playing field.

The grant-in-aid as a mechanism of public administration is very old in America, starting in the nineteenth century with federal land grants to railroads, colleges, and state governments. After adoption of the federal income tax in 1913, grants were made in cash, but usually with strings attached. By 1970 over $25 billion in federal grants was being made to state and local governments, a figure that surpassed $100 billion in 1985, $200 billion in 1994, and $300 billion in 2001. Today nearly 17 percent of federal outlays are in the form of grants, with 32 percent of state and local expenditures coming from this source.[16]

Table 4-1 shows the top ten granting agencies of the federal government, ranked by number of grant programs directed to state, local, and tribal governments. The grants of these agencies account for 552 of the total of 591 federal grant programs, the remainder administered by agencies not in the top ten. In addition, some 337 other federal grant programs are meant for nonprofit groups or individuals—for example, to fund research projects and fellowships. State governments also make grants, both to their localities and to private organizations, and the aggregate dollar amount transferred by these state grants exceeds the national government's total. About 70 percent of state grant funding comes from state revenues, with the rest constituting "pass-throughs" of funds obtained from Washington.[17]

The wide range of federal grant programs can be seen in table 4-2, where they are ranked by dollar size. By far the biggest is Medicaid, whose funds are dispensed by the Centers for Medicare and Medicaid Services (CMS), formerly known as the Health Care Financing Administration. As Daniel Williams has noted, CMS is the ultimate "steering" bureaucracy in that it releases hundreds of billions of dollars each year without delivering any services. It contracts with the Social Security Administration for the enrollment of eligible Medicare beneficiaries. Regional intermediaries then process claims and deal with health care providers, most of whom are in the private sector. Medicaid, by contrast, is administered through the fifty state governments. They, in turn, deal with intermediaries and providers. As Williams points out, this complex arrangement creates many implementation difficulties, including accountability. When provider and advocacy groups criticize the federal government for having inflexible regulations, Medicaid intermediaries say the states are the problem, Medicare intermediaries say Social Security is the problem, Social Security and the states say CMS is the problem, and CMS says it has oversight responsibilities only and does not administer the services. All are right! The problem is caused not by any one of these actors but by the system.[18]

Table 4-1 Top Ten Federal Granting Agencies, 1998

Agency	Number of grants	Obligations (in $millions)
Department of Health and Human Services	155	155,275
Department of Education	100	21,474
Department of the Interior	58	1,788
Department of Agriculture	55	18,784
Department of Commerce	39	622
Department of Justice	38	4,410
Environmental Protection Agency	36	3,100
Housing and Urban Development	33	23,733
Department of Transportation	19	29,331
Department of Labor	19	7,447

SOURCE: David R. Beam and Timothy J. Conlan, "Grants," in *The Tools of Government: A Guide to the New Governance*, ed. Lester M. Salamon (Oxford: Oxford University Press, 2002), 347.

Table 4-2 Twenty Largest Federal Grant Programs, 1998

Program	Obligations (in $ billions)
Medicaid	104.8
Highway Planning and Construction	21.9
Temporary Assistance for Needy Families (TANF)	16.7
Section 8 Rental Certificate Program	8.1
Title I Grants to Local Education	7.4
National School Lunch Program	5.9
Head Start	4.3
State Children's Insurance Program (CHIP)	4.2
Child Support Enforcement	4.1
Women, Infants and Children (WIC)	3.9
Special Education Grants to States	3.8
Foster Care Title IV-E	3.5
Community Development Block Grants (CDBG)	2.9
Public and Indian Housing	2.9
Federal Transit Formula Grants	2.7
State Administration for Unemployment Insurance	2.5
Federal Transit Capital Investment Grants	2.3
Social Services Block Grant	2.3
Rehabilitation Services–Vocational Rehabilitation Grants to States	2.2
Public Housing Comprehensive Grants	2.2

SOURCE: David R. Beam and Timothy J. Conlan, "Grants," in *The Tools of Government: A Guide to the New Governance*, ed. Lester M. Salamon (Oxford: Oxford University Press, 2002), 348.

Despite these complexities, however, the public good is eventually served. Medicare and Medicaid make hospitalization affordable to millions of Americans and contribute greatly to the health of the nation. So, too, do other grant programs listed in the table. Highway planning and construction grants created and maintain the vast interstate highway system. Temporary Assistance for Needy Families (TANF) allows welfare reform to proceed without leaving those affected in the lurch. The National School Lunch program feeds 25 million children daily. Head Start gives 900,000 underprivileged children a chance annually to succeed in both school and life. Other grant-related achievements have already been mentioned: birth weight increases associated with the WIC program in chapter 1, many of the statistical "accomplishments of America" discussed in chapter 2, and the U-shape-causing enhancement of minority education described in chapter 3.

The key to success in this massive grant superstructure of American federalism is that funding flows take place in huge quantities. At the same time, the system's complexity makes the jobs of both donor and recipient bureaucracies difficult. For the bureaucracies that give out the money, the principal problem is that they do not directly control the activities that achieve goals for which they are accountable; responsibility is divorced from action to some extent. The more hands through which the funds pass, the more opportunities arise for their ineffective use or misuse. For example, recipient governments may employ grants to free up local monies already dedicated to the funded task. This "fungible" aspect of grants means they may not truly serve the intended purpose. Innumerable audits, reviews, and evaluations are needed, consuming valuable staff time and expertise up and down the implementation chain. The initial review of applications and release of funds ahead of legal deadlines is itself a major burden. Grant program offices run the risk of becoming mesmerized by the paper flow rather than serving the higher ends being pursued. Public administration becomes a matter of carrying out cyclical routines rather than directly affecting the world.

The job of the recipient bureaucracy is also made more difficult, although of course without grant funds it may or may not be able to act at all, depending on the nature of the program. At this receiving end, too, great time and expense go into writing grant applications, compiling periodic reports, and submitting annual reapplications. In some programs, considerable uncertainty may exist as to whether the funds will come through each year and in what amount. Delays in obtaining this assurance create difficulties with planning and staffing. Bureaucrats turn away from the substance of their work to scrounge for funds, spending much time lobbying in the state capital or Washington to maintain contacts there. In the final analysis, the program's future becomes hostage to the mercies of donor officials. A danger thus exists that informal signals sent by headquarters officials may become the program's shaping force, not the wishes or needs of the local citizenry. Block grants and waiver programs help in this regard, but they cover only part of the system.

Two additional patterns of intergovernmental administration create special problems. One is detailed *supervision* by a bureaucracy at one level of the federal system of counterpart bureaucracies at a "lower" level. A federal-state example is the Social Security Administration's supervision of disability determination by state rehabilitative services departments. Another is supervision of state employment commissions by the Federal Unemployment Insurance Service and the U.S. Employment Service. (Note in table 4-2 the grant program for state administration for unemployment insurance. When in chapter 2 we examined statistics on unemployment compensation error-rate and timeliness, they had been collected in this nationally supervised setting.) There are state-local examples as well, such as oversight by state social service departments of county welfare departments, by state auditing offices of city and county treasurers, and by state waterworks boards of local water plants.

Typically, intergovernmental supervision of this kind includes detailed fiscal control and the laying down of requirements for record-keeping, statistics-gathering, personnel practices, and program evaluation. In many instances, administrative manuals are provided that closely guide day-to-day work, with updated pages distributed periodically. The main advantage gained by the supervising agency from this arrangement is getting the work done in a decentralized way, yet according to essentially uniform standards. Also, costs are saved if field employees are paid less. For the supervised bureaucracy, the outcomes may include less discretion to adapt to local conditions, funding that is inadequate to cover rising workloads or indirect costs, and morale problems caused by unfavorable pay differentials compared to headquarters.

The second distinctive pattern of intergovernmental administration involves *mandates.* These are legal requirements placed by one government on another, such as on state and local governments by the national government or on localities by the states. Catherine Lovell and Charles Tobin conducted an inventory of federal and state mandates imposed by legislation or regulation on one city and one county in each of five states: California, North Carolina, New Jersey, Washington, and Wisconsin. A total of 223 direct orders were counted from the federal level and 3,268 from the state.[19]

These mandates may consist of commands attached to grants, or they may be stand-alone instructions. They may impose requirements with respect to administrative procedures, reporting requirements, and personnel practices. Some do not require positive action but restrict it, such as placing caps on tax powers, for which California is famous. The mandates may apply to specific bureaucracies—for instance, by a requirement that all county health departments provide outpatient mental health services. Alternatively, they may apply to all departments in a cross-cutting way, such as obligations regarding discrimination, the handicapped, and bilingual education. Sometimes crossover sanctions are in effect, which means that noncompliance under one grant jeopardizes other grants too. As a consequence, these mandates can become administrative straitjackets for the bureaucrats who are subject to them. Also, if unfunded, they can leech resources from the substantive core of programs. In 1995 Congress passed the Unfunded Mandate Reform Act, but its effect on slowing the growth of new federal mandates has been limited.[20]

In short, the intergovernmental grant system enables devolved governance in a continent-sized country, balancing competing needs to meet national problems on the one hand and preserve state and local autonomy on the other. But the system also makes the work of the bureaucrats more difficult and uncertain. Some academic observers advocate alternate models of intergovernmental administration that stress mutual interdependence among the actors in the federal system. Instead of the top-down message of "compliance or no money," they propose that grants be reconceived as an opportunity for negotiation, bargaining, and collaboration among equally respected parties. Only the future will tell if this idea catches on.[21]

When Public Action Is Dispersed

Just as implementation would be easier if bureaucracies did not have to work with other bureaucracies, it would also be simpler if nongovernment outsiders were not participants. But neither is the case. American public administration is distinctive by world standards in the degree to which private organizations are brought in to carry out programs. When operating the colonial post office, Benjamin Franklin hired men with horses and wagons to carry the mail along the Post Road. The collection of taxes was "farmed out" to thick-skinned individuals eager for a commission, and landowners with extra room in their houses were paid to take in orphans. In a similar way, many of the activities of present-day government are given over to businesses and nonprofit organizations to perform. When this kind of devolution happens, bureaucracy's role changes from direct doer to procurer of implementers and payer of bills. It makes agreements with and issues grants to community groups, and it works with other diffuse systems of implementation. Public administration becomes public action, dispersed to private parties outside the government.

As a measure of the magnitude of dispersed public action in the United States, Paul Light estimates that the total federal workforce is approximately doubled when one includes jobs created by contracts and grants.[22] This kind of extension of government's reach also occurs at the state and local level. The consequences of the pattern are great, for both the bureaucracy and the nation, as the complexity of implementation is increased another order of magnitude beyond that created by the intergovernmental system. Issues attendant upon government's proper scope and role are raised. The distribution of power within the process of governance is affected.

Yet this form of "indirect" administration is different from what we saw with respect to intergovernmental grants. While the connection between responsibility and control is similarly strained, in this situation one bureaucracy is not working with another bureaucracy but with a private entity. Ties to the constitutional framework and legal authority are not as strong. In this relationship governments are not so much sovereigns as signatories to contracts and agreements.[23] Bureaucrats deal not with counterpart officials but with businesspersons and group spokespersons, who enjoy in their capacity as private citizens constitutional rights protecting them from government. Moreover different organizational incentive systems, cultures, and normative orientations are thrown together. For their part, government agencies pay homage to an ethos of the public interest, while corporations are in business to make money, and community service organizations are advancing a variety of causes. Hence conflicts are inevitable and coordination not easy. The effectiveness of many government programs rests on how it all works out.

Because of differences between dispersal of public action to business contractors on the one hand and to nonprofit organizations on the other, these two arrangements must be considered separately. We begin with outsourcing to contractors, a practice that has grown vastly in size and scope in recent decades. In 1998 the federal government spent $177 billion per year—about 15 percent of federal spending—on procurement, $103 of which was for services, with the remainder for goods and for construction. In 1999 state and local governments together spent $1,750 billion for procurement, 41 percent of their aggregate total expenditure.[24]

Almost everything imaginable is contracted out: the development and testing of new weapons systems, the design and installation of information systems, the operation of social-service programs, road engineering and construction projects, and the operation of training centers. In the military arena, private suppliers maintain and support bases at home and operate communications systems, repair helicopters, and rebuild devastated economies in war zones. As we saw in chapter 3, municipalities in the Los Angeles area outsource street-sweeping, custodial services, refuse collection, payroll preparation, traffic signal maintenance, asphalt overlay, tree-trimming, and grass-mowing. Contractors also administer foreign aid projects, run prisons, operate fire departments, catch speeders on television cameras, and tow away cars. Even use of private collection agencies by the IRS has been considered. "Government work," ever the topic of ridicule at cocktail parties, is plenty good enough for a giant segment of corporate America.

The employment impact of this work is not lost on America's communities. The regional economies of Seattle, San Diego, Houston, Norfolk, and many other cities depend heavily on federal dollars. When the 1990s high-tech bubble burst in the Washington, D.C., metropolitan area, contract business in information technology and homeland security took up the slack. Large defense contractors, such as Lockheed Martin, General Dynamics, Northrop Grumman, and Raytheon, employ thousands of people around Washington, not because their plants are nearby—they are not—but because this is "where the action is" in terms of obtaining requests for proposals (RFPs), submitting proposals, renegotiating contracts, and carrying on the informal politicking necessary to keep abreast of developments at the Pentagon and elsewhere in the government. Also, tens of thousands of smaller "beltway bandits" surround the nation's capital, contracting to produce every conceivable product for government, from writing computer software programs to the preparation of training manuals.

There are good reasons for the existence of "the contracting state." One is that many goods and services required by government demand skills not available in-house, or at least not in sufficient amounts. Another is that investors, not taxpayers, should make the huge investments in plant and equipment not permanently needed by government. A strictly political factor is that outsourcing permits politicians to claim that government is "getting smaller" even as budgets continue to climb.

It would be easy to assume that contracting out reduces the complexity of implementation, since it is now done by others for a fee. But, as with grants, implementation complexity is made worse by contracting out. Again the reason is that bureaucracy's control over what happens is one step removed. If the prime contractor has subcontractors, it is two steps removed. If the subcontractors themselves have subcontractors, it is three steps, and so on.

As Pressman and Wildavsky taught us, the complexity of joint action is best understood over the passage of time. To illustrate with a hypothetical example, if a social services department hires a company to create a new system of tracking deadbeat fathers, it can give specifications for the system but cannot foresee unanticipated problems. It must rely on its contracting officer being kept sufficiently informed during the implementation process that difficulties are brought to the surface before they create inordinate delays or add-on costs. But if this kind of supervision is to work adequately, the government's contracting officer or that person's technical representative must possess a detailed knowledge of the system and must be placed at a position in the hierarchy where he or she can intervene before it's too late. The problem with the first of these requirements is that a relative absence of in-house competency on the subject may be the reason the contract was let in the first place.

A real-life case of increased complexity, and a tragic one indeed, was brought to light by the *Columbia* space shuttle disaster of 1 February 2003. The National Aeronautics and Space Administration (NASA), long under leadership with a pro–private enterprise bias, in 1996 turned over all day-to-day operations of the shuttle program to a joint venture of aerospace firms, Lockheed Martin and Boeing. Called the United Space Alliance, this company in turn let 2,240 contracts to subcontractors. The contracted work specifically included safety inspections, with NASA personnel performing general "insight" but not direct oversight. While the companies were docked for safety infractions, they also were awarded bonuses for on-time performance and allowed to keep 35 percent of any savings they generated. The report issued by the Columbia Accident Investigation Board indicted NASA's overall culture for an overconfident and careless approach to safety engineering. In addition, the board cited the problem of poor communications and lack of internal coordination. While the work of the contractors was not specifically criticized (except for a flawed model of foam damage), the report said that giving over shuttle management to a private corporation rendered "an already problematic safety system simultaneously weaker and more complex."[25]

Yet, as we know, the outsourcing movement has an ideological impetus behind it. At its center is blind faith in the superior efficiency of the private sector. Does contracting out actually produce significant savings? While contractor employees may be paid less, the contractor must earn a profit and the government must pay for contract solicitation, award, administration, and appeal. Much empirical evidence has been presented on the matter. As mentioned earlier, Graeme Hodge examines 129 studies and reports that in the areas of cleaning, maintenance, and refuse collection, 6- to 12-percent savings seem to occur, but for other services, no significant cost reductions are noticeable. Donald Kettl indicates that in surveys of local government most jurisdictions report savings—a result he attributes mainly to a greater freedom to reduce wages, cut fringe benefits, and hire and fire more easily. Jeffrey Greene compares two sets of cities, six that contract out widely and six that do not. The contracting group tends to be more efficient by his measures, although statistical differences are not always significant. When he ranks the twelve cities in order of productivity, contract cities are both the best and the worst, with full-service cities ranked in the middle, leading him to the conclusion that no clear pattern emerges from his data. Another scholar, George Boyne, analyzes more than twenty empirical studies of efficiency and contracting. About half support the efficiency thesis, but several of the studies seem methodologically flawed. Boyne contends that the private-efficiency thesis is not so much disconfirmed as untested.[26]

But in the eyes of many, there is no need to test the thesis. It is accepted as a matter of moral certitude. When I was a twenty-five-year-old intern with the Bureau of the Budget (now the Office of Management and Budget), I was assigned to the "Competition with Business" program, begun two years earlier under Bulletin 55-4. It was based on President Eisenhower's deeply-held belief that government should not engage in commercial-type activities. My mentor and I would take the government shuttle to the Pentagon to tell DoD officials that the president wanted them to turn over the army's ice cream plants and shoe repair shops to private enterprise. They would solemnly and politely agree to take care of the matter, but nothing ever happened. What later dawned on me is that it may be quite important for armies to know how to make ice cream and repair shoes, especially in the field during wartime.

Years later Eisenhower's anticompetition program was transformed by OMB Circular A-76 into a complex exercise whereby the performance of selected government departments was in effect compared to a theoretic ideal: "the most effective organization." If it fell short of that ideal, bids were solicited from private enterprise. The in-house department could, however, compete for the bid as well. Lengthy studies were done at great cost, mainly at Department of Defense facilities. Much to the chagrin of contractor associations and conservatives in Congress, when the bids were let out, the government won about half the time. As a result, the rules were later changed to penalize government bidders, "to level the playing field."[27]

In 1997 chagrin over the bidding success of government had cause to grow. A $250 million information technology contract was put out for bid by the Federal Aviation Administration (FAA) for "ICE-MAN" (Integrated Computing Environment Mainframe and Networking), a system expected to perform the FAA's payroll, personnel, and flight-safety functions. The private IT community was stunned when the contract was won not by one of their own but by a revolving-fund entity of the Department of Agriculture, the National Information Technology Center (NITC) located in Kansas City, which underbid by nearly 15 percent IBM, Unisys, Lockheed Martin, and other big players in private industry. As ICE-MAN has come on line in recent years, its users have expressed overwhelming approval of the results.[28]

As discussed in chapter 3, the core of the case for outsourcing is the notion that by purchasing from the private sector, government benefits from the advantages of a competitive marketplace in terms of price and quality. But this assumes that competitive producers exist for the items needed. Many things government buys, however, are not "off the shelf" or commonly produced, such as new weapons systems or ways to combat homelessness. In many areas of the country, few competent firms, if any, may know more about a local social or economic problem than do existing bureaucracies. In my own town, the contracting out of refuse collection drew only one bid, leaving the town council with no legal alternative but to accept it. Once a working relationship has been achieved in these less competitive situations, moreover, the contract is likely to be renewed automatically without careful review.

Issues other than efficiency and costs are involved in contracting. Hodge notes that literature on the subject often mentions problems of corruption, such as favoritism to campaign contributors in contract decisions and contractor kickbacks to officials. Kettl adds that conflicts of interest are a constant problem, as illustrated by a case in San Francisco where a manager who had been hired from a consulting firm awarded contracts to his former company. In the federal government, contractor abuses have also been uncovered, such as leasing equipment at an inflated rate from a company owned by one's spouse and charging living expenses to corporate expense accounts. Kettl goes so far as to say that some of the worst waste, fraud, and abuse in government has, ironically, been perpetuated not by the government itself but by its private contractors, with the bureaucrats receiving blame for not having detected it.[29]

David Van Slyke has studied the privatization of social services at the state level, and one of his conclusions is that excessively close ties between government officials and contractors can forestall true competition among bidders for contracts. He learned that relationships between agency managers and private providers "bordered on incestuous," allowing key organizations to be "wired into the system." An example of such wiring is provided by an investigation by *Washington Post* reporters into a bankrupt company hired to house convicted juveniles in the District of Columbia. The investigated company, Re-Direct Inc., came to public attention after six of its teenage charges had been murdered and a seventh had committed a murder. It was found that Re-Direct had been started by a teacher in a previous District program for troubled teenagers (who also sat on contract-review panels) and a supervisory social worker employed in its Youth Services Agency. Together they had created a new company for the purpose of making a bid on pending juvenile care contracts with which they were connected. Not surprisingly, they won. Absent significant oversight or agency control, Re-Direct took care of boys and girls over a period of four years, leading to what the *Washington Post* termed "deadly consequence."[30]

Insider connections in contracting out are not limited to the state and local levels of government. Following the 1991 Persian Gulf War, Defense Secretary Richard Cheney commissioned a Pentagon study on how best to support postwar military activities in the region. Brown and Root, an Idaho-based construction company, was given a contract to conduct the study, the outcome of which was a proposal to delegate all support logistics to a single contractor. The plan was adopted, and Brown and Root was then picked to implement its own plan. Later, Cheney became chief executive officer of Brown and Root's parent company, the Houston-based oil giant Halliburton. He remained in that position for five years and then resigned to run for vice president in 2000. A year later, Brown and Root won another long-term contract to provide a wide range of contingency services to the military in the event of overseas deployment. This deal provided the basis for winning several contracts—totaling $183 million by October 2003—to support Operation Enduring Freedom, which centered on Afghanistan following September 11th. Next, in the aftermath of the invasion of Iraq, Operation Iraqi Freedom was launched, and from it Brown and Root secured contracts with an aggregate value of $1.7 billion as of October 2003. In 2002–2003 the price of Halliburton shares rose by half, and the conglomerate's bottom line moved from red ink to black. While Vice President Cheney had dropped all direct financial ties to the company, he retained stock options and still receives deferred payments for services previously performed.[31]

Sharing Power, the title of Kettl's landmark book on contracting, points to his contention that the most important feature of contracting out by government is that it concerns not the details of management but the fundamentals of governance. When governments transfer duties to private parties, they also transfer power to them. Far from being arms-length purveyors of goods and services, contractors are insiders who participate actively in policy implementation. It is not unusual for numerous consultants or contractor representatives to meet with many fewer government employees to develop program or strategic plans. Contract employees hired to assist in program management sit in government offices once occupied by civil servants. In government office buildings, large spaces filled with office cubicles designed for civil servants are occupied instead by contract personnel. They not only perform the work but fashion ties to elected officials and external constituencies that give them clout in shaping that work. Because of endemic staff shortages in government, contract employees are turned to for confidential duties at the heart of the institution, such as preparing plans and even voting in meetings. Increasingly, this makes public management not a matter of internal leadership alone, but of keeping tabs on contractor activities as well. Once again, rather than simplifying administration, privatization complicates it.[32]

In addition to the business contracting mode of dispersed public action that we have been discussing, other quite different types exist. Each possesses its own set of complexities and implications.

One is the use of nonprofit organizations as surrogates for government. In this implementation mode, nongovernmental organizations deliver public services to citizens, such as needle exchange programs for drug abusers, counseling for AIDS victims, therapy for the disabled, protection of abused women and children, and shelters for the homeless. The organizations receive grant or contract funding from government, supplemented by private contributions that are encouraged by the tax code. The sources of public funding are often second- or third-hand, such as those channeled through state agencies or municipal block grants. Hence the relatively removed nonprofit organizations frequently operate with great autonomy, in effect being accountable only to their own boards. Even this check is sometimes undercut by the influence of a charismatic leader who represents the social cause pursued.

This form of public action has many advantages. It permits approaches to local problems that are uniquely tailored to local conditions. It creates space for active engagement by members of the community in activities to improve that community's quality of life. Volunteers help staff the programs, creating opportunities for forming bonds as well as saving money.

The other side of the picture is that since government is to some extent a sponsor and funder of the activity, it retains a moral if not legal responsibility for the quality of services rendered. But because its relationship to the program is so remote, government cannot assure quality. Executive directors and board members control programs. If members of the community are dissatisfied, they may have no practical avenue for redress beyond the organization itself. A lack of professional competence within the organization can go unnoticed for some time. A study of eighteen community-based development organizations in El Paso found that most had remarkably primitive systems of financial planning and management and very few full-time staff.[33]

One of my students, Michelle Murphy, conducted a "twin" study on this topic, comparable to the paired bureaucracy studies reviewed in chapter 3. She examined two community development organizations in different states. They were similar in size, purpose, and organization, and both received federal funds. One had a diverse and expanding program, highly active board members, a variety of funding sources, and a solid community reputation. The other was more limited in its program, more passive in its style, less financially secure, and relatively unknown. In other words, the outcome of nonprofit devolution "all depends." Key factors she identified as necessary to the success of such ventures were the style of the director, the activism of board members, and the extent of connection with the community.[34]

In addition to its uneven nature, service delivery by this mode can encounter intense political controversy. In a recent article, Sheila Kennedy and Wolfgang Bielefeld discuss implementation of President George W. Bush's "Charitable Choice" initiative to channel federal funds to faith-based organizations for provision of social services. They point out that even though sectarian agencies have been doing this work for decades, the presidential attention stirred up new debate on the subject. Civil libertarians saw the initiative as a fresh assault on separation of church and state. The religious right warned that funds should not go to Islamic or Scientology churches. African American pastors worried that "government shekels" might be accompanied by "government shackles." As Kennedy and Bielefeld point out, "Caught in the middle are public managers, who must make the legislation work in the face of significant administrative challenges."[35]

In addition to contracting out and working through nonprofit organizations, three other forms of dispersed public action have emerged: public-private partnerships, collaborative networks, and private organizations that perform public services. From the standpoint of degree of privatization, the government's role diminishes successively in the three forms.

In public-private partnerships, two or more parties span the boundary between government and the private sector to take on a joint project or set of activities. Although the term is sometimes applied to any long-term government collaboration with private organizations, more strictly speaking it describes a situation in which the two parties share the costs, risks, and benefits of a common undertaking. Examples include such arrangements as when real estate developers and a city government build a combined shopping mall–city hall, or when, as happened at Virginia Tech, a university, the state Department of Transportation, and the automotive industry joined hands to create an experimental road test-bed. In this situation, the asymmetric donor-recipient relationship is replaced by a joint venture among equals. A sharing of decision-making power and control, as well as financing, is established.

The concept carries on its face an almost "motherhood-and-apple pie" image, in that it hardly seems possible to question the teaming together of diverse organizations in a desirable common venture with each participant making its contribution. The practice generates its own set of complexities, however. The partners do not merely strike a deal, they create a common entity. Authority and resources must be actually shared, differences resolved, and trust built. Technical knowledge of another's realm must be appreciated if not mastered. Relationships must be embedded in the routines of the organizational culture so that they persist over time. Conflicting institutional values do not have to meld, but they must become compatible. Investors must still make profits and satisfy stockholders, while bureaucrats cannot stray from their charter or the Constitution. As Richard Ghere points out, such close partnership requires many capabilities that are not easy to come by. Bureaucrats representing the public in such arrangements must be able to accomplish many things: balancing competing values without sacrificing vital principle, recruiting an infusion of capital without giving away the store, cultivating astuteness in bridging world views, and reconciling entrepreneurial strategies with a dedication to the public good.[36]

The collaborative network differs from this pattern in that whereas the partnership contemplates a defined project carried out in close association, the network constitutes a loose framework for ongoing collaboration in an area of common concern. It may or may not involve a central node of authority. Members of the network typically come from multiple sectors and represent a wide array of stakeholders. Governmental entities may or may not be members, but typically tasks of public concern are taken on. While one member may take the lead, the ideal is to give all members equal standing. The aim is to arrive at decisions following authentic collaboration rather than legislature-like pressures and maneuvering.

Hence, in this model of dispersion no single party has outright control—including the government. The bureaucrats must abide by the collective outcome. They may want to reject the outcome but are pressured by the structure of the arrangement not to do so. Hence it is not surprising that most networks facilitate consensus rather than adopting new policies. For example, bodies known as State Rural Development Councils are composed of representatives of varied public and private entities concerned with agriculture and economic development. They pursue ways to solve common problems on this front and remove barriers to action. A water-quality network in Tillamook County, Oregon, brings together representatives of the EPA, state agencies, lumber mills, paper plants, and farmers to develop water management goals and monitor water quality. The National Quality Forum in Washington, D.C., coordinates the collaborative work of approximately one hundred organizations concerned with health-care-quality measurement and reporting.[37]

The final category of dispersed public action to be considered is that in which private organizations perform public functions. This is nothing new—the New York Stock Exchange is a famous example. Two particularly noteworthy types have emerged in recent years. One is the Business Improvement District (BID), an organization created to stimulate the revitalization of downtown commercial and entertainment areas. More than four hundred of these entities exist in cities across the country. Although their legal forms differ, their activities tend to include installing pedestrian-scale infrastructure, producing festivals and tourist maps, collecting refuse and removing graffiti, operating parking garages, regulating sidewalk vending and begging, and mounting unarmed security forces. Each BID is controlled by a board of property owners elected under a voting system that is weighted by asset value. It can tax its membership, administer a budget, and hire a bureaucracy—in other words, it can be a private government.[38]

The second type is the Transportation Management Association (TMA), which is created to improve transportation systems and facilities in major metropolitan areas and central business districts. Over one hundred exist, two-thirds of them in California. With rare exception, they are entirely private associations or have a partnership link with government. Their membership normally includes property owners, developers, employers, and local governments. Funds are raised from corporate membership fees, weighted by number of employees, that are supplemented by occasional government or private grants. Activities include monitoring traffic flows and commuter times, encouraging alternative work schedules, promoting ride-sharing and carpools, operating shuttle services or sidewalk circulators, and, in a few instances, lobbying for urban transit. While TMAs work closely with government in many instances, their decisions are not necessarily made in consultation with elected officials or bureaucrats.[39]

Solve Those Problems!

American bureaucracy, despite facing no-win situations and the complications of federalism and dispersed action, is supposed to "solve problems." At the beginning of this chapter we mentioned that the Progressive notion of inevitable problem-solution can lead to false expectations, for identification of a problem is itself no guarantee that a solution exists. Some of our society's problems can be corrected by government. An example in my own region is a road into North Carolina whose sharp curves make it very dangerous to drive. That highway can be rebuilt, if the right decisions are made and sufficient funds become available. For other problems, however, full correction of the problem may not be possible. A perfect example in the current era is terrorism: we can combat and prepare for terrorist acts, but total elimination of the threat is impossible. Another illustration is the international spread of infectious disease. Because of microbial adaptation, jet travel, mega-cities, and human contact with animals caused by land-clearing, the incidence of thirty-five diseases has exploded worldwide over the past three decades. SARS, West Nile virus, Hantavirus, Ebola, Nipah, Hendra, and AIDS cannot be halted by any conceivable set of government programs—the most to hope for is some degree of control.[40]

Unfortunately for the reputation of government, when such "missions impossible" are identified and scheduled for performance by the body politic, people are not likely to accept that success may not be obtainable. Citizens, legislators, and advocates don't politely say, "OK, you're right. The problem can't really be solved. Just do your best." Instead, the critics concede nothing; they demand solutions even more resolutely; if solutions are not forthcoming, they seek enemies and scapegoats—and a good candidate for both is often bureaucracy.

What is a "problem"? It is something we do not like—a pain, a difficulty, an injustice, a misfortune, a shortcoming, a gap, a vexation, a tragedy, a discomfort, a scandal, a disaster. An important point here is that these dislikes are *subjectively* defined. Problems are derived from people's feelings about conditions, not the conditions themselves. In the case of some difficulties or disasters—dangerous highways and terrorist attacks being good examples—almost everyone sees them as problems. Hence, taking collective action is a clear matter of common concern. For less commonly agreed-upon problems, however, the element of subjectivity is more apparent. For example, are violent video games a problem? Radon gas in basements? Gays in the Boy Scouts? Prayers at commencement? It all depends on your point of view.

Hence, while death-trap highways, terrorist attacks, and infectious diseases are instantly discernible as problems, other difficulties or injustices *can* become problems. This happens when political candidates, elected officials, concerned citizens, injured parties, or activist groups take the initiative to bring attention to their issues and persuade others that public action is needed. The issues then go on the government's agenda, so to speak. Examples of this process are legion, famous ones being the civil rights movement to place racism on the agenda and the Green movement to put the plundered environment there.

If enough pressure is generated to impel action on the agenda item, a law may be passed, a regulation adopted, an executive order issued, or the mayor may simply tell the city manager, "Do something about that!" At this point the bureaucracy must swing into action and actually attempt to solve the problem. As the stage of agenda formation shifts to the stage of administrative accomplishment, as the bureaucracy takes over from publicists and politicians, the harsh realities of altering human behavior and intervening in the physical environment must be confronted. And the job may not be easy. In fact, it may be impossible.

But that does not mean that nothing can be done. What may indeed be possible is suggested by the name of that street I mentioned at the beginning of the chapter: Progress can be made. This is bureaucracy's rightful objective when it is handed a Mission Impossible. What I mean by progress is steady, forward movement. We cannot wipe out racism forever, but we can take significant steps against it every day, in and out of government. Smog, lead, and nonpoint pollution of streams cannot be eliminated, but they can be lessened—significantly—by hard, concerted effort. Terrorism cannot be "destroyed" in a "war," but it can be fought tooth-and-nail over the years in small ways and big, all across the country and the world. The same is true with AIDS, SARS, the West Nile virus, and Ebola. That this kind of progress ultimately produces results is, in the final analysis, the lesson of chapter 2's table of Accomplishments of America (see table 2-9).

The crucial point, then, is that despite the exaggerations of political rhetoric and hyped expectations of the media, bureaucracy's task is less to solve problems than to make good progress on them. In most instances, this concept is best redefined as making *headway* on problems, not ending them. The reason for this inconclusiveness lies not in bureaucracy's timidity or weakness or ineptitude, but in the kinds of tasks it is assigned. Generally, these problems have two characteristics. First, they are of a mass rather than a confined nature—that is, changes must take place in many places, in many things, and in many people. Second, they are not of a type wherein change can be achieved through the workings of the market on an automatic self-interest basis. This means that organized efforts must be mounted that combine the following minimal ingredients: (1) integrated or at least coordinated public action, (2) the backing of legal authority, (3) an infusion of funds that can be flexibly deployed, and (4) a determination to mount a concerted campaign over the long haul. When this combination is institutionalized, we have the essence of bureaucracy.

The theme of this chapter has been that bureaucracy as institutionalized in America is given particular handicaps in making good progress. These handicaps are not restricted to the United States—both the assignment of contradictory tasks and the conflicts manifest as "red tape" are universal. But the stretched-out, devolved nature of American administrative implementation is not universal. The intergovernmental grant system requires thousands of individual bureaucracies to interact with each other. Dispersal of public action to the private sector introduces many added complexities and uncertainties. Moreover, these devolutions to the Greek cross of implementation borne by America generate a variety of economic and social forces that are powerful indeed. Making good progress with such a system requires bureaucratic institutions that are strong enough to counter the great pressures exerted by the self-interest of corporations and the subjectively identified causes of social and community actors, not to mention the agendas of partners, collaborators, and urban business and transportation interests. Ask the impossible of bureaucracy? Easy!

Chapter 5 Looking Closer at Those Bureaucrats

The United States has roughly 21 million bureaucrats, if the term is used to mean civilian government employees of all types at all levels. Who are they? What are they like? Do they wear green eyeshades? Do they sit at desks all day and shuffle papers? Are they mostly white males? Are they mostly liberal Democrats? Do they order people around and enforce rules to the letter? Are they empire builders? Do they sabotage policies they don't like? These are some of the questions we'll strive to answer in this chapter.

As to the specific question of whether they wear green eye shades, the answer is no. They wear instead the sunglasses of hurricane pilots, the helmets of firefighters, the Smokey-the-Bear felts of state troopers, the magnification glasses of neurosurgeons, the sealed hoods of toxic-substance investigators, and the baseball caps of ordinary citizens.

Moreover, most bureaucrats don't sit at desks all day. If they do, they are working at computer terminals rather than shuffling papers. And, if you call them at their desks, they may be elsewhere in the office conferring with fellow employees—or out of the building talking to community leaders. A bureaucrat's principal workplace may not even be a desk at all. It may be a noisy schoolroom, a quiet museum, the ward of a veterans' hospital, the home of a family suspected of child abuse, a border crossing with Mexico, a reconstruction site in Iraq, or an interstate highway crowded with drivers doing 85.

That is to say, our stereotypes of what a bureaucrat is like and does are, for the most part, dead wrong. "The popular impression of a civil servant is like an outdated photograph," writes John Weaver, with "as little relationship to today's government worker as one of his baby pictures."[1] One is hard-pressed to think of a job bureaucrats don't do. They drive snowplows, stock rivers, examine patents, negotiate contracts, deliver mail, jail criminals, inspect meat, fight terrorism, inspect mines, prepare budgets, make grants, do research, negotiate treaties, and much more.

Their Representativeness

We begin a closer look at these bureaucrats by seeing how similar or different they are from the rest of us. Half a century ago Norton Long pointed out that the federal civil service importantly supplements the U.S. Congress as an instrument of representation. One of several intertwined themes of his argument was that recruitment into the American civil service is relatively open.

Unlike civil service practices in many countries, bureaucrats in the United States come from all social levels, groups, and regions of the nation. This means, Long said, that the bureaucracy substantially mirrors the makeup of the national population, more so than do the members of Congress.

> If one rejects the view that election is the sine qua non of representation, the bureaucracy now has a very real claim to be considered much more representative of the American people in its composition than the Congress. This is not merely the case with respect to the class structure of the country but, equally significantly, with respect to the learned groups, skills, economic interests, races, nationalities, and religions. The rich diversity that makes up the United States is better represented in its civil service than anywhere else.[2]

Such representative diversity cannot and should not replace the official representation provided by Congress and other elected bodies, of course. Elections form the larger framework for political responsiveness and accountability in a democracy. The fact that legislators must be reelected in order to stay in office remains a key link in the concept of popular sovereignty. But other linkages between citizens and government can and must exist, and one can argue that one of the more important is the fact that the characteristics of citizens running the government mirror the characteristics of the citizens served by that government.

Following World War II, when the British Labour Party took over from Churchill's Conservatives, many intellectuals wondered whether an elitist civil service in Whitehall could properly serve the new socialist regime. This questioning of whether the bureaucracy was *adequately* representative launched a large body of scholarship on the matter. Studies of the higher civil service in Europe and Japan tended to show that graduates of certain schools or members of certain professions dominated the bureaucracy's top echelons. In several developing countries, persons from particular regions or ethnic groups were found to be in control of the bureaucracy, at the expense of the rest of the population.

Kenneth Meier used a statistic known as the Gini index to measure bureaucratic representation on a comparative national basis. In this measure, 0 indicates perfect demographic mirroring and 1 means totally imperfect. For all federal civil servants in the United States, Meier found that on the variable of occupational status of one's father, the index score was .12; for educational level and age, .11; for region of birth, .13; and for birthplace size and current income, .25. With respect to high-level civil servants around the world, the father's occupational status score was .47 in the United States, compared to .53 for Britain, .66 for Denmark, .78 for France, .82 for Turkey, and .89 for India. Meier concludes, "The United States civil service does indeed mirror the American people as a whole."[3]

Since Meier's work, more data have become available. With respect to income level, the earnings of bureaucrats are comparable to those of the rest of the workforce, at least in terms of averages. In 2000, American government employees at all levels earned an average of $40,228 in wages and salaries, compared to $38,612 for workers in private industry. (Adding in fringe benefits makes the difference greater: $50,782 versus $45,613.) As for level of education, that of bureaucrats was somewhat higher. In the same year (2000), 41 percent of federal government employees had a college education or better, compared to 30.4 percent of the overall civilian labor force.[4]

With respect to political views, using national survey data James Garand and associates compared policy attitudes and voting behavior of government employees at all levels in the United States to those of the general public. They found that on thirty measures of general political attitudes, ten showed the bureaucrats to be more liberal than other respondents to a statistically significant degree. Of forty-eight variables called "feeling thermometers" (questions deemed capable of revealing underlying political attitudes), bureaucrats' responses on seventeen showed a liberal bias. Among thirty-four spending questions (in which respondents were asked if government spent too much, too little, or just the right amount), the results on nine indicated a statistically significant support by the bureaucrats for more spending—for space, health, education, crime, science, defense, the environment, student aid, and the needs of African Americans. With respect to voting, Garand found that in half the indicators government employees were shown to have voted significantly less often for Republicans than had other Americans.[5]

In an article published in 1990, Gregory Lewis specifically set out to test whether bureaucrats are or are not like ordinary Americans in social attitude in several areas of public policy. Drawing on annual national survey data, he compared the general public's sentiments on several matters—first, to those of "all" bureaucrats, including government employees at all levels of government except postal employees and schoolteachers, and then to those of "top" bureaucrats, defined as government managers and professionals. The results are shown in table 5-1.[6]

Within a point or two, bureaucrats as a whole are shown to be identical with the general public in their concerns about crime, drugs, the environment, welfare, and the condition of the cities. Their views are similarly close on capital punishment, premarital sex, school busing, and fundamentalist religion. Overall, comparability outweighs contrast: statistically significant differences occur between the public and all bureaucrats in only fifteen of forty-four items. For example, government employees are more pro-defense and pro–space exploration, less hostile to divorce and to pornography, more committed to free speech, and less opposed to homosexuality and to interracial marriage. As for top bureaucrats, they have generally the same configuration as all bureaucrats, except that they are more liberal on such matters as abortion, capital punishment, extramarital sex, and women's place in society—differences that can likely be accounted for by the managers' and professionals' higher levels of income and education. A *Washington Post* article reporting on

Table 5-1 Attitudes of the American Public and Public Employees (in percentages)

		Bureaucrats	
	The public	All	Top
Government spends too little on:			
Halting crime	65	67	64
Improving education	65	61	61
Improving health	62	64	64
Dealing with drug addition	62	63	61
Improving the environment	61	63	61
Welfare	39	40	38
Problems of cities	39	40	38
Condition of blacks	32	31	28
The military	21	25	16
Space exploration	14	17	19
Foreign aid	5	4	2
Own taxes too high:	66	62	62
Would favor law:			
Legalizing abortion	38	42	52
Making divorce harder	54	48	45
Making pornography illegal	42	37	33
Keeping marijuana illegal	80	80	74
Requiring gun permits	73	70	76
Would allow public speech:			
By a homosexual	70	80	88
Against all churches	68	80	89
Claiming blacks inferior	60	67	76
By admitted communist	60	72	82
Advocating military rule	57	65	77
Dealing with crime:			
Approve death penalty	77	77	70
Courts too lenient	87	84	81
Approve wiretapping	21	30	32
Police shouldn't strike citizens	24	20	15
Religious attitudes:			
Is fundamentalist	32	33	25
Attends church weekly	30	29	32
Is strong religious member	44	42	43
Prays daily	56	53	46
Sex attitudes:			
Premarital sex wrong	27	26	26
Extramarital sex wrong	74	70	62
Homosexuality wrong	75	69	59
Attitudes toward women:			
Married women should work	80	84	86
Woman's place is at home	24	20	12
Would vote for woman for president	86	90	93
Men better suited for politics	36	35	31
Racial attitudes:			
Accept interracial home dinners	81	88	98
Ban interracial marriage	26	17	11
Blacks should not be pushy	58	49	29

continues

Table 5-1 *(continued)*

	The public	Bureaucrats All	Bureaucrats Top
Favor open housing laws	52	55	54
Favor school integration	92	96	98
Should bus schoolchildren	25	24	23
Would vote for black for president	86	90	90

SOURCE: Gregory B. Lewis, "In Search of the Machiavellian Milquetoasts: Comparing Attitudes of Bureaucrats and Ordinary People," *Public Administration Review* 50 (March/April 1990): 220–227.

Lewis's findings summarizes them this way, quoting in part from an earlier edition of this book:

> Although government bureaucrats are sometimes negatively portrayed as "fear-ridden, yet arrogant, incompetent yet ominous, milquetoasts yet Machiavellians," in reality, the attitudes of bureaucrats and those of the rest of the population are remarkably similar on major public and personal issues.[7]

Still, not all bureaucrats think the same, and region of the country is one source of difference. Robert Watson surveyed top nonelected officials in four administrative program areas in the municipalities of one state, Alabama. As the figures presented in table 5-2 show, he found them balanced in party affiliation but emphatically conservative in ideology. The planners were even more to the right than those in public works, parks, and budgeting, curiously enough. Watson also noticed that it was the few liberal civil servants, more than their conservative colleagues, who said they did not try to impose their personal views in administering programs. He concludes that the study questions, in one state at least, "the old adage that bureaucrats are liberal activists who resent or are uncontrollable by elected officials."[8]

Other data reinforce the notion that the political views of bureaucrats vary by the policy focus of the department in which they serve. In a study of the voting behavior and political attitudes of federal careerists in the Senior Executive Service, Stanley Rothman and Robert Lichter contrasted those working for "traditional" agencies, such as the departments of Commerce, Agriculture, Treasury, and Justice, with those in "activist" agencies, including the

Table 5-2 Party Affiliation versus Ideology of Bureaucrats (in percentages)

Political Party		Political Ideology	
Strongly Democrat	16.0	Strongly conservative	40.2
Weakly Democrat	10.1	Weakly conservative	17.8
Independent	32.1	Neutral	28.9
Weakly Republican	10.4	Weakly liberal	3.7
Strongly Republican	17.0	Strongly liberal	3.7
Other	7.9		

SOURCE: Robert P. Watson, "Politics and Public Administration: A Political Profile of Local Bureaucrats in Alabama," *Administration and Society* 29 (May 1997): 189–200.

departments of Health and Human Services and Housing and Urban Development, as well as environmental, civil rights, and consumer agencies. The second group tended more often than the first to vote for Democratic presidential candidates and to favor liberal causes. At the same time, Rothman and Lichter point out that the liberalism in these liberal-leaning agencies was generally tame and not radically antibusiness in nature:

> Our findings give scant support to those who see the bureaucracy as hostile to business or other traditional institutions. Senior civil servants as a whole are indeed somewhat more liberal than most Americans. However, they are considerably less disaffected from traditional American values than their conservative critics contend. Moreover, while key bureaucrats in the activist agencies are somewhat more liberal than those in the traditional agencies, the differences are not large enough to explain the "adversarial" behavior of which businessmen complain.[9]

Turning from political views to levels of political participation, the Garand study mentioned earlier found that with respect to voter turnout, the bureaucrats participated in the political process more fully than did citizens as a whole—and to a significant degree. Similarly, an analysis of national survey data by Gene Brewer and Sally Selden found that government employees are more likely than other citizens to belong to civic, social, and community groups. They are also more likely to vote, support a candidate, or be involved in political organizations. These findings are interpreted as particularly significant in view of the fact that in their methodology Brewer and Selden held constant age and ideology.[10]

As for the fundamental political values held by bureaucrats, William Blair and James Garand inquired whether bureaucrats are different from other citizens with respect to their commitments to democratic principles and political tolerance. They concluded, among other things, that government employees are more likely to uphold the rights of political and social minorities and to support gender and racial equality. They also note that bureaucrats are more supportive of the federal government, but only by 2 points on a 100-point scale. For some years the IRS has noted the propensity of federal employees to pay their taxes on time. In 1996, 7 percent of government workers failed to file a tax return or owed back taxes, compared to 9 percent of taxpayers as a whole. For 2001 these percentages were, respectively, 2.8 and 5.2 percent.[11]

So far, our discussion of bureaucratic representativeness has not incorporated race and sex. In America, however, these variables are at the heart of discourse over representative bureaucracy. Americans can be proud that the civil rights revolution and the women's movement that originated in this country are now spreading to much of the world. To what extent have the ideals of racial and gender equality permeated government employment here in the United States?

As one might expect, the passage of time has seen major changes. Half a century ago, racial minorities were greatly underrepresented in American public employment, as were women. Bureaucracy, like business, was essentially a white, male preserve. In 1940 the percentage of federal employees who were black stood at 4.2; in 1950, it was 9.3. Not until 1960 did the figure reach the approximate proportion of African Americans in the population, at that time about 11 percent. In subsequent decades the proportion rose well above that level, and it has stayed there since. As for gender, in 1939, 19 percent of the federal workforce was female. By the end of World War II, the figure had reached 37 percent, but after the war it dipped back to 24 percent. During the 1960s upward movement began again, but it was not until 1978 that the wartime level was again reached.[12]

The extent of more recent progress, for both minorities and women, can be seen in table 5-3, which shows federal executive-branch employment percentages over the 1990–2000 decade, as well as percentages in the resident population for 2000. The proportion of African Americans in the federal executive workforce in 2000 was 17 percent, substantially more than their representation in the population as a whole. Percentages of other minorities continued rising somewhat, with Asians and American Indians also exceeding their proportions of the population by that year. Only Hispanics remain behind. Taken as a whole, minority employment in the federal government stands at about 30 percent, which is very close to perfect representation of the population. As for women, their proportion in the bureaucracy rose from 43 to 45 percent—6 points below their proportion in the population. State and local governments, meanwhile, reached identical levels. By 1999, 30 percent of their aggregate workforce consisted of members of racial minorities, with 45 percent being female.[13]

Overall proportions of minorities and women in the public workforce answer only one aspect of the question of these groups' representation in government work. The other is how far up they rise in the hierarchy of power. What about management and executive positions?

Table 5-3 Government Employment and Resident Population by Race, Ethnicity, and Sex (in percentages)

	Federal Executive Branch						Resident Population
	1990	1992	1994	1996	1998	2000	2000
African Americans	16.6	16.6	16.7	16.6	16.7	17.0	12.8
Hispanics	5.4	5.5	5.7	6.1	6.4	6.6	11.8
Asians[a]	3.5	3.7	4.1	4.3	4.5	4.5	4.1
Native Americans[b]	1.8	1.9	2.0	2.0	2.1	2.2	.9
All minorities	**27.3**	**27.8**	**28.4**	**29.1**	**29.6**	**30.2**	**29.6**
Women	43.1	43.5	43.9	44.0	44.4	45.0	51.1

SOURCE: U.S. Office of Personnel Management, *Federal Civilian Workforce Statistics: Demographic Profile of the Federal Workforce As of September 30, 2000* (May 2001), table 1-1. (Postal employees are not included.) Percentages of the resident population are from *Statistical Abstract of the United States: 2001*, 13, 295.

a. Includes Pacific Islanders.

b. Includes Alaska Natives.

Data on the attainment of upper-level jobs in the federal civilian work-force by racial and ethnic minorities and women are given in table 5-4. The category at the top of the table, employees at senior pay levels, is the most restrictive group of those shown. Minorities are very substantially underrepresented in this group, with Hispanics more so than blacks. Still, the proportions of both minorities rose dramatically in this category over the ten years, far faster than in the federal workforce as a whole. The proportion of women at senior pay levels more than doubled over the decade. The other two categories shown in the table are successively less restrictive. The position of minorities improves in each case but more gradually, with African Americans exceeding their presence in the population in the administrative category. The percentage of women in these categories rose as well, reaching a percentage in the administrative category about the same as their presence in the executive branch as a whole.[14]

In other words, over the past ten years or so, *many* more minorities and women than before have risen to senior positions in the federal bureaucracy. These changes have made a visible impact on the face of Washington. In the Patent and Trademark Office, for example, blacks and Asians constitute 37 and 13 percent of the staff, respectively, with whites at 47 percent. In celebration of this diversity, the organization annually sponsors a Community Day of international games and foods. In another place where this change is manifest, the proportion of female attorneys in the Justice Department rose from 6 percent in 1970 to 32 percent in 1993. During the Clinton administration, nine of the top fifteen jobs at Justice were held by women, including that of attorney general.[15]

Table 5-4 Federal Employees at Senior, Professional, and Administrative Levels by Race, Ethnicity, and Sex (in percentages)

	1990	2000
GS and related grade groupings at senior pay levels:		
Minorities	7.7	13.5
African Americans	4.7	7.1
Hispanics	1.5	3.3
Women	11.1	24.4
Upper categories of white-collar workforce:		
Professional category		
Minorities	17.4	21.8
African Americans	7.2	8.7
Hispanics	3.5	4.4
Women	33.7	40.7
Administrative category		
Minorities	20.1	25.9
African Americans	12.3	15.2
Hispanics	4.6	6.2
Women	38.3	44.1

SOURCE: Office of Personnel Management, *Federal Civilian Workforce Statistics*, tables 1.2, 1.4, 1.5, and 1.7.

In state and local government, progress in moving minorities and women to the top has been even better, although the statistical categories used are not identical to those for the national government. In 1999, 17.6 percent of "officials/administrators" were members of minorities, of which 11.1 percent were black and 4.2 percent Hispanic. Women occupied 34.5 percent of these jobs. In the same year, 25.7 percent of those classified as professionals were minorities, with 14.9 percent black and 5.8 percent Hispanic. Fifty-four percent were female, higher than the ratio of women in the population. As for women at the very top of state government, Angela Bullard and Deil Wright examined the gender of names of state agency heads and calculated that from 1964 to 1990 the proportion of female names rose from 4 to 19 percent. It is probably much higher now.[16]

In another study of state civil servants, Vernon Greene, Sally Selden, and Gene Brewer computed a composite measure of bureaucratic representation that incorporates proportionate presence *and* hierarchical rank, achieved by weighting upper-level employment. They found that among men, Asian Americans scored highest, followed by whites, African Americans, American Indians, and Hispanics. Among the women, the order was Asian Americans, African Americans, whites, American Indians, and Hispanics. According to this measure, women generally tend to be underrepresented, although the degree differs by ethnic group.[17]

Some data are available on how minorities have fared in the public sector versus the private. Evidence exists that African Americans, in particular, have benefited from employment in government as compared to business. In 2001 they occupied 16.2 percent of the jobs in the total public administration field, covering all levels of government, whereas in the private economy's agriculture, manufacturing, and services sectors they held, respectively, 3.6, 10.1, and 12.6 percent. Even in 1980, when fewer African Americans were rising to the top than today, blacks were getting good jobs in government more readily than in the private sector.[18] As table 5-5 shows, this was especially so for female African Americans.

The *Washington Post* compiled figures on African American employment in the Washington, D.C., metropolitan region in various occupations. The

Table 5-5 African American Employment in the Public and Private Sectors, 1980 (in percentages)

	State & local govt.		Private sector	
	Technical & professional	Managers & administrators	Technical & professional	Managers & administrators
Males	3.8	3.6	2.4	2.0
Females	6.2	2.1	2.6	1.1

SOURCE: Nelson C. Dometrius and Lee Sigelman, "Assessing Progress toward Affirmative Action Goals in State and Local Government: A New Benchmark," *Public Administration Review* 44, no. 3 (May/June 1984): 244.

analysis was not intended to differentiate between the private and public sectors, but it had implications in this regard. In 1990, blacks constituted 18 percent of government managers and 18 percent of postal managers but only 10 percent of the civil engineers and 7 percent of the lawyers. The *Post* concluded that while "blacks continue to surge into public jobs . . . in numbers large enough to create a solid, visible presence," the black middle class is "finding it hard to break out of government jobs and into the top ranks of the private sector."[19]

Peter Eisinger collected minority advancement data on the New York City government, compiling a sample of the nearly 10,000 officials, administrators, and professionals who work for the city's Human Resources Administration. He discovered that whereas exactly half of the white members of the sample came from middle-class backgrounds, less than a quarter of black members did; most of the latter group grew up in working-class or impoverished homes. To attain these positions, Eisinger reasons, the African Americans as a group had moved farther upward than the whites in terms of social mobility. Moreover, for those blacks who happened to have siblings working in the private sector, their brothers and sisters tended to be at a lower level of responsibility. Eisinger concludes, "local government employment plays a more significant role for blacks than for whites as an intergenerational avenue to higher status."[20]

A considerable literature has developed on whether minority public administrators perform differently than whites in the positions they hold. Researchers have been interested in knowing whether in their work they favor the interests and viewpoints of their own race, a concept referred to as "active" representation. In a study of the federal Farmers Home Administration (now Rural Housing Service), Sally Selden found that districts of the agency that employed more minorities granted proportionately more loans to minorities. Also she found that minority FHA county supervisors tended to be more supportive of the interests of minorities than their white colleagues were.[21]

In 1974 Adam Herbert advanced the thesis that minority public administrators, sensing a hostile white environment in their organizations, feel special compulsions to prove that they are team players in order to be promoted. Two decades later, Herbert's thesis was revisited by Sylvester Murray, Larry Terry, Charles Washington, and Lawrence Keller, who surveyed mostly African American higher civil servants in the federal government. These authors found that most respondents in the sample perceived that they are expected to be loyal to institutional patterns but also to act as agents of change. Also, most said that they recommended and advocated pro-minority policies. At the same time, they felt the need to make compromises when agency policies were in conflict with their views, a balancing act perceived as acceptable to their organizations. Murray and associates conclude, "The American administrative state, especially at the national level, is making progress on its commitment to a diverse but highly educated corps of civil servants."[22]

To sum up, America's bureaucrats are by no means members of a closed elite. Federal employees have somewhat more income and education than most Americans, but the differences are marginal. As for political beliefs, bureaucrats are somewhat—not drastically—more liberal than other Americans, with variation by hierarchical rank, section of the country, and type of organization. Also, bureaucrats are more likely than other Americans to vote, to pay their taxes on time, to join political and social organizations, and to uphold principles of minority rights and social equality.

As for the extent to which American bureaucracy is representative from the standpoint of race, ethnicity, and gender, we found that decades ago minorities and women were glaringly absent from the public service. But significant if uneven gains over the decades produced a situation at the turn of the century wherein government employment was 30 percent minority and 45 percent female. For African Americans in particular, government had become a prime vehicle of upward mobility, and for some years their proportionate employment in government has surpassed their ratio in the population. At the same time, however, the representation of blacks and women at the upper levels of responsibility has not been proportional, although this ratio is also improving. When minority public administrators attain higher positions, they seek to advance minority interests, but this "active" representation is tempered by a recognized need to accept agency policy as well.

Their "Personality"

Our closer look at bureaucrats continues by examining an idea that also has roots in the past century—the notion that, if we *really* look closely at bureaucrats, we find not ordinary human beings but a special kind of person who thinks and acts in certain ways. The reason? Their "bureaucratic personality."

The basic contention is that the structure of bureaucracy itself produces a distinctive mentality or personality. This idea sprang originally from Max Weber's sociological characteristics of bureaucracy: full-time, appointed, career employees who labor in a hierarchy under a regime of specialization and rules. In chapter 1 we noted expectations of pathological behavior seen as deriving from the Weberian model, and in chapter 3 a myth of determinism. The expectation in this instance is that, whether by self-selection in entering bureaucratic employment or by socialization once having got there, the bureaucrat possesses a particular turn of mind and pattern of conduct. While the so-called bureaucratic personality is most often associated with government, some theorists also see signs of it in big private organizations.

This school of analysis began in earnest with a famous article by Robert Merton, "Bureaucratic Structure and Personality," published in 1940. Merton argued that at least four principal traits of the bureaucratic personality are produced by bureaucratic organization. First, the specialized nature of bureaucratic work causes "an inadequate flexibility in the application of skills." This is said to occur because an extreme narrowness in scope of work does not allow the functionary to be capable of adapting to ever-changing conditions. Second, the need for reliability and discipline in bureaucratic output causes officials to overemphasize the importance of rules. They then forget the initial reason for the rules, and, by a "displacement of goals," enforcement of the rules surpasses in importance the policy objectives the organization is ultimately trying to achieve. "An extreme product of this process of displacement of goals," wrote Merton, "is the bureaucratic virtuoso, who never forgets a single rule binding his action and hence is unable to assist many of his clients."

Third, Merton charged, the lengthy career of the bureaucrat makes him or her cautious, conservative, and protective of an entrenched position. Too much is at stake to take any chances with innovation or risk. Finally, the general application of rules to individual cases creates an impersonal, categorical mode of thinking that ignores the humanity and individuality of clients. "The personality pattern of the bureaucrat is nucleated about this norm of impersonality," Merton contended. Accompanying it is an arrogant and haughty manner, stemming from the formal authority with which the bureaucrat is vested, as well as the lower-level official's psychological need to compensate for an inferior position within the organization by exhibiting superiority to those outside it.[23]

Others have elaborated on and extended Merton's thesis. Anthony Downs, in his well-known book, *Inside Bureaucracy,* propounds a "Law of Increasing Conservatism." By this he means a tendency for bureaucrats to become change-avoiders as they grow older and remain fixed in their positions. They seek to hang on to the power they have and avoid the risks of rocking the boat. They also play rigidly by the rules so as to evade blame by their superiors in case of mistakes.[24]

In a related claim, Charles Peters argues that the protections of a civil service career attract individuals who lack confidence, competence, drive, and courage; the consequence is a contagion of bureaucratic timidity. Says Peters,

> As we begin to climb the administrative ladder, a dominant personality type does emerge (or maybe it's that a certain element in civil servants' personalities comes to dominate as they climb the ladder), and an excess of caution is certainly one of its characteristics. . . . Civil servants are too often mother's little boys and daddy's little girls who have learned to expect security without having to earn it.[25]

Guy Benveniste contends that bureaucrats live a life of fear because of conflicting tensions on the job. On the one hand, they face an increasingly uncertain world that is impossible to predict; on the other, they are told by their organizations to act as if they could control, plan and anticipate the future. Because of this unresolvable tension, bureaucrats live in fear of being caught committing errors and thereby jeopardizing their careers. They respond by playing defensive games, which include minimizing and avoiding risks, inventing false risks, manipulating evaluations, stressing protective documentation, and deliberately doing nothing.[26]

Joseph Bensman and Bernard Rosenberg paint a more complex picture. They state that bureaucrats must remodel their prior personalities in order to fit the employing organization's norms. This produces an erosion of personal identity, which causes some bureaucrats to lose interest in their work and perform duties perfunctorily. In others, it sets the stage for the replacement of personal relationships by organizational ties or, alternatively, the identification of egos with uncompromising adherence to the rules.

To complicate matters further, Bensman and Rosenberg also deduce that a sense of powerlessness in the large and subdivided organization may lead instead to a blatant disregard of the rules, in a kind of rejectionist syndrome. Still another anticipated reaction is redirection of personal resentments against clients and subordinates, thus acting as a tyrant toward inferiors while being a sycophant to superiors. Anxious "to project those qualities which will be the most pleasing to others," the bureaucrat adopts a synthetic personality and performs as a "poseur" rather than a sincere individual. Furthermore, as he or she sees others being equally deceptive, interpersonal trust evaporates. One of several potential outcomes to this situation is a craving to rise in rank at any cost. Hence, within the prevailing atmosphere of insincerity and distrust, ambitious bureaucrats become Machiavellian infighters capable of lies, betrayal, and ruthless tactics of interoffice conflict.[27]

To yet another theorist of bureaucracy, Frederick Thayer, the underlying psychological culprit of bureaucracy is hierarchy. Said to have been invented some 6,000 years ago when the left side of the brain became dominant, the social concept of hierarchy was invented (along with an external god and legitimated authority). Hierarchy leads to several forms of alienation, or types of separation within the individual. These include loss of control over decisions about work; similar noncontrol over what is produced; severance of authentic relations with coworkers; and, finally, separation from oneself, caused by detachment of work activity from personal purpose. Bureaucracy, according to Thayer, is truly "impersonal" in the sense that it denies free and equal personhood and makes bureaucrats into repressed nonpersons who perform in roles, not as themselves.[28]

Probably the best-known analysis of the bureaucratic personality is that of Ralph Hummel, whose book, *The Bureaucratic Experience*, now in its 4th edition, has been a mainstay of college courses in public administration for over a quarter-century. In order to provoke classroom discussion, it is often assigned to students to be read in opposition to *The Case for Bureaucracy*. (At the risk of debunking some good academic lore, despite our intellectual disagreements Ralph and I are close friends.) Hummel summarizes his position as follows:

> Bureaucracy gives birth to a new species of inhuman beings. People's social relations are being converted into control relations. Their norms and beliefs

> concerning human ends are torn from them and replaced with skills affirming the ascendancy of technical means, whether of administration or production. Psychologically, the new personality type is that of the rationalistic expert, incapable of emotion and devoid of will. Language, once the means of bringing people into communication, becomes the secretive tool of one-way commands. Politics, especially democratic politics, fades away as the method of publicly determining society-wide goals based on human needs; it is replaced by administration.[29]

Unlike some of the critics mentioned earlier, Hummel admits that there are good bureaucrats who do exciting work, get the job done, and are endowed with lively minds and personal courage. The problem, according to Hummel, is that within the bureaucratic setting these qualities are repressed or at least made very difficult to exert. More broadly, the problem with bureaucracy is that of modernity itself. As civilization's most important modernizing force, bureaucracy is seen as central in bringing to the fore modernity's antihuman consequences.

Concrete manifestations of the bureaucratic personality are multiple in Hummel's view. When bureaucrats deal with clients, they approach them not as unique human beings but as cases that must fit defined characteristics. In dealing with outsiders, bureaucrats are taught to deploy incomprehensible, power-imposing language rather than to engage in mutual and meaningful dialogue. The bureaucrats themselves are eviscerated psychologically by being subject to organizational pressures that wage war on their human instincts. Their consciences are replaced by the will of superiors, and their freedom of action is circumscribed by rules and jurisdictional boundaries. Instead of exploring future possibilities in a creative manner, they carry out tasks according to a protocol devised in the past. Completion of tasks is then evaluated not by their newness or imagination but by measurement against a preset quantitative standard. The overall outcome, argues Hummel, is that the bureaucrat's individual human identity is undermined and individual human potential not realized.[30]

Many more pieces of published writing could be cited in this area, but let us stop here to ask, To what extent does the "bureaucratic personality" really exist? Are bureaucrats *always* inflexible, rule-bound, conservative, timid, arrogant, manipulative, alienated, cold, controlling, incomprehensible, and unimaginative? Do they, more than the rest of us, even *tend* to have those traits? What do we really *know* about how bureaucrats behave from research on the subject?

Perhaps the best-known empirical study—and partly for that reason one of the most controversial—is a project done many years ago by Melvin Kohn. In it he attempted to measure the personal consequences of employment in a bureaucracy, no matter whether private or public. Kohn's inquiry extended to the employee's personal values, social orientation, and intellectual functioning. A national sample of 3,101 men employed in civilian occupations was surveyed by structured interview. The extent to which the respondents were employed in a bureaucratic milieu was identified by the respective organization's number of supervisory levels and number of employees, with more of each denoting more bureaucratization. Variables examined for the effects of bureaucratization were the extent to which value is placed on conformity to external authority; the degree to which social orientations of an authoritarian, legalistic, and noninnovative nature are exhibited; scores on form perception and problem-solving intelligence tests; and analysis of the use of leisure time.

With all this complexity in research design, Kohn's main finding was simple: correlations of bureaucratization with these factors were notably small. Even more interesting, the directions of correlation *consistently contradicted* what the bureaucratic personality is supposed to be like!

> Men who work in bureaucratic firms or organizations tend to value, not conformity, but self-direction. They are more open-minded, have more personally responsible standards of morality, and are more receptive to change than are men who work in non-bureaucratic organizations. They show great flexibility in dealing both with perceptual and ideational problems. They spend their leisure time in more intellectually demanding activities.[31]

Kohn looked for mediating variables that might explain why bureaucrats are more self-directed. The only possible candidate seemed to be level of education. More bureaucratized organizations employ more educated individuals, who then display the orientations found. Another speculation by Kohn is that the nature of bureaucratic jobs may actually challenge independent and creative people. Supervision may be tighter with more layers of hierarchy, but protection is greater from arbitrary actions of superiors. In brief, "bureaucracy may hold a special attraction for self-directed, intellectually flexible men who are receptive to innovation and change."[32]

In a somewhat similar study, Charles Bonjean and Michael Grimes interviewed some 332 independent businesspersons, hourly workers, and salaried managers residing in a town of 11,000. One part of the data collected established the extent to which the respondents' personal work environment was bureaucratic in nature, as measured on scales of authority, procedures, specialization, written rules, and impersonality. Then personality tests were administered to the respondents, designed to reveal the extent to which alienation of six different kinds was experienced. These were powerlessness in the sense of feeling controlled by unfathomable forces; normlessness in terms of being unaware of clear standards; isolation from supportive social groups; anomie or generalized alienation from others; self-estrangement; and a sense of separation from society. Scores on these dimensions were then correlated against the bureaucratization variables. The principal finding: "a relative absence of significant relationships." Of 101 intercorrelations examined, only 18 were statistically significant. Of these, only one concerned managers—a positive association between extent of written rules and anomie.[33]

In a study of the relationship between bureaucratization and powerlessness in the public schools, Gerald Moeller and W.W. Charters examined twenty school systems in the St. Louis metropolitan area. These systems were rated on extent of bureaucratization by a panel of experts. Forty teachers from each district were then surveyed on their personal sense of power over such matters as choosing textbooks, exerting influence over policy, and selecting teaching partners. Contrary to expectations, teachers from more bureaucratic schools showed a *greater* sense of power than did those from less bureaucratic institutions. Differences in mean scores were substantial and statistically significant.[34]

Dennis Organ and Charles Greene conducted research on aspects of bureaucratization and alienation in three corporate research and development divisions. They surveyed 247 senior scientists and engineers and their peers to see how such professionals were affected by "formalization," that is, the extent to which standard practices, policies, and job responsibilities are prescribed in writing. It was found that their degree of alienation, measured on a 5-point scale, was *inversely* related to formalization. The reason, the researchers suggest, is that formalization reduces role ambiguity, reinforces external norms, and clarifies professional contributions. In short, "by providing the professional with a great scope and clearer context for self-expression in work, formalization may prevent self-estrangement."[35]

John Clayton Thomas and Victoria Johnson examined alienation among urban hospital workers. They set out to ascertain the extent to which such workers felt oppressed or dissatisfied from having to deal with so many indigent patients, but without enough resources to handle them. Upon analyzing 259 questionnaires obtained anonymously from all staff levels at a Midwestern hospital, they found not overwhelmed employees but individuals who seemed to be coping quite well. While 51 percent agreed that "my department has rules for everything," only 14 percent indicated that they were dissatisfied because of insufficient opportunities for independent thought and action. Among the low-level service workers, less than half agreed with the statement, "I get the respect I deserve for my work as a public employee." Nonetheless, no less than 100 percent marked "I feel a sense of pride" from working in the hospital.[36]

Clarence Stone and Robert Stoker looked for signs of alienation among employees of local housing authorities and community development agencies. They gathered questionnaire data from 479 employees of such organizations, and some of their results are shown in table 5-6. Note in that table that with respect to perceived powerlessness, half or more of the respondents disagreed with statements related to having no say in the organization or

Table 5-6 Local Public Employees' Feelings about Their Jobs (in percentages)

	Strongly agree	Agree	Not sure	Disagree	Strongly disagree
Employees like me do not have any say about what the agency does.	17	25	2	42	14
There is little the typical employee can do to bring about change in this agency.	15	34	2	40	10
Employees like me can change things in the agency if we work at it.	12	54	3	26	4
Agency officials do not care much about what people like me think.	11	25	3	51	10
It is difficult to remain an idealist in this job.	20	54	2	22	2
There are many disappointments in a job like mine.	16	51	3	37	3
I often come home with a feeling of satisfaction about my job.	15	56	1	23	4

SOURCE: Clarence Stone and Robert Stoker, "Deprofessionalism and Dissatisfaction in Urban Service Agencies," paper presented to the annual meeting of the Midwest Political Science Association, Chicago, 1979, 47–48. Data supplied by Professor Stone.

having no ability to change it. To the contrary, two-thirds felt that, with effort, changes could be brought about. Also, most rejected the notion of uncaring officials. Although most conceded that idealism is difficult and admitted that disappointments are many, over 70 percent saw themselves as coming home at night feeling a sense of satisfaction.[37]

David Nachmias studied the perceived capacity to effect change at the national level of government. He examined data from a survey, conducted by the Office of Personnel Management (OPM), of the attitudes of federal employees. One item tapped fear of change by asking for reactions to the statement, "When changes are made in this organization, the employees usually lose out in the end." Of the 13,000-plus surveyed, 35.2 percent answered "agree" or "strongly agree," while 46 percent indicated "disagree" or "strongly disagree." In response to the statement, "It is really not possible to change things around here," 37.6 agreed to one extent or another and 50.3 percent disagreed. Interestingly, longer-tenured, higher-ranked, and older bureaucrats were significantly more optimistic about change than were their shorter-term, lower-level, and younger colleagues.[38]

We recall from the beginning of this section that inflexibility and an obsession with rules were Merton's first two characteristics of the bureaucratic personality. John Foster examined all studies he could find that tested empirically for rule rigidity among bureaucrats. His review included studies relevant to rule compliance and proceduralism in the private and public sectors, as well as pertinent attitudinal surveys and observational studies. Foster then asked, "What then have we learned about the nature of rule rigidity in organizations over the half century since Merton's essay alerted us to this potentially serious dysfunction of bureaucratically dominated societies?" His answer was as follows:

> Certainly not enough. Yet we can conclude that, at this time, there is virtually *no* empirical evidence to support the mechanistic simple rigidity model, as Merton may have anticipated when he called for further study in his original essay. Rule rigidity actually may be reasonably rare. Certainly the "bureaucracy yields rote rule adherence" aphorism should be dropped from our texts, lectures, and conventional wisdom.[39]

To sum up, numerous empirical studies strongly refute the concept of a unified, pervasive bureaucratic personality characterized by inflexibility, conservatism, alienation, timidity, ruthlessness, uncaring haughtiness, and all the other ominous features cited by theorists ranging from Merton to Hummel. In fact, behaviors of these kinds do not even seem to exist as tendencies, let alone totalities. Kohn and Bonjean-Grimes report almost no confirming evidence of the posited relationships between organizational structure and member behavior. While all of us have experienced individual instances of bureaucrats who are rule-obsessed, like to push people around, and have the creative imagination of a cement block, this says nothing about the proportionate frequency of such attributes. They may even be rare, as Foster concludes about rule rigidity. An even more surprising possibility is raised by Moeller-Charters, Organ-Greene, and to some extent Kohn, who found relationships among the relevant variables to be the very opposite of what is predicted. Thus the bureaucratic personality model may not be merely incorrect, but wrong by 180 degrees. Indeed, the research of Thomas-Johnson, Stone-Stoker, and Nachmias encountered bureaucrats who are proud, not repressed. They felt not powerless, but able to make a difference.

One is reminded of another personality stereotype, the "military mind." Fred Reed once wrote the following about this model of organizational behavior: "It exists: closed, narrow, explosive, combative, redolent of a hostility not associated with any discernible cause. Maybe these men really were dropped on their heads. The salient point about the military mind is that few officers have it."[40]

Their Motivations

We focus now on one particular dimension of the behavior of bureaucrats, the motivational patterns they bring to their work. To begin our exploration of this topic, we refer to a theory of bureaucracy mentioned in chapter 1. According to a concept advanced by public choice economists, bureaucrats are driven by a desire to expand government programs and budgets. This "budget maximizing" model is most often associated with William Niskanen, although others espouse it as well.[41]

Such a model of bureaucratic motivation comes naturally to market economists, for they tend to assume that the principal motivator of human action is the desire to optimize the satisfaction of personal preferences through rational action. This desire influences both consumers and producers, not to mention investors, and the public choice school assumes that the same motivation drives bureaucrats. Just as corporate executives seek to maximize net corporate income (and hence their personal wealth), government administrators are seen as acting to maximize their department's budgets or appropriations. More funds lead to higher rank, power, and salary for the officials, or so it is assumed. Such budget-maximizing conduct is assumed to take place regardless of the needs of clients or of the public as a whole. Bureaucrats are thus expected to lobby for and support program expansion regardless of conditions. Such "spending advocacy" goes far to explain, it is said, why government seems to keep on getting larger, eating up additional taxes, and removing more of the economy from the effects of efficiency-creating market forces.

The budget-maximizing thesis has been tested in a number of ways. In a recent study, Julie Dolan conducted a survey of members of the federal Senior Civil Service, asking their views on government spending in specific policy areas. She replicated questions given to members of the general public in other surveys that begin, "If you had a say in making up the federal budget this year, for which of the following programs would you like to see spending increased and for which would you like to see spending decreased?" This permitted her to compare civil servants' views with those of the overall population, as Gregory Lewis did in his survey of social attitudes (see table 5-1, p. 87). The results of Dolan's survey are given in table 5-7.[42]

One overall finding by Dolan is the very reverse of what one might expect: SES executives are more conservative than the public on spending for almost all policy issues, with the exceptions of foreign aid and protection of the environment. While this finding runs contrary to an "out of control" budget-maximization preference, Dolan speculates that the real reason may

Table 5-7 Support for Increased Federal Spending in Certain Policy Areas (in percentages)

	General Public	Members of Senior Executive Service		
		All executives	HHS executives	DoD executives
Dealing with crime	69.3	44.0	40.5	57.1
Public schools	67.6	53.4	65.9	42.9
Health care	64.1	31.6	52.5	23.5
Homelessness	57.2	31.5	37.5	25.2
AIDS research	56.1	33.7	33.0	31.1
College financial aid	54.5	30.9	41.0	20.8
Child care	51.9	34.0	47.5	24.4
Social Security	47.2	7.3	11.9	3.4
Environmental protection	41.1	45.4	48.8	31.9
Assistance to blacks	27.4	13.4	24.3	7.7
Aid to big cities	26.4	11.4	15.0	4.3
Defense programs	17.5	6.9	0.0	15.1
Welfare programs	10.8	6.3	19.5	1.0
Food stamps	10.2	5.8	20.0	1.0
Foreign aid	5.4	22.5	11.9	25.2

SOURCE: Julie Dolan, "The Budget-Minimizing Bureaucrat? Empirical Evidence from the Senior Executive Service," *Public Administration Review* 62, no. 1 (January/February 2002): 45, 46.

be that these respondents are more realistic and sophisticated than the overall population.

In an observation more directly relevant to the budget-maximizing model, Dolan notes that the spending attitudes of top executives in the Department of Health and Human Services are less generous than those of the public in program areas the department itself supervises, such as health care, AIDS research, and child care; again there is an exception: welfare programs. Likewise, civilian executives in the Defense Department are more conservative than the public on defense spending. Dolan sees these two sets of differentials as directly refuting the budget-maximizing thesis. They question, she believes, "the assumption that bureaucrats uniformly prefer larger budgets." "In sum," Dolan concludes, "the budget-*minimizing* tendencies of federal administrators reported here suggest that self-interest is not as powerful a motivator as previously believed, and they suggest we should revise our theories about self-interested bureaucrats inflating government budgets for their own gain."[43]

Economists André Blais and Stéphane Dion organized a conference of scholars intended to test the Niskanen model. A segment of Niskanen's theory is a bureaucratic "left effect" in voting, that is, a tendency for government employees to vote for parties and candidates that support bigger government and larger budgets. To test this left effect empirically, Blais, Dion, and colleague Donald Blake examined data on forty-three elections held in eleven countries from 1953 to 1988. A significant voting bias of this kind was indeed detectable in several of the countries, even when other variables, such as the impact of labor unions, were accounted for. In a later book dealing with Britain, France, Canada, and the United States, these same authors arrived at a similar conclusion, although the effect was less pronounced at executive levels than among public employees generally. These findings are consistent with the modest liberal bias found among bureaucrats mentioned earlier in this chapter.[44]

The overall conclusions of the budget-maximizing conference were not particularly supportive of Niskanen, however. While bureaucrats seem systematically to seek higher budgets each year, they were not shown to have benefited very much, because of declining personnel costs as a proportion of overall costs. Also, salary compression and automatic grade-step increases diluted any direct, personal payoffs. Moreover, while bureaucrats have a substantial impact on budget outcomes, it became clear that politicians exert extensive autonomous influence in this realm as well. Opening up the possibility of an alternative, unselfish motive, Blais and Dion speculate that "bureaucrats may seek increased budgets because of their values, regardless of their self-interests." Some evidence even exists, they said, to support the notion that "many civil servants are mission-minded" and are "committed to improve the quality of service to the public."[45]

British political scientist Patrick Dunleavy has extended reappraisal of the public choice literature to include group action as well as voting theories and bureaucratic conduct. He concludes that while economic explanations for political behavior hold promise for further research, they must be rigorously tested. Their validity will not be established by formal modeling alone, he warns. As for Niskanen's budget-maximizing thesis, Dunleavy pronounces that it is not borne out at the micro level of bureaucratic behavior, the management level of network activity, the macro level of overall government spending, or the policy level of privatization steps. "The existing empirical support for budget-maximizing models is scanty in the extreme," he concludes; "it is hard to see their popularity as founded on anything but an intuitive faith in their message or an ideological predisposition to accept them without testing."[46]

In a book entitled *Working, Shirking, and Sabotage,* which deals with the question of control of bureaucrats, John Brehm and Scott Gates continue the dialogue over economic theories of administration. In the largest sense, the book sets out to compare economic explanations of bureaucratic behavior with those rooted in public administration and organization theory. The authors' overall conclusion is that the public administration theories are less unified but the economic theories are less convincing. The framework of the book is principal-agent theory, according to which superiors (such as elected officials) enter into contract with inferiors (such as bureaucrats), in order to instruct them on what to do under conditions of inferior information on their part.

The title of the Brehm-Gates book refers to three proposed models of bureaucratic conduct. One is that civil servants do, in fact, actively and reliably pursue the official goals they are assigned ("working"), as is predicted by presumably naïve public administration theory. A second is that bureaucrats will not actively pursue the goals if they disagree with them or if they are simply lazy ("shirking"). This is the expectation of principal-agent theory, which anticipates that agents will pursue their own self interest if they can get away with it. The third possibility is that bureaucrats will actively undermine policy goals they do not approve of ("sabotage"), as is also predicted by principal-agent theory.

To test these and related hypotheses empirically, the authors draw on OPM surveys of federal workers, computer simulations, studies by others of police behavior and state regulators, and their own survey of social workers in Durham County, North Carolina. From OPM data that shows federal bureaucrats would like to earn higher pay, Brehm and Gates admit they might be tempted to budget-maximize. Realistically, however, this incentive is largely inoperable, they conclude, because of the constraints of governmental budgets and public personnel systems. Brehm and Gates then look for evidence as to whether federal bureaucrats are motivated to work at all. Another economics theory, the leisure-maximization model, predicts that they will not. The authors conclude that, to the contrary, federal civil servants actually work very hard: "An image of bureaucrats as lazy and indifferent, propagated by politicians, the public, and even some scholars, is wholly inaccurate."[47]

In seeking to understand why bureaucrats actually work hard, Brehm and Gates turn to their Durham County survey, the source of data presented in table 5-8. From it they identify two kinds of motivators, "functional" and "solidary." The functional incentive is personal identification with the inherent importance of the work, a factor tested in the top five items of the survey. The solidary motivator is the reinforcing influences of liked and respected coworkers, gauged in the lower five items. The percentages in the table show the potential force of both motivators. Also noticed by Brehm and Gates is that the social workers took paperwork home at night (not a sign of shirking), seldom fudged paperwork or bent the rules (not examples of sabotage), and responded significantly to the needs and desires of citizens (a nonobligatory form of work).[48]

The central conclusion of Brehm and Gates is that bureaucrats are mainly influenced by who they are. And who they are leads not to shirking and sabotage but to conscientious, dedicated goal-seeking. Rejecting the innate skepticism of principal-agent theory, they conclude as follows:

> Ultimately, our data and our models turn the phraseology, if not the meaning, of principal-agency theories around: Bureaucracy works in the United States because of "principled agents." We found that federal employees consider themselves to be hard workers, an opinion shared by their supervisors. We found that social workers and police officers rarely engaged in policy sabotage and were highly professional and strongly influenced by principles that cohere with the

Table 5-8 Functional and Solidary Preferences of Durham County Social Service Employees (in percentages)

	Strongly disagree	Disagree	Neither agree nor disagree	Agree	Strongly Agree
The things I do in my job are important to me.	0.0	0.7	2.9	52.2	44.2
Doing my job well makes me feel good about myself.	1.5	0.0	2.9	38.7	46.9
I care little about what happens as long as I get a paycheck.	41.3	49.3	7.2	1.4	0.7
A person enters this profession because he likes the work.	2.2	13.0	27.5	39.9	17.4
It's encouraging to see the high level of idealism in this field.	7.6	22.9	26.7	36.6	6.1
A person gets the chance to develop good friends here.	4.3	5.1	29.7	50.7	10.1
Working hard on my job leads to respect from coworkers.	2.9	23.9	23.9	40.6	8.7
This department is really very impersonal.	6.8	45.1	29.3	14.3	4.5
My colleagues know how well we all do in our work.	1.5	16.1	15.3	55.5	11.7
Sometimes I go along with my coworkers even if it's not what I want.	5.1	23.5	14.7	52.9	3.7

SOURCE: John Brehm and Scott Gates, *Working, Shirking and Sabotage: Bureaucratic Response to a Democratic Public* (Ann Arbor: University of Michigan Press, 1997), 89, 108.

> mission of their organizations. We found that citizens and interest groups could be influential in the policy process, with greater marginal effect than some political elites. Scholars, as well as the public and politicians, need to credit bureaucrats for being public servants, for working as hard as they do, and for being as responsive as democratic government demands.[49]

We conclude this discussion of bureaucratic motivation by summarizing the literature that compares the mindsets of government employees and private-sector employees. Recently Hal Rainey and Barry Bozeman published an overview of the private-public comparative literature, part of which concerns workplace motivation. They point out that in over a quarter-century of scholarship much empirical evidence has accumulated. Moreover, the findings of this research have tended to converge, creating substantial confidence in their validity.

One conclusion seems to be, say Rainey and Bozeman, that despite earlier reports to the contrary, public-sector employees tend to express somewhat higher levels of general work satisfaction than do their private-sector counterparts. Another is that bureaucrats do not seem less motivated than business workers. They do, however, seem to have a different composite of motivational influences. Particularly at the level of management, public employees "place higher value on public service; on work that is beneficial to others and to society; on involvement with important public policies; and on self-sacrifice, responsibility, and integrity." While it is true that intersector differences are not always great and that many people in private business also are committed to community service, Rainey and Bozeman say, "the evidence suggests that things are not necessarily so bleak in the public bureaucracy."[50]

A recent study by David Houston applies multivariate statistical tests to comparative public-private workplace motivation, drawing on General Social Survey data for 1991, 1993, and 1994. It confirms earlier findings that public employees place less importance than their private counterparts do on higher pay and more value on the substantive importance of the work being done. Intrinsic motivators such as feelings of accomplishment outweigh extrinsic ones such as high salaries and short work hours. Dennis Wittmer, in another study, arrived at the same conclusion when comparing managers in the two sectors. He also found leaders of nonprofit organizations to be motivated by factors similar to those associated with public-sector managers.[51]

In summary, the elegant models of market economists do not lead us to an understanding of what makes bureaucrats tick. Civil servants would like better pay, of course, as well as a promotion and a pat on the back when it is due. Occasions arise when they would love to ignore the instructions of their political chiefs. But what really activates bureaucrats is a belief in the inherent worth of their agency's mission, the social reinforcement effects of their professional environment, and the concept of public service. As for the paranoid suspicions of budget-maximization and principal-agent theories, they can be safely transported to the landfill of unusable models for public administration.

Their Lesser-Known

We conclude this closer look at America's 21 million bureaucrats by shifting from theories and research to actual people. At the beginning of this chapter we sought to break some stereotypes of bureaucrats by listing some of the diverse places where they work and what they do. We now take another step in the direction of bringing the bureaucrats to life. Let's meet some living ones—using real names, real people, and real work. The following are some vignettes featuring such lesser-known bureaucrats.[52]

Randy J. Aden is a supervisory special agent with the FBI. He is in his early fifties and rides a Harley. He graduated from the University of Nebraska and has an M.P.A. from California Lutheran University. Aden's office is on the fifteenth floor of the Federal Building in West Los Angeles, where he heads the Sexual Assault Felony Enforcement Unit, or SAFE. Its mission is to enter sex-oriented chat rooms on the Internet in order to flush out sexual predators who cross state lines to victimize children. Most such predators are white men who want to talk with female teenagers about sex and their fantasies. Aden and his fellow agents pose as willing teens in order to lure suspects to a meeting place where they take them into custody. The unit's offices are off-limits to outsiders because of the sexually disturbing materials it deals with. Asked to name what he looks for in new members of SAFE, Aden lists a strong work ethic, imagination, resourcefulness, skill at thinking on one's feet, and a sense of humor.[53]

Evelyn Fields is director of the National Oceanic and Atmospheric Administration Corps (NOAA), a 233-member organization that is the smallest of the government's seven corps of commissioned officers. Holding the rank of rear admiral, Fields successfully countered attempts made during the Clinton years to disband the corps in order to promote "management efficiencies." A black woman in her early 50s, Fields grew up in the port city of Norfolk, Virginia, and graduated from Norfolk State College. Starting her career as a cartographer in NOAA's Atlantic Marine Center, she rose through the ranks, was commissioned, and became the first woman to command a U.S. government ship at sea for an extended period. She oversees a staff of 700, fifteen research ships, and fourteen aircraft. Commenting on her success, Fields says, "The fact that I'm female is nice; the fact that I'm black is nice; but I don't think those were the reasons I was selected."[54]

Mary Margaret "Meg" Falk is director of the Office of Family Policy at the Pentagon. She graduated from Marygrove College in Detroit and got an M.P.A. from Wayne State University. On the morning of 11 September 2001 she was meeting with her staff when Flight #77 slammed into the building. After telling her staff to call home to report that they were all right, she got on the phone without consulting anyone and proceeded to set up a family assistance center in a hotel in nearby Crystal City. She and her staff rented computers, set up telephone lines, and began taking calls from worried relatives of Pentagon workers. A building diagram was drawn to indicate what rooms were likely to have been in the destroyed area. Contacts with the press were coordinated and the privacy of affected families protected. Falk received a public service award the following June.[55]

Arthur R. Eberhart and *Dwight E. Adams* are section chief and assistant director, respectively, of the FBI's laboratory division. In 1999 they combed shallow graves in Kosovo to obtain forensic evidence for the indictment and later trial of Slobodan Milosevic and others. They and their coworkers took photographs and made sketches at the site of a massacre of 124 Albanians. They discovered children who had died from blunt-force trauma, adults with slit throats, bodies buried beneath dead cattle, and even terrified victims still alive. As the work progressed, whole families stood by, hoping to identify loved ones. "It was very emotional," said Eberhart, recalling the fear in the eyes of a boy to whom he gave candy. Adams was told by a woman that her husband had been wearing a Chicago Bears jacket and carrying a watch with a broken face. His body turned out to be unidentifiable, but Adams recognized the jacket and watch, which he gave to the woman. "Yes, yes, yes, you found my husband," she said.[56]

Cheryl Bertoia is director of ice operations for the National Ice Center, a small organization in Suitland, Maryland, that is funded by the Coast Guard, the navy, and NOAA. A geographer by training, Bertoia and her staff track sea ice around the world by means of data received from satellites, buoys, ships, meteorological models, aerial ice reconnaissance, and shore station reports. Digital images are produced of ice patterns all around the world and placed on the Internet. Software packages embodying these images are delivered to navy and Coast Guard ships, commercial vessels, foreign governments, and the scientific community. Although most of the observed ice is stationary, movement by icebergs forty miles across is sometimes detected. More important is the monitoring of thousands of break-off fragments, which are dangerous to shipping because they lie low in the water.[57]

Celia Yette is a service representative for a Social Security office in Petersburg, Virginia. An African American, she was born in 1970 with stunted arms and deformed feet from the effects of the drug thalidomide, which had been prescribed for her pregnant mother. Despite all expectations to the contrary, Yette succeeded in graduating from high school and earning bachelor's and master's degrees in English. After working as a call-center phone representative, she obtained her job with Social Security, where she carries out her duties by using her right foot to manipulate papers and dial the phone. She greets staring clients with aplomb, answers their questions about claims, and processes their cases with dispatch. "My goal is to be a blessing to anyone that comes into the office with questions," Yette says. "I wanted to be someone who contributed to society." In her spare time, at the church she attends, Yette tutors people in English and helps them prepare for the GED examination.[58]

Gayle Hannah is postmaster in Oriskany, a tiny rural crossroads in Botetourt County, Virginia. The office occupies a wooden building 8 feet wide and 16 feet long, just off Route 615. Hannah has been in charge of this fragment of public administration since 1991. Each business day at 11 a.m. she opens the office, raises the American flag on the pole out front, dampens the stamp sponge with bottled water (there is no plumbing), and empties mail from the drop box outside the door. Soon neighbors trickle in to pick up their general delivery mail, buy a few stamps, or just chat. Aside from the church in town, this is the community's social center. Around noon, the mail carrier from Eagle Rock drops off the day's few pieces of incoming mail, and in a few moments Hannah sorts it into the cubicles. At 1 o'clock she closes her books for the day, lowers the flag, and locks up.[59]

Each of us will have different reactions to these vignettes about lesser-known bureaucrats. Here are some of mine. Randy Aden seeks imaginative people with a sense of humor to help him outwit sexual predators on the Internet—probably the last kind of person he would want to recruit is the "bureaucratic personality" whose creativity has been smothered. Rear Admiral Evelyn Fields is not only an African American but a woman as well—and living proof that the upper reaches of American bureaucracy are becoming more open to both genders and all races. Meg Falk did not obey the "Law of Increasing Conservatism" when she dumped the rulebook and threw caution to the winds to create the 9/11 assistance center. To suggest that Arthur Eberhart and Dwight Adams were stereotypical bureaucrats, incapable of emotion and devoid of will, while digging in the graves of Kosovo would be absurd. At the National Ice Center, Cheryl Bertoia is not playing defensive games or committing policy sabotage but showing what a principled agent does to meet her agency mission of keeping the sea lanes safe. Celia Yette at the Petersburg Social Security office is motivated not by expectations of material rewards or personal gain but by an altruism that is further ennobled by her own life situation. The neighborly postmaster Gayle Hannah is hardly an arrogant, haughty bureaucrat—or a budget-maximizer for that matter.

We conclude this chapter with a second set of vignettes. These focus not on lesser-known bureaucrats but on lesser-known citizens whose lives have been affected by the work of bureaucrats.

Barbara J. Mann has a house in Portsmouth, Virginia, next to a city water tower that was leaking and flooding her yard. Grass around the tower could not be cut because of standing water, and the mosquitoes were multiplying. Because the city used the property to store pipe and gravel used for street repair, Mann called the city's director of public utilities, James R. Spacek, to report the problem. Although only the tower itself and not the land below it fell under his department, Spacek apologized for the whole mess and accepted responsibility for correcting it. In the meantime, he gave her a phone number so that she could call him day or night in case of further problems. Mann proceeded to get the leaking tower repaired and coordinated with Street Maintenance to remove the pipe and gravel, with Parks and Recreation to mow the grass, and with Environmental Control to spray insecticide on the grounds. Mann reports that every time she tried to call Spacek, he was always personally available.[60]

Jennifer R.S. Grogan resides in a small city in Massachusetts. When she and her husband moved there from another state, they had to transfer their car registrations, so Grogan went to the local Department of Motor Vehicles to do so. She had no problem registering her own car but could not complete the procedure for her husband's car since, the clerk explained, he was not present to sign the application. Grogan explained that her husband worked some distance away and could not be reached for two days. Without batting an eye, the clerk said, "Go outside, get your husband's signature and bring it back to me." When Grogan said again that her husband was not outside the building, the clerk calmly repeated the instructions, twice. Dumbfounded by the apparent breakdown in communication, Grogan did not realize until after she had left the building what the clerk had meant. She went behind a tree, signed her husband's name, and returned the form to complete the transaction.

Robert L. Iverson is a doctor who practices in suburban Detroit. Suddenly finding that his wife was missing, he notified the police, who immediately put out a bulletin. Unfortunately, his wife's car was soon found on a side street in a bad part of town with her body inside. In the days following, the media publicity surrounding the case depicted Iverson as the prime suspect. Nevertheless, the investigating detectives showed him respect and courtesy, despite the doctor's outbursts of outrage and frustration. They administered a polygraph test in a calm voice and kept him informed on the progress of the case. Eventually two suspects were arrested and confessed to the crime. In a newspaper op-ed piece, Iverson wrote, "The people constituting the 'thin blue line,' who go in harm's way in our community, are superb and dedicated. I forever will be indebted."[61]

Charles Tolchin of Washington, D.C., was diagnosed with cystic fibrosis at the age of five. At the time, being such a young victim of this genetic lung and digestive disease suggested that his life would end by the age of eight. Taken into the National Institutes of Health as an experimental patient, Tolchin was given new inhalants and new antibiotics and was taught recently-developed techniques to cough up mucus. These advances permitted him to survive to adulthood, and eventually he became healthy enough to undergo a lung transplant. Its success permitted him to skip five hours of respiration therapy a day and to live a normal life for many years. Looking back on his years under the care of NIH doctors, he recalled in particular a Dr. Milica Chernick, who always warmed her stethoscope before applying it to his chest. Tolchin credited his new life to the brilliance, dedication, and heartening enthusiasm of the doctors and scientists at NIH. Charles Tolchin passed away 7 August 2003, at the age of thirty-four.[62]

Wayne Slusher, of Roanoke, Virginia, noticed signs of dementia in his father. In happier years his father had often said that if anything ever happened to him, he wanted to be taken to the VA hospital. When Mr. Slusher's condition reached the point where hospitalization was inevitable, the son obeyed his father's wishes and took him to the Veterans Medical Center in Salem, against the advice of friends. Leaving his father in this institution that first night was extremely hard, but in the ensuing weeks Slusher realized that the doctors, physician's assistants, nurses, and social workers there were doing everything possible to alleviate the suffering of advanced Alzheimer's disease. Along with the family, members of the VA staff were by his father's side at the end. This hospital, says Slusher, "is full of immensely compassionate, caring professionals who could not have done more for my father. We think, too, perhaps they do not get recognition and praise from the community as often as they should."[63]

Colbert I. King is a journalist in Washington, D.C. In the summer of 1957, while in high school, he got a temporary job in the sub-basement mailroom of the Department of Agriculture building in Washington. It was his first true work experience, and because of it he learned what it means to arrive at work on time and do the work assigned, even if it is unpleasant. On his mail runs, the young African American noticed that as he climbed higher in the building, occupants of the offices looked less and less like him. During that summer, civil rights debates were going on in Congress. As he thought about his future, it was encouragement from the older black men in the mailroom—along with family support—that spurred King to go to college. "No one wanted me to remain in the sub-basement," he recalls. He went on to a career that included the military service, the Foreign Service, and the Senior Executive Service. Government employment is not the Promised Land, says King, but it "has been a source of opportunity and a gateway to the middle class for racial minorities and women."[64]

Again, I know you have your own thoughts about these vignettes, but let me offer a few. In James Spacek, Barbara Mann encountered not a bureaucratic personality who would quibble over jurisdictional boundaries, but a public employee who made a point of solving her entire syndrome of water tower problems. Jennifer Grogan, in trying to register her husband's car at the DMV, ran into a clerk who helpfully winked at the rules in the name of common sense, rather than a bureaucratic virtuoso who never forgets a single rule and hence does nothing. When Robert Iverson was being investigated for his wife's murder, he encountered not psychological domination or controlling language, but regard for his feelings as well as his rights. At NIH, Charles Tolchin met not coldly rational experts, but doctors who warmed stethoscopes and found ways for him to live. At the VA hospital, Wayne Slusher realized that his father's last days were being spent not among synthetic poseurs or repressed nonpersons, but in the care of humane professionals. In the sub-basement mailroom of the USDA, Colbert King confronted not alienated resentment from his coworkers, but encouragement to seek new opportunities. Not bad, bureaucracy!

Chapter 6 Bureaucratic Bigness and Badness Reconsidered

An old debate in antitrust policy is whether "bigness is badness." At issue is whether bigness in corporations is itself a sin—or whether to be bad requires actually committing anticompetitive acts, such as predatory pricing. That distinction is never drawn in public debates on government bureaucracy, where it is always assumed that bureaucracy is both big and bad, and sinful on both counts. In this chapter we reconsider all such assumptions.

The Size of Bureaucracy

If anything is associated with bigness, it is government bureaucracy. Its huge size is often given, by conservatives and liberals alike, as one of the principal problems of bureaucracy. A newspaper feature writer describes bureaucracy as "a brontosaurus of unimaginable size, appetite, ubiquity and complexity." At the federal level alone, the reporter says (and mostly understates), the giant beast owns 413 buildings, leases 228 million square feet, operates 450,000 automobiles, and owes trillions in debt.[1]

The total number of government employees *is* very big. Rounded off, some 21 million civilians work for the public sector in the United States: 2.9 million in the national government, 4.9 million in state governments, and 13.1 in local governments. Together they constitute roughly 15 percent of the civilian workforce. Added to this civilian total are about 1.4 million military personnel on active duty.[2] In absolute numbers the American bureaucracy is probably the fifth largest in the world, perhaps smaller than what is found in only China, India, Indonesia, and Russia.

Moreover, U.S. public employment has grown significantly over the country's history. In 1941 it was roughly 5 million, and in 1957 about 8 million. In relative terms, government employment at all levels was 10 percent of total civilian employment in 1948 and 14 percent in 1964. In the past forty years this percentage has remained remarkably stable, in the range of 15 to 17 percent.[3]

Yet despite such large overall dimensions and past growth, the effective size of the bureaucratic brontosaurus is a more subtle matter than first appears. This, by the way, is also true with real dinosaurs. As those who have made cinematic visits to Jurassic Park know, these fascinating beasts that once roamed the earth came in many shapes and sizes. Not all were enormous—some were actually the size of birds. In fact, today's birds are believed to be their distant relatives.

A similar observation can be made about bureaucracy. When we look at different types of administrative agency, shape and scale vary greatly. As for the matter of size, it could be argued that what really counts to us as citizens is the bigness of government offices or facilities where we visit or work. After all, we don't experience bureaucracy in terms of grand organizational totals but the nature of the places where we actually go. When I visit my local post office, for example, the scale of employment I experience is quite different from the entire U.S. Postal Service, with its 850,000 employees.

When we adopt this concrete perspective, how big is bureaucracy? Put another way, what proportion of government facilities is comparable to a mature brontosaurus rather than to more bird-like creatures?

Table 6-1 shows the range of scale by number of employees in one important and sometimes notorious bureaucratic function, welfare and social services. All citizens experience this breed of dinosaur at some point in their lives. The data given in the table cover the entire country, providing employment ranges for two types of social service agency, the public welfare offices of local

Table 6-1 Size of Public Welfare and Social Security Offices

	Local public welfare		U.S. Social Security	
Number of employees	Number of offices	Cumulative percentage	Number of offices	Cumulative percentage
1–9	798	42.6	164	18.0
10–19	186	52.6	334	54.7
20–29	91	57.4	154	71.6
30–39	76	61.5	64	78.6
40–49	67	65.1	31	82.0
50–59	61		18	
60–69	35		22	
70–79	38		11	
80–89	37		11	
90–99	30		8	
1–99	**1,419**	**75.8**	**817**	**90.0**
100–199	172		54	
200–299	103		13	
300–399	52		7	
400–499	24		4	
500–599	20		0	
600–699	21		3	
700–799	12		3	
800–899	9		0	
900–999	5		0	
1–999	**1,837**	**98.1**	**901**	**98.9**
1,000–1,999	23		8	
2,000–2,999	10		2	
3,000–3,999	2	100.0	0	100.0
Total	1,872		911	

SOURCE: U.S. Census Bureau, *Compendium of Public Employment*, 1997, table 13; and U.S. Office of Personnel Management, *Biennial Report of Employment by Geographic Area*, 1998, table 5.

governments and the field offices of the U.S. Social Security Administration. The figures are geographically based in that they pertain to offices located in individual counties and independent cities. For this reason, the numbers must be taken as approximate, in that if one county or city contains more than one office, size is exaggerated. On the other hand, when the staff of an office serve more than one rural county, size is understated. To some extent, the two types of error cancel each other out.[4]

Looking first at local public welfare offices, we see at the top of the table that 798 out of 1,872 bureaucracies, or 42.6 percent, employ only 1 to 9 individuals—these places are indeed bird-like in size. As one moves down the table, the proportional frequencies of larger sizes are shown: on a cumulative basis, 52.6 percent, or slightly over half of the offices, employ fewer than 20 persons; 65.1 percent have staffs of fewer than 50, and 75.8 percent have fewer than 100 employees. In other words, most public welfare bureaucracies are in the small-to-modest size range. Only 2 percent have more than 1,000 employees.

The Social Security offices for which data are available are even smaller by these measures, even though the percentage with under 10 employees is substantially lower. Well over half of the 911 offices employ fewer than 20 workers, and over 80 percent fewer than 50. Ninety percent have staffs of under 100 individuals. In the whole country, only ten offices employ 1,000 workers or more.

Is this degree of smallness an exception? Is there something peculiar about the social services area that keeps its office staffs small? In the previous edition of this book, I analyzed employment size ranges for all federal civilian agencies except intelligence organizations on a geographic dispersion basis; the results, though now a decade old, are probably still valid for the most part. They indicate that a tendency toward small scale prevails all across the government and is often even more pronounced than shown in table 6-1. Fifty-two percent of field units employed fewer than 5 individuals and 69 percent 10 persons or less. Just under 93 percent of the facilities had staffs of under 100. In a separate analysis of local government employment, based on jurisdiction rather than geographic size, I found that 30,000 out of the more than 80,000 local governments employ fewer than 25 people, three-quarters have fewer than 50 workers, and 85 percent fewer than 100.[5]

Even if almost all bureaucracies in the United States are paltry-sized dinosaurs, there are some big ones, too, as the data at the bottom of table 6-1 indicate. They are located, as one would suspect, in large urban areas. We must also keep in mind that agency headquarters, where organizations are run but ordinary citizens rarely venture, are generally on a much larger scale. Nearly 10,000 work at the Baltimore headquarters of the Social Security Administration, for example, and in Washington, D.C., the Department of Veterans' Affairs maintains a staff of 5,000, while the Department of the Treasury employs 15,000. Military installations around the country can also employ large numbers, including the 9,000 civilian naval personnel in Norfolk and over 20,000 at San Diego. At the local level, big city public employment can add up as well, reaching 450,000 in New York City and 100,000 in Los Angeles County. In short, some bureaucracies are definitely brontosauri.[6]

Growth, Aging, and Badness

A major reason for the popular notion that governmental bureaucracies are invariably huge is the belief that they have an endemic, inexorable tendency to grow. Thus, the implicit reasoning goes, with the passage of time bigness will surely appear. Being as aged as it is, bureaucracy *must* be bloated. Moreover, as the bigness gets bigger, the badness must get worse. We examine such possibilities.

The standard introductory course in management or public administration spends a half hour or so on Parkinson's Law. C. Northcote Parkinson was a whimsical Englishman whose experiences in the British War Office taught him that "work expands so as to fill the time available for its completion." (The BBC created a musical version of The Law, scoring its overture for typewriters.) In a delightful scenario, Parkinson tells us how civil servants, imagining themselves to be overworked, want the assistance of subordinates. But since subordinates are potential rivals to those who appoint them, two are installed rather than one so that they can countercheck one another. Eventually, the subordinates appoint their own pairs of helpers, and the organization proceeds to mushroom in size. By means of explicit but mysteriously grounded formulas, Parkinson predicts that staff expansion "will invariably prove to be between 5.17 and 6.56 percent, irrespective of any variation in the amount of work (if any) to be done." [7]

Is this good fun designed to brighten an otherwise dull lecture, or is there something to it? Do bureaucrats conspire to create jobs out of petty self-protection? Does bureaucracy, for whatever reason, steadily and inevitably expand, even if not by Parkinson's rates?

Certainly many believe it does. Citizens witness the escalation of government budgets and tax assessments each year. Despite temporary surpluses, federal deficits easily balloon. Conservatives suspect crass vote-buying by liberal politicians who promise new programs to every constituency, forcing the creation of new bureaucracies. Liberals envision rampant corporate welfare, causing drains on federal budgets in the form of subsidies, tax expenditures, and bailouts. Others assume that because of the influence of the military-industrial complex, the Defense Department is always more plush than it needs to be. Everyone has reasons to be convinced of an inflated and ever-growing bureaucracy, with or without Parkinson's Law.

In addition, students of organization have spun out a number of theories supporting chronic bureaucratic expansion. Their arguments focus on internal organizational needs and processes. One of the earliest is Anthony Downs, who claims that "all organizations have inherent tendencies to expand. What sets [government] bureaus apart is that they do not have as many restraints on expansion, nor do their restraints function as automatically." He advances many reasons for this view: Growth is attractive to organizations because by means of it they increase the power, income, and prestige of leaders and recruit better new personnel. In addition, expansion reduces internal conflicts and enhances the probability of long-term survival. Government agencies are particularly susceptible to unimpeded growth because a lack of competitive market pressures excuses officials from the need to weigh the marginal costs and returns of further spending.

Like most theorists of organizational growth, Downs believes that many bad things happen as the bureaucracy expands. These include "wasted motion," or nonproductive effort given over to supervising others instead of performing tasks. Also, authority is delegated or "leaked" from the top, and, consequently, powers of control and coordination significantly erode. What follows is an attempt to counteract declining control by imposing ever more elaborate staff-monitoring systems. These only introduce rigidity, however, by creating more rules, requiring more reports, and stimulating operating units to spend more time evading control. The end result is that administrative operations become, according to Downs, rigid, ossified, and incapable of fast or novel action. "Thus the bureau becomes a gigantic machine that slowly and inflexibly grinds along in the direction in which it was initially aimed. It still produces outputs, perhaps in truly impressive quantity and quality. But the speed and flexibility of its operations steadily diminish."[8]

Any line of reasoning that posits bureaucratic growth as inevitable and its consequences as undesirable leads to a concept of decay. Here organization theorists invariably turn to biological analogies of aging and the life cycle. Downs himself is no exception, and his famous "life cycle of bureaus" is memorized by all students of organization theory. It goes roughly like this: Entrepreneurial zealots agitate so as to create new bureaus, usually by breaking them off from old ones. These new bureaus then seek to achieve autonomy early so that they can pass an "initial survival threshold." Rapid growth at this stage attracts "climber" bureaucrats who promote even faster expansion for career reasons, spawning an "accelerator effect." Eventually, however, young bureaus run into obstacles and slow down, with the consequence that the climbers jump ship and "conservers" take over. This creates a "decelerator effect." But instead of shriveling up or dying, such aging bureaucracies live on almost interminably, ever expanding while continuing to suffer the ravages of age. Meanwhile, officials themselves become older and more conservative, as career stakes escalate and reasons mount not to rock the boat.[9]

Another well-known model of aging in public administration is Marver Bernstein's life cycle of regulatory commissions. Although specifically tailored to this form of bureaucracy, it parallels Downs's theories in several ways.

Bernstein contended that these commissions—for example, the Federal Communications Commission or Securities and Exchange Commission—go through four phases: Gestation, Youth, Maturity, and Old Age. *Gestation* is dominated by the battle for statutory enactment, waged in order to bring order or reform to a miscreant industry. *Youth* is characterized by a crusading attempt to implement the new law by recruiting staffs of smart young lawyers. As soon as reformist interest recedes, however, the interests who are being policed begin to penetrate the agency. In *Maturity*, open conflict is replaced by settled procedures and the policeman role changes to one of concerned manager and supporter of the regulated industry. During *Old Age*, political support from the legislature and executive narrows, and "capture" of the commission by regulated groups becomes complete. Bernstein holds out the faint possibility of subsequent revival of these gerontological wrecks, but this difficult step requires a genuine scandal or emergency. No regulatory function has ever been eliminated—he wrote before the era of deregulation—meaning that Old Age will not terminate until an unplanned upheaval occurs.[10]

In chapter 5 we discussed budget-maximizing theories of the public choice theorists, in particular William Niskanen. These are indirectly pertinent to the discussion of employment growth in bureaucracy, since additional appropriations can and will be used to hire more staff. However, since government contracts out so much of its work and engages in other kinds of dispersed public action, budgetary growth and employment expansion do not necessarily coincide.

Some public choice writers expect staff escalation nonetheless. Oliver Williamson contends that bureaucratic managers create ever-larger staffs in order to elevate their own rank in the hierarchy. Large employment numbers help to guarantee organizational survival by making dismantlement even more unthinkable. Gordon Tullock predicts that ambitious bureaucrats, dissatisfied by the distorted information flows they receive from subordinates, compensate by creating ever bigger executive cadres, which because of their size are even more error-prone.[11]

Much of the conceptual underpinning of public choice theory as related to bureaucracy is based on the notion that public organizations lack the discipline of the market, as suggested by Downs. Niskanen refers to government agencies as "monopoly bureaus." The assumption here is that since bureaucracies face no competition in the free enterprise sense, they do not adhere to the business ideal of constantly increasing productivity and cutting costs. With pressures to stay lean and mean removed, so the argument goes, agencies tend inevitably to flabbiness and sloth. Some years ago Vincent Ostrom indicted public administration as facing an "intellectual crisis" because of its inattention to needed competition among bureaucracies. He proposed to address the crisis by restructuring bureaucracy to the extent possible in the form of small-scale, competitive, and internally democratic service enterprises.[12]

These theories, then, present a dark, depressing picture with respect to bureaucratic growth and aging. Agencies are seen as not facing adequate incentives or restraints to keep themselves young, slim, and hip. They are portrayed as subject to inevitable enlargement and deterioration over time. The economics version of this hypothesis is that bureaucracies are fatally flawed by lack of immersion in the cleansing discipline of the competitive market. The corresponding biological scenario is the anthropomorphic life cycle, in which the deterioration of aging is inevitable. But unlike human aging, the outcome is not eventual death but a state of everlasting bloat. The brontosaurus lives on forever, growing ever bigger and more ponderous.

We have already presented data showing that smallness, rather than hugeness, is the hallmark of the bureaucracies encountered by citizens. Let us now explore what the data indicate about the growth of bureaucracies over time and its consequences.

Table 6-2 shows civilian employment over several decades in the departments and other leading agencies of the national government. If we follow the figures for each bureaucracy over the five points in time, what do we find? Frequent growth, yes. But close examination shows that this is by no means always the case. Twenty organizations are listed and four decades covered, with seven data cells empty because the organizations did not yet exist. This creates a total of 73 ten-year change opportunities. Of these, 43 showed expansion, 2 stability, and 28 contraction. Thus in 30 of the cases, or 41 per-

Table 6-2 Civilian Employment in Selected Federal Agencies, 1960–2000 (in thousands)

	1960	1970	1980	1990	2000
Departments					
Agriculture	98.7	114.3	129.1	122.6	104.5
Commerce	33.8	36.1	48.6	69.9	47.7
Defense	1,047.1	1,169.2	960.1	1,034.2	676.3
Education			7.4	4.8	4.8
Energy			21.6	17.7	15.7
Health and Human Services	61.6	110.2	155.7	124.0	62.6
Housing and Urban Development	11.1	15.0	17.0	13.6	10.3
Interior	56.1	71.7	77.4	77.7	73.8
Justice	30.9	40.1	56.3	83.9	126.0
Labor	7.1	10.9	23.4	17.7	16.0
State	38.0	40.0	23.5	25.3	28.0
Transportation		67.0	72.4	67.4	63.6
Treasury	76.2	90.7	124.7	158.7	143.5
Veterans' Affairs	172.3	169.2	228.3	248.2	219.5
Other agencies					
Environmental Protection Agency			14.7	17.1	18.0
General Services Administration	28.2	37.7	37.7	20.3	14.3
NASA	10.2	30.7	23.7	24.9	18.8
Postal Service	562.9	721.2	660.0	816.9	860.7
Small Business Administration	2.2	4.4	5.8	5.1	4.2
Tennessee Valley Authority	15.0	23.8	51.7	28.4	13.1

SOURCE: *Statistical Abstract of the United States: 1976*, 249, 250; *1992*, 330; *2001*, 319.

cent, the prediction of constant bureaucratic growth was not realized. After 1980 particularly, numerous instances of decline occurred, due to such pressures as conservative policy trends, budget cuts, administrative reorganization, and increased contracting out.[13]

In table 6-3 we use the same kind of data to examine growth in state bureaucracies. Time-series employment data are given for two major administrative departments in every state of the union: the welfare or social services department and the highway or transportation department. The figures are for three points in time, 1987, 1993, and 2000, creating 100 opportunities for six-year growth for each department. Analysis shows that welfare departments expanded 59 times, contracted 31 times, and remained stable 10 times. (Because of the 100 base, these figures are also percentages.) In the highway departments, the frequencies are 39, 50, and 11, respectively. In other words, the continuous-growth thesis was not sustained 41 percent of the time in welfare or 61 percent of the time in highways.[14]

Yet the real importance of these figures to citizens and taxpayers is not the up and down movements in isolation, but changes in relation to pertinent external factors such as changing demands and conditions—in other words, bureaucracy's "market." In absolute numbers, the biggest growth over the forty years covered in table 6-2 was the Postal Service's increase of nearly 300,000 employees, which seems a gigantic number. If, however, changes in postal employment are related to the actual volume of mail handled, the picture looks quite different. Between 1960 and 2000 the mail volume more than tripled, and if it had not been for productivity increases during that span of years, the postal workforce would have had to grow even faster, by a significant factor. However, the number of workers needed to move a billion pieces of mail, a measure of productivity, was more than halved in that period, decreasing from 8,838 in 1960 to 4,334 in 2000.[15]

We are told that the quality of bureaucracies and the effectiveness of their performance are to deteriorate over time, both as growth proceeds and as age produces deterioration but not death. Empirically, we can test for the adverse effects of growth and aging on organizations in two ways: by cross-sectional comparisons among organizations of differing size and age, and by longitudinal comparisons of identical organizations over time. Let us review studies employing both methods.

We begin with cross-sectional studies. In a study of local government bureaucracy in North Carolina, James Christenson and Carolyn Sachs surveyed by mail members of the public in 100 counties of that state. Respondents were asked to rate the quality of various county services, such as libraries, schools, law enforcement, parks, and medical services. Approximately 8,900 questionnaires were returned and used to construct a "quality of services" index. Scores on this index were then correlated against the number of public employees in the county. The resulting coefficient was .48; in other words, those who perceived superior services tended to live in counties with more

Table 6-3 Employment in State Welfare and Highway Departments, 1987–2000 (in thousands)

	Welfare departments			Highway departments		
State	1987	1993	2000	1987	1993	2000
Alabama	4.0	4.6	3.8	4.0	4.3	3.8
Alaska	1.4	1.7	1.7	2.8	2.9	2.7
Arizona	2.9	5.5	5.6	1.1	3.3	3.0
Arkansas	2.7	3.4	2.2	3.9	4.0	3.9
California	3.0	3.4	3.7	15.3	19.3	21.0
Colorado	1.3	1.3	1.9	3.0	3.1	3.0
Connecticut	4.0	4.6	4.8	4.2	3.8	3.6
Delaware	1.7	1.8	1.7	1.3	1.4	1.6
Florida	6.4	10.2	13.9	8.6	11.3	10.3
Georgia	6.2	8.2	9.4	6.3	6.1	6.0
Hawaii	.9	1.2	.8	.8	.9	1.0
Idaho	1.1	1.8	1.7	1.6	1.8	1.7
Illinois	12.2	12.2	14.3	8.7	8.8	8.3
Indiana	1.9	5.2	5.0	5.6	4.8	4.3
Iowa	3.5	3.3	2.8	3.0	2.9	2.9
Kansas	2.8	1.7	2.7	3.5	3.6	3.4
Kentucky	5.5	4.7	6.7	6.6	5.6	5.5
Louisiana	5.4	5.8	5.5	5.5	5.6	5.5
Maine	1.9	1.9	2.0	2.7	2.8	2.7
Maryland	6.7	7.5	7.4	5.2	5.0	4.7
Massachusetts	8.6	6.4	7.5	5.0	4.6	4.3
Michigan	13.3	13.0	13.4	4.1	3.8	3.1
Minnesota	1.6	1.7	2.6	5.0	5.0	5.2
Mississippi	2.7	3.3	3.1	3.1	3.4	3.3
Missouri	6.0	7.1	8.2	6.1	6.5	6.4
Montana	1.1	1.2	1.5	1.7	1.8	2.0
Nebraska	2.7	2.8	2.8	2.2	2.4	2.2
Nevada	.7	1.0	1.0	1.4	1.4	1.6
New Hampshire	1.0	1.3	1.4	2.0	2.0	1.9
New Jersey	5.6	5.8	6.0	9.0	8.2	7.5
New Mexico	1.8	1.4	1.6	2.7	2.7	2.3
New York	8.0	8.1	6.7	14.3	15.1	13.1
North Carolina	1.1	1.2	1.4	11.2	13.0	11.9
North Dakota	.4	.2	.4	1.1	1.1	.9
Ohio	1.8	2.0	2.1	8.6	9.0	7.2
Oklahoma	6.3	6.8	6.3	3.7	4.2	3.0
Oregon	3.5	4.4	5.7	4.0	3.4	3.5
Pennsylvania	10.7	10.2	12.0	14.1	12.8	13.8
Rhode Island	1.7	1.6	1.6	1.0	1.0	.8
South Carolina	4.5	4.8	5.0	4.6	5.2	4.9
South Dakota	1.1	1.1	1.0	1.3	1.3	1.0
Tennessee	5.2	4.5	5.3	5.0	4.8	4.6
Texas	13.1	22.9	20.7	15.1	13.7	15.3

(continues)

Table 6-3 *(continued)*

	Welfare departments			Highway departments		
State	1987	1993	2000	1987	1993	2000
Utah	1.8	2.7	3.2	1.6	1.8	1.8
Vermont	.8	1.2	1.2	1.1	1.1	1.0
Virginia	1.7	2.4	2.1	10.7	11.3	10.4
Washington	3.6	7.2	5.5	5.5	6.4	6.6
West Virginia	2.5	2.5	.1	5.7	5.7	5.1
Wisconsin	1.5	1.2	1.4	1.9	2.2	1.9
Wyoming	.6	.3	.8	1.5	1.9	1.8

SOURCE: *Statistical Abstract of the United States: 1976*, 249, 250; *1992*, 330; *2001*, 319.

employees. Christenson and Sachs conclude that their study "supports the proposition that a greater number of public employees results in a higher perception of quality in public services. In the provision of services, the quantity of employees and the quality of services go hand in hand."[16]

Another cross-sectional comparison dealing with North Carolina was conducted by the Research Triangle Institute's Center for Population and Urban-Rural Studies. Instead of examining citizen opinions of government services, it collected program performance measurement data. The study covered eighty-seven communities within the state. Levels of effort, effectiveness, and performance by town and city governments in four areas were measured: fire protection, police protection, street maintenance, and garbage collection. The communities were stratified in six population-size ranges, with the differences between them sufficient to reflect much variation in size of municipal bureaucracy. Table 6-4 shows some of the resulting comparative measurements.[17]

We see that by no means were larger communities, with their larger bureaucracies, performing more poorly. To the contrary, the productivity of police in

Table 6-4 Program Measurement Data, North Carolina Communities, by Size

	Under 2,500	2,500–3,999	4,000–7,999	8,000–19,999	20,000–49,999	Over 50,000
Average fire response time (minutes)	3.6	4.4	3.2	1.8	3.7	2.7
Fire property loss per capita ($)	73	10	20	15	14	16
Average police response time (minutes)	3.6	3.8	3.4	3.2	4.0	3.8
Crime clearances per $1000 spending	.27	.27	.27	.52	.38	.51
Street miles maintained per street employee	3.1	2.4	4.1	4.6	4.7	4.1
Households served per garbage collection employee	213	249	208	289	312	329

SOURCE: Research Triangle Institute, Center for Population and Urban-Rural Studies; and North Carolina Department of Natural Resources and Community Development, Division of Community Assistance, "Comparative Performance Measures for Municipal Services," December 1978.

terms of clearing crimes and of refuse collectors in serving households was substantially greater in the bigger municipalities. Smaller towns were less impressive with respect to fire loss sustained per capita and street miles maintained per employee. Fire and police response times seemed unrelated to community size.

A final cross-sectional study focuses on organizational age rather than size. In one of the many "Aston" studies of intercorrelation of organizational variables conducted by social scientists at the University of Birmingham in England, D. S. Pugh and associates examined fifty-two organizations located in the English Midlands. Most were private firms, but eight government departments were included in the sample. These organizations varied in age from 29 to 170 years. The variable of age yielded few meaningful correlations against other factors. Age had no significant association with organizational size ($r = .16$), for example, or with a combined variable called "structuring of activities" that includes extent of specialization, standardization, and formalization ($r = .09$). This is hardly compatible with theories of expansionism or increased complexity or rule elaborateness as organizations age. The investigators did discover one reasonably high correlation with age, its relationship to "concentrations of authority"—the statistic was, however, in the opposite direction to what one would expect ($r = -.38$). In other words, older organizations, instead of engaging in greater attempts at coordination and control, were characterized by more decentralization and autonomy and less standardization of personnel procedures.[18]

Turning now to longitudinal research, Howard McCurdy employed the Downs life-cycle theory to examine the history of the National Aeronautics and Space Administration (NASA). He sought to discover, using archival and questionnaire data, whether, following its creation in 1958 and the first moon landing in 1969, NASA subsequently followed the life-cycle pattern of organizational decline and ossification, aided and abetted by an ever-older and more conservative management. He concluded that the predicted effects occurred with respect to average age, recruitment and promotion, control systems, and managerial attitudes, but with important caveats. One was that agency professionals continued to be innovative, maintaining faith in the underlying norms of their original test-and-exploration culture. Another was that the "aging" characteristics were the result not only of internal processes but of conditions imposed from the outside—such as increased scrutiny and restriction from Congress and the White House. Also, for political reasons, NASA was forced to contract out much of its work, converting engineers into contract administrators. (Indeed, following the *Columbia* tragedy in 2003, it was discovered that contractor engineers had conducted a superficial initial assessment of wing damage during the ill-fated shuttle's liftoff.)

McCurdy concludes that while this case study does not discredit decline theory, it suggests the need for some refinements. Even in steady-state or declining organizations, he says, entrepreneurial conditions can be created and the social status of the agency can be raised, thus attracting innovative people.

Conversely, actions that reduce status or make for dull work—such as contracting out—may promote administrative proliferation and conservatism.[19]

An empirical test of Bernstein's life-cycle thesis was conducted by Kenneth Meier and John Plumlee, who developed a series of quantitative measures related to congressional and presidential support of agencies, cross-recruitment of personnel between the regulators and the regulated, and various manifestations of organizational rigidity. Time-series data on these variables were gathered from the year of origin for eight federal regulatory agencies. On political support, Meier and Plumlee discovered that appropriations, personnel, and budgetary growth rates tended to be high early in the history of the agencies, but primarily because they were starting from scratch. Later, the rates did not consistently decline, but instead fluctuated. On cross-recruitment, it was found that appointments from industry usually decreased with age, rather than increased, as Bernstein's model would predict. In like manner, retirement of agency leaders to the regulated industry usually became less frequent with time. "None of the data unambiguously support the contention that regulators and the industry form a more symbiotic relationship as time passes," Meier and Plumlee conclude. "In most cases the data directly refute the hypothesis."

As for the contention that aging produces rigidity, Meier and Plumlee found that the proportion of agency leaders with legal training tended to increase as time passed (the legal profession may wish to take issue with this measure of rigidity). The age of top executives rose over time for several agencies, but slowly. No important relationships were found between organizational age and the variables of leader turnover, percentage of top appointees without prior substantive expertise, end-of-year case backlogs, and number of cases handled per employee. The authors conclude that "the future does not look bright for an aging theory of regulatory agency decay."[20]

As we have noted, life-cycle theorists do not abide by their organic metaphor with complete faithfulness, since they do not see death as inevitable. In fact, they regard bureaucratic death as nearly impossible. Yet they may wish to change their minds after glancing at that enormous cemetery of the federal government, Appendix B of the *United States Government Manual*, where one finds well over a thousand "Federal Executive Agencies Terminated, Transferred, or Changed in Name Subsequent to March 4, 1933." Robert Stein and Kenneth Bickers calculate that between 1971 and 1990 an average of thirty-six federal programs were eliminated each year. In the late 1990s, a "CyberCemetery" was founded at the University of North Texas to preserve the web sites of defunct federal bureaucracies. By 2002, fifteen agencies and commissions had been electronically buried there, including the Office of Technology Assessment, the Advisory Commission on Intergovernmental Relations, and the National Partnership for Reinventing Government.[21]

Herbert Kaufman has studied this matter of bureaucracy's mortality. He tracked survival and termination in sub-units of the ten civilian departments of the federal government in existence in 1973, plus entities of the Executive Office of the President then extant. Tracing administrative survival forward from 1923, Kaufman found that 148, or 85 percent, of the 175 organizations existing at that point were still alive in 1973—fifty years later. Twenty-seven had been terminated, mainly by internal departmental action. Kaufman calculates that the death rate of government organizations is about half that of business firms—27.6 per 10,000 versus 56.8.

Investigating the causes of bureaucratic death, Kaufman concluded that the major reasons for it are program competition, changes in leadership and policy, obsolescence, and completion of mission. Whether age itself is a cause of death—or a means of survival—remains an open question, he says. A faint tendency exists for younger organizations to expire more easily than older ones. Still, a comparison of the ages of dying and surviving organizations shows little discernible difference. Although aging organizations supposedly become more rigid and hence could become more vulnerable, the fact that older units do not experience a higher death rate "casts doubt on the allegation of inevitable sclerosis. Organizational old age does not seem invariably to bring on greater rigidity."[22]

In conclusion, data from the real world of bureaucracy cast serious doubt on prominent theories purporting to explain its growth, deterioration, and death. Bureaucracies are often not very big to start with, and they do not expand in size unendingly over time; indeed, they often contract. When bureaucracies do grow, they do not necessarily outpace the tasks they are assigned, and they do not necessarily deteriorate; in fact, in some cases bigger bureaucracies actually work better than smaller ones. Also, the supposed ravages of time are not as universal or imperative as many would have us believe. Nonetheless, bureaucracies do die, a realization that makes great common sense yet flies in the face of beliefs that bureaucracies simply control themselves without external interference. We now turn to the subject of bureaucracy's power.

The Political Power of Bureaucracy

The founding scripture of public administration in America, an essay written by the young Woodrow Wilson in 1887 when he was teaching at Bryn Mawr, states that administration "is removed from the hurry and strife of politics." Although a germ of truth lies in these words, anyone who has entered the portals of a bureaucracy or a public administration classroom knows that bureaucracy is indeed a highly political part of any government. Politics is played not only in bureaucracy but by it. Making reference to this fact, my late colleague Norton Long left another classic statement for the field: "The lifeblood of administration is power."[23]

The political power of bureaucracy is an enduring topic that has preoccupied political scientists, political commentators, and other scholars of public administration for generations. In the minds of most observers, the issue is not whether bureaucracies have power but the magnitude and ominous nature of that power. Bureaucracies are seen as too influential, too unchallenged, and subsequently dangerous. Bureaucrats are thought of as assuming a preeminent, even unchecked role in the formation and execution of public policy. Some critics, such as Robert Michels, whom we encountered in chapter 1, contend that, in the final analysis, bureaucracy is incompatible with democracy.

The deductive case for why bureaucracies are too powerful can be made on at least four grounds. First, the Weberian organizational form seems to be an inherently powerful instrument because of its properties: its unified hierarchy concentrates control, its high degree of specialization provides great expertise, its permanent records accumulate vast quantities of information and officially interpret the past, and its tenured workforce cannot be removed and hence is not accountable. Second, the principal function of public administration, the implementation of law and policy, puts bureaucracy in the position of representing the sovereign majesty of the state to citizens in concrete, everyday terms. To them, the state *is* bureaucracy. Third, the technical nature of modern administration means that legislators and other elected officials must delegate discretionary authority or even rule-making power to the bureaucrats, who thus are "legislators" of sorts. Fourth, from the standpoint of principal-agent theory, information asymmetry favoring the agents gives them the ability to outmaneuver their principals and pursue their own objectives. Moreover, as conditions change, the contract between them gets out of date, giving agents added opportunities to veer from policy or otherwise be disloyal.

To what extent do these deductive arguments hold up empirically? Let us examine the best available scholarship on the subject.

Joel Aberbach and Bert Rockman interviewed 476 federal executives in three periods: in 1970 during the Nixon Administration, in 1986–1987 under President Reagan, and 1991–1992 during the senior Bush presidency. Their sample included both partisan political appointees ("principals") and higher civil servants ("agents"). Reviewing the three periods, the researchers conclude that the civil servants in all three of these Republican administrations were not composed of left-leaning liberals alone but included plenty of solid Republicans. In other words, the civil service in these periods seemed to take on the political coloration of its masters. Aberbach and Rockman cite this as "evidence of considerable responsiveness in what is sometimes characterized as an insulated institution."[24]

Cornell Hooten studied the dynamics of bureau response to external political guidance in the Urban Mass Transportation Administration and Food and Nutrition Service during the Carter years. One thing he could not help but notice in both agencies was that the bureaucrats made a point of stressing the precise wording of formal directives and legal definitions. In other words, they took their "contracts" seriously. More generally, he found that while careerists certainly harbored personal opinions on policy, for the most part they worked actively and regularly on behalf of political executives. In doing so, however, they were not blindly obedient. Instead, they judiciously weighed the internal and external factors that were likely to affect outcomes, including the extent to which the institution possessed the needed expertise or capacity. Any resistance to policies from the top was usually based on the perceived realities of the situation, not personal disagreement. On occasion the bureaucrats would make a point of warning superiors, for their own good, of political land mines that lay in wait along the pathways of contemplated policy.[25]

Irene Rubin studied budget and program cutbacks in five federal agencies during the Reagan years, a time that was most uncomfortable for the career civil service. During this period she uncovered little evidence of foot-dragging in the implementation of the new policies. The only exception was anonymous reports to the inspector general at the Department of Housing and Urban Development (HUD), where one of the great scandals of the Reagan years was eventually uncovered. "In short," Rubin concludes, "the agencies were much more controllable when it came to cutback and new policy initiatives than one might have imagined."[26]

In another study of bureaucratic policy responses to the incoming Reagan administration, Marissa Martino Golden conducted in-depth interviews with current and former high-level civil servants of the National Highway Traffic Safety Administration (NHTSA), the Food and Nutrition Service, the Civil Rights Division of the Justice Department, and the Environmental Protection Agency (EPA). Inspired by the organizational response typology of Albert Hirschman, she sought to find out whether the careerists reacted to Reagan's new appointments and conservative policy shifts by leaving (exit), dissenting (voice), supporting actively (loyalty), or merely tolerating (neglect).[27]

At the NHTA, Golden found that while bureaucrats disputed decisions by the new administration to reduce vehicle recalls and rescind regulations on airbags and bumper heights, few left the agency and most passively supported the changes philosophically as an outcome of the election. At the Food and Nutrition Service, the new administration sought greater program accountability and productivity. At that time also, ketchup was named as a vegetable in the school lunch program, a step much ridiculed by the press. Several liberal-leaning civil servants resigned or were forced out, but those who remained accepted the right of the newcomers to change things. The ketchup flap, incidentally, was set off by a leak to the press from an advocacy group, not by the bureaucrats (who perhaps should have leaked it themselves).

At the Civil Rights Division, Reagan appointees sought to eliminate affirmative action, terminate racial quotas and timetables, and end school busing. Career attorneys in the division were emphatically opposed to these policies and accordingly voiced their strong opposition in personal conferences with the assistant attorney general, who listened carefully but did not accept their views. Some attorneys left. Those who remained continued with their work, but did not recommend investigations they knew would be turned down.

As for the EPA, during the Anne Gorsuch directorship, the career bureaucrats were ignored and walled off from policymaking. Some overt dissent took place among the bureaucrats, even guerilla warfare at the lower ranks. Several people were forced to leave or left voluntarily. Those remaining kept quiet. Some leaks and whistle blowing occurred, but most careerists regarded this as contrary to professional integrity, and the violators were ostracized. In sum, in these four agencies Golden found substantial exit and voice, some neglect, a little sabotage, but mostly resigned loyalty. She concluded, "upper-level career civil servants are more responsive than resistant to the president and his appointed deputies."[28]

Dan Wood and Richard Waterman examined the relationships of eight regulatory bureaucracies to their external environments in the 1970s and 1980s, using time-series modeling techniques intended to identify the causal effects of outside stimuli. The agencies studied were the Interstate Commerce Commission (ICC), the Equal Employment Opportunity Commission (EEOC), the Federal Trade Commission (FTC), the Nuclear Regulatory Commission (NRC), the Food and Drug Administration (FDA), the NHTSA, the Office of Surface Mining (OSM), and the EPA. The agencies' policy behavior was measured by numbers of specific regulatory actions, for example operating certificates issued (ICC), litigation actions taken (EEOC), consent decrees obtained (FTC), safety violations found (NRC), inspections done (FDA), engineering evaluations completed (NHTSA), cessation orders given (OSM), and litigation referrals made (EPA). The data were analyzed on a monthly or quarterly basis, permitting a fine-tuned, time-sensitive longitudinal study.[29]

The external stimuli held against these measures for possible causal effects were from the presidency, Congress, courts, and larger political environment. Both one-time stimuli were identified, such as the appointment of a new administrator or passage of a new law, and stimuli over time, such as a trend in budget reductions, a spate of congressional investigations, or a rise in press attention. The analysis sought to model dynamic interactive effects between the agency and its environment. The modeling technique was repeated until the best statistical fit emerged, and quantitative findings were evaluated in light of archival data and follow-up interviews. From their study, Wood and Waterman concluded that "instructions" received from principals usually came from many sources, including the president and congressional committees. Responses to these signals definitely took place, often very fast. Yet the bureaucrats sent out their own policy signals to the external environment as well. The outcome was an integration of numerous past and current democratic preferences. Bureaucracy's contribution was to add to this representation a pressure for rational action. At the end of the day, Wood and Waterman conclude,

> American public bureaucracies are not slow, omnipotent, or unresponsive to public preferences. Furthermore, they are not out of control, as most citizens and some scholarly literature have suggested. Politicians regularly control bureaucratic outputs using various instruments provided for under the current government framework.[30]

What does this research tell us? One point might be that, unlike the Prussian state in which Max Weber lived, the American bureaucracy does not overawe its citizenry and does not possess, to use Weber's term, "overtowering" political power. In the United States we have a Constitution, Bill of Rights, separation of powers, and a culture that is instinctively suspicious of government. Yet American bureaucrats certainly exercise administrative discretion, and they often possess information not independently available to their political superiors. Still, at the crucial time following displacement of the ruling party, the studies reviewed found that a high degree of compliance to a new political order generally occurs. This may not be accompanied by joy or enthusiasm, but to an impressive degree bureaucracy is respectful of the election's verdict. Leaks, whistle-blowing, and sabotage are minimal. In some instances the bureaucrats may see themselves shifting their own political views in the direction of the new administration's orientation. In any case, the formal texts of statutes and other written mandates handed down are taken seriously. At the same time, basic acceptance of new policy signals does not mean that bureaucrats are blindly obedient to their new political masters. They ardently and openly disagree with them on policy when they believe it is misguided from the standpoint of ethics, feasibility, or impending land mines. The bureaucrats also continue to advocate their private positions in the appropriate places.

To sum up, bureaucracies are checked but not chained. They are responsive to external political control but not politically supine. They react not merely to static instructions but to changed circumstances. They not only implement policy but shape and advocate it. Bureaucrats are loyal to new regimes yet do not simply keep quiet when they disagree. They accept election results and, in that sense, adhere to Wilson's politics-administration dichotomy. At the same time, they draw from Long's lifeblood of power to advance ideas they think are right.

The Political Contributions of Bureaucracy

Brian Cook, in his book *Bureaucracy and Self-Government*, argues that traditional thinking about the role of bureaucracy in a democratic polity is shortsighted. While it is true that public administration's main function in a democratic polity is to carry out the laws and wishes of elected officials and the public, he states this should not be its only function. A purely "instrumental" interpretation of the role of administration, says Cook, should be supplemented by what he calls a "constitutive" role. In it, higher public ends are independently pursued by public administration. Bureaucracy is actively "formative" as well as reactive in the policy process. The administrative apparatus is regarded as not merely a tool of the elected regime but an integral part of the governing order.[31]

Several elements comprise Cook's constitutive notion, and I shall attempt to summarize them in my own words. One is that public administration offers to democratic governance what might be thought of as a steady hand on the tiller. That is, in political deliberations it stands for the need to preserve continuity, be temperate, and retain system integrity. When drafting new regulations, for example, bureaucrats will remind the politicians that group consultation, due process of law, and the effects of existing statutes must be incorporated into the product. Another contribution of public administrators is to bring definition to vague policy concepts advanced by lawmakers, such as the phrases "multiple use" of natural resources and "managed growth" in urban development. In so doing, the bureaucrats enter the realm of not just how to do it but what to do.

Then too, bureaucracy institutionalizes and hence advocates key values with which it is imbued, such as basing action on analysis (rationality) and considering long-term future effects (planning). In this way, administration enriches the processes of collective social learning. Finally, bureaucracy adds to the vitality of democratic life in several ways. These include sponsoring forums for public deliberation, facilitating understanding among competing groups, encouraging a willingness to join in collective action, and promoting an ethic of citizenship and sense of community.[32]

In pursuance of this point, Cook takes exception to something that was said in earlier editions of *The Case for Bureaucracy*. He states that a metaphor I used for bureaucracy's discretionary role does not convey the magnitude of what he calls the constitutive role. In the passage to which he refers, I had written that bureaucracy is not like the raging river whose floodwaters will invade the land unless every hole in the levee is plugged, meaning that not every external check on bureaucracy need be complete for democracy to be safe. A better counteranalogy, I continued, is "the vessel at sea, which is subject to numerous influences of wind, current, and radioed commands from shore, but still sets its own immediate course. Only in this way will the vessel get safely to shore to unload its cargo of effective public policy."[33]

Cook believes that in the analogy I did not go far enough in portraying the rightful role of bureaucracy, which he expands as follows:

> For example, ships at sea do not just receive messages radioed from shore; they send them as well. The information on conditions and the captain's judgments contained in such messages may result in alterations to the commands about the course to take, or even at what port to call. Furthermore, on long voyages, ships may make many ports, and the interactions between crews and residents may be the grist for more information and judgment communicated to ship owners and users, which again may alter both strategies and objectives. On the long voyages of the eighteenth and nineteenth centuries, in which a ship's cargo might have

> included live plants and animals, the cargo itself would have grown or declined, but certainly it would have been transformed, partly on the basis of the good or poor efforts of the crew.[34]

Cook then goes on to point out that administrators do not just decide on the mode and timing for the delivery of prepackaged policies, but develop further both the substance of programs and strategies for their implementation, often without much legislative guidance. "It might even be best to abandon the vessel-at-sea metaphor altogether," he concludes, "because it depicts an isolation from politics and the public lives of the citizenry that is not the experience of most public administrators."[35]

Let me respond to Cook's criticism by endorsing his position. I am happy to have my metaphor revised or scrapped entirely. More important, I would like now to amplify my own vision of the bureaucrat's role in governance. I have no qualms about charting a more explicitly purposive and politically significant role for public administration, as long as it remains constrained by the law and by elected officials. As we learned in chapter 1, bureaucracy was initially installed in the world's first modern republics as a tool to carry out public needs identified by the people's representatives. That point should not be forgotten or set aside. This means that administration's larger contributions to the polity will augment, not replace, its basic instrumental function. We just learned in this chapter that bureaucracy responds reliably to elected regimes, a democratic asset that cannot be sacrificed. At the same time, bureaucracy is by no means a puppet to its masters, allowing room for actions that strengthen democracy rather than weaken it.

Figure 6-1 identifies six contributions beyond the mere enforcement of laws that American bureaucracy now makes to the political system, presenting them in a matrix to show their interrelationships. The columns signify that the contributions operate in two ways: enhancing the system's capacity to function and increasing the degree to which collective action is sustainable over time. The three rows indicate what is affected by these

	System capacity	Action sustainability
Resources	Fueling the system	Sustaining the missions
Decisions	Making elections count	Intervening in policy
Citizens	Fostering upward mobility	Promoting civic participation

Figure 6-1 Political Contributions of Bureaucracy

contributions, that is resources, decisions, and the citizenry. We discuss each cell of the matrix in turn.

Fueling the System

The first contribution derives from bureaucracy's role in generating funds for the work of government. Obviously, governments cannot operate without money. Many governments around the world are chronically crippled because of inadequate revenue systems. One reason for writing a new American constitution in 1787 was to correct such a defect at the national level.

Not only is it impossible for bureaucracy itself to function without adequate government income, the same is true for all public activities, including the holding of elections and the operations of legislatures and courts. While enforcing tax laws may be construed narrowly as an instrumental function of public administration, that characterization fails to capture the activity's enormous and fundamental importance. Raising public revenue constitutes laying the very basis for all else that goes on in the polity. Just as the Constitution and laws form the legal foundation for our democratic republic, tax collection lays the fiscal foundation.

Although governments at all three levels of American federalism collect taxes, the national government is of supreme importance, for it raises more than 70 percent of the total. As noted in chapter 4, state and local governments depend on Washington for nearly a third of their revenue. The Internal Revenue Service (IRS) is at the heart of this fiscal achievement. Although its conceptual roots go back to Alexander Hamilton, the modern IRS was created during the Truman administration. It is the leading collector of public revenue in the world, drawing more than $2 trillion annually from the earth's richest economy. Although the IRS also collects corporate, employment, estate, and excise taxes, the core of its mission is enforcement of the individual income tax. This activity is governed by a highly complex revenue code, enacted by Congress and made more elaborate every year. The agency's 100,000 employees process more than 125 million returns annually. Accomplishing this each year makes the IRS the fuel tank for our democracy.[36]

Yet keeping that tank filled is unpopular. The private tax "farmers" of the eighteenth century were despised members of the community. In our own time the acronym *IRS* conjures up images of mid-April discomfort at the very least, and in some circles Nazi-style authoritarianism. Politicians champion tax cuts by implying that tax revenue is wasted and that the people know best how to spend their money. In the latter 1990s a concerted campaign was launched against the IRS by Republican candidates for president and by the Republican chairman of the Senate Finance Committee. A "restructuring and reform" act passed in 1998 was designed to make the agency more efficient, responsive, service-oriented, and pro-taxpayer. Despite a number of problems with the statute, substantial improvement in IRS operations was thereafter detected by the public, as evidenced by the rise in its ACSI ratings (noted in chapter 2).

At the same time, Charles Rossotti, the IRS commissioner who carried out the changes, observed that while taxpayer rights and computer improvements were important, they must not overshadow the need to hire enough auditors and revenue agents to enforce taxpayer compliance, especially by high-income individuals. Lacking sufficient personnel, the agency is unable to pursue 60 percent of identified tax debts or investigate 79 percent of cases where offshore bank accounts or other abuse-suggestive tactics are used, he complained. Even the lead spokesman for "customer service" at the IRS realized that, whether the customers like it or not, democracy's fuel tank must be filled and filled fairly.[37]

Sustaining the Missions

Charles Rossotti is not alone in promoting his agency's mission; as noted in chapter 2, such advocacy is often done by bureaucracy. Critics of government consider this a bad thing, denouncing it as empire building, personal self-aggrandizement, or an attempt to hang on to outdated activities of government. Yet in this book we have seen that bureaucratic growth is not inevitable, since appropriation increases commingle with cutbacks. Indeed, fiscal starvation is not unknown in government; this is literally seen in some state penitentiaries, where wardens are reducing prison food rations to save money. Another illustration is local law enforcement agencies that are charged with new antiterrorism responsibilities but not given the funds to carry them out. To compensate for this shortfall, several charitable foundations have been created to raise money for police departments.[38]

In chapter 4 we noted how many of the problems assigned to bureaucracy to "solve" require dedicated, ongoing work over many years. In fact, many problems cannot be eliminated at all, and progress must be measured in terms of making continuous headway over a long time. Yet the political support needed to attack problems this way almost inevitably erodes. As issues fall from fashion, programs dealing with them become vulnerable to more faddish causes in the competitive battle for resources. This does not mean that public needs in the area are declining; in fact, they are probably increasing because of demographic and economic growth. But because the resource environment of bureaucracy is not a market but a political arena, new income does not automatically accompany citizen need or want—it must be obtained through political advocacy. While interested clientele groups or legislative committees may help with this political process, the bureaucracy's own leadership and institutional credibility remain the most telling factors.

In effect, bureaucracy becomes the "keeper" of its missions, which otherwise can easily fall through the cracks of a fragmented political system. It is here that Long's "lifeblood of power" is important. Use of political power for sustaining core missions is not undemocratic; to the contrary, democratic purposes are being fulfilled. The agency and its program, whether it be a public health department, school district, police department, or agricultural research station, exists not because it simply has connections or a will to survive, but because its work is essential to the people. Yet the public may not think of it this way unless the mission is suddenly suspended, as happened with partial closure of the federal government in 1995. True, some bureaucratic missions truly go out of date, which is why there are many "deaths" in the bureaucracy.

A long view puts sustained missions in perspective. Paul Light once surveyed 1,000 historians and political scientists, asking them to identify the federal government's greatest achievements during the second half of the twentieth century. Among other things, they came up with expanding civil rights, reducing contagious disease, ensuring the safety of food and water, and building the interstates. Bureaucracy had a crucial role in all of these achievements, and none would have been possible without a steady, sustained mission underway over many decades.[39]

Making Elections Count

What I mean by this contribution to system capacity is the ability of bureaucracy to make democratic elections meaningful. Free elections, democracy's most important decision point, are a sham if it becomes impossible for non-incumbent candidates or opposition parties to win and then follow through with implementation of their proposed programs. Unfortunately, the lack of this capacity plagues many otherwise open political systems around the world. Their bureaucracies are either unable to shift gears when regimes change or are insufficiently competent to mount new programs.

Allow me to elaborate on this point from a personal standpoint. In the 1960s my wife and I went to Puerto Rico in connection with my new teaching job at its university's School of Public Administration. As it happened, we ended up living across the street from the famous Roosevelt Brains Truster and former governor of Puerto Rico, Rexford Guy Tugwell. I became interested in researching the history of public administration on the island, which by that time had attained a reputation as the best in the Caribbean basin. Delving into the subject, I discovered that many of its institutions had been created in the 1940s, when Tugwell served as the last appointed governor. At that time, a populist political reform movement was gaining ascendancy, led by the charismatic politician Luis Muñoz Marín, who would later become the island's first elected governor. Muñoz was determined to take power in the island's legislature away from a coalition of conservatives, who for decades had dominated island politics on behalf of a colonial elite and who retained their seats by buying votes from the poor. In the 1940 election, however, the rural peasants took the risk of no longer voting for cash but placing their trust in Muñoz's party instead.

The island's bureaucracy was at the time a small, inert enterprise, rife with nepotism and favoritism. When Tugwell insisted that a competent public service based on merit, training, and good leadership would be essential to the success of the reform program, Muñoz reluctantly agreed, and with the governor's guidance a total reshaping of the island's public administration took place. As it turned out, Muñoz's party remained in office for many years, eventually completing one of the most successful cases of planned socioeconomic development of our time. Moreover, ever since, the island has benefited from a healthy competition among political parties, numerous turnover elections, and an honest electoral process. With a competent and responsive bureaucracy permanently in place to assure that whatever party won would be able to carry out its program, democracy prospered along with the Puerto Rican people.[40]

Intervening in Policy

A purely instrumental view of bureaucracy pretends that it carries out policy only and does not make it. This, of course, is untrue. Not only is it impossible to separate policymaking from policy implementation, but bureaucrats frequently have influence on policy formation as well—if for no other reason than they usually know more than anyone else about how best to achieve policy objectives.

By policy intervention I refer not to policy-making influence, however, but to the more active role of adopting or countering policy under selected circumstances of short-term, critical importance. Such circumstances are rare, but they do occur. I regard such interventions as not antidemocratic because they sustain decision frameworks already in effect. I have two examples to offer.

One is the conduct of New York City bureaucrats on 11 September 2001. Upon hearing that the World Trade Center had been hit, the director of the city's Office of Emergency Management immediately told police to close off all streets below Canal. He also ordered that all Manhattan tunnels and bridges be closed and that the harbor be sealed. The city's commissioner of transportation, realizing that all means of external communication to the political leadership had been cut off, suspended ferry and bus schedules and deployed the freed-up vessels and vehicles to evacuate lower Manhattan. Two other administrators, the deputy director and trainmaster of the PATH commuter train to New Jersey, were in the underground station below the twin towers when the first aircraft hit. Sizing up the situation, they ordered a loaded incoming train to skip the WTC stop and return to New Jersey and then instructed another train to unload in New Jersey and return to Manhattan for evacuation purposes. This quick action effected the removal of 3,000 people from the scene of disaster.[41]

My second example comes from the time of extended debate during the months prior to the 2003 war on Iraq. An issue in contention at one point was whether Osama bin Laden's al Qaeda terrorist network was linked to Saddam Hussein's regime. For a time the Bush administration portrayed the two as closely intertwined, offering yet another rationale for the war. This position was softened, however, after newspapers quoted unnamed CIA analysts and FBI investigators as saying that senior administration officials were exaggerating the strength of the evidence of such a connection. Then, a few days later, a taped bin Laden broadcast came to light, and the administration portrayed it as clearly demonstrating bin Laden's strong support of Hussein. Again mentioning unnamed sources, the papers noted that in the tape bin Laden had gone out of his way to show contempt for Hussein and members of his Baath Party, whom he termed "infidels."

Did these behind-the-scenes bureaucratic contacts with the press constitute unconscionable "sabotage" of the agenda of the president and his advisers? Those in the White House probably thought so. At the same time, however, these interventions by lower-level agents induced the leaders to back off from untenable positions that would have been exposed later. Even though the bureaucrats were "off-message" from the Bush standpoint, their actions allowed retreat from shaky limbs before they were sawn off.[42]

Fostering Upward Mobility

Over time, bureaucracy has done much to make it possible for the "left out" members of the population to improve their lives and enter the middle class. I refer here not to the outcomes of programs specifically set up for this purpose, such as welfare, social services, and economic development. I mean instead the side-effect consequences of large-scale institutions created to achieve other public purposes, specifically, the public schools, the armed forces, and the bureaucracy itself as a source of employment. The aggregate contribution of these institutions to upward social mobility in our society has been enormous. By allowing millions of Americans to become more active citizens and reach for a higher station in life than they would otherwise have attained, these enterprises have greatly benefited the capacity of our democratic political system.

The educational and socialization functions of the public schools lay the foundation of a successful and effective citizenry. The most striking attributes of the American public school system are its original egalitarian roots and its later enlargement of educational opportunity for nonwhites. When established in the nineteenth century, the system was revolutionary in that it provided free education for all social classes. This democratic parity distinguished it from most educational systems yet developed, wherein those destined for the trades were separated from those headed for university. Then, in 1954, the nation began a long journey toward racial equality in the schools that is still not complete. Yet it is important to note that underprivileged minorities have increasingly benefited from being in school. Between 1960 and 2000, the proportion of the African American population over twenty-five who had graduated from high school increased from 20 percent to 78 percent. For Hispanic Americans, this figure was 32 percent in 1970 and 57 percent in 2000. The augmented influx of new immigrants in recent years has created another great clientele for upward mobility; in 2000 nearly 20 percent of enrollees in American elementary and high schools were foreign born or had a foreign-born parent.[43]

The armed forces constitute another great egalitarian mixer and upward-mobility processor for the society. I vividly recall my own experience at army boot camp, where people from all walks of life were bound together by having to run the same gauntlet. In both wartime and peacetime, millions upon millions of young men have been deeply affected by the experience of military service. Some have, for the first time in their lives, had enough food to eat and adequate clothing to wear. The intensive training recruits receive has added to educational levels. In the military, as in the schools, racial segregation was practiced until it was ended in the years after World War II. In more recent decades, women have joined in this socially transforming process. For many in the armed forces, of both sexes and all races, the experience has turned them into leaders, as an increasingly diversified officer corps has been formed to lead the diverse enlisted ranks. These men and women then take their leadership skills into the civilian society upon leaving the military.

Employment in the civilian bureaucracy also offers a significant source of upward mobility in the population. Salaried government employment itself may be thought of as admission to the middle class. The key point here is that opportunities for advancement within the civil service make it possible to rise upward. Agency programs of educational assistance and in-house training add to these possibilities. As noted in chapter 4, members of racial minorities generally fare well in government employment. Over the decades, minority percentages in the federal executive branch have risen significantly, with African Americans, Asian Americans, and American Indians now exceeding their proportion in the population. Also, advancement upward seems to be faster than in the private sector, and over time senior jobs in the federal government are being increasingly filled by minority and female occupants. We recall that Evelyn Fields started out as a cartographer in NOAA, only to rise through the ranks to become a rear admiral and the first black woman to command a government ship at sea. Celia Yette graduated from an hourly job in telemarketing to a professional position in the Social Security Administration. Colbert King was once a mail boy in the subbasement of the USDA building, later becoming a military officer, diplomat, government executive, and now a senior columnist in Washington.

Promoting Civic Participation

A final political contribution by bureaucracy is to civic engagement in our democracy. In various ways, bureaucracy encourages citizen involvement in community organizations and in the political process. The resultant additions to "social capital," as some call it, reinforce the democratic system's sustainability by forming bonds among people, promoting community and political activism, and building trust in others and in the political process. While many other institutions and forces also contribute to social capital, bureaucracy's role is not insignificant in this regard. (Indeed this was one of Cook's points; see p. 129.)

A number of scholars have conducted empirical studies whose conclusions bear on this idea. Theda Skocpol and her coauthors studied the nationally organized clubs, lodges, advocacy groups, religious associations, and service organizations that were so important in nineteenth-century America. Skocpol points out that these institutions were modeled after the government's own federal structure. Along with a national headquarters, most such groups had organizations in each state and, within them, local or regional chapters. A key factor that made this national network possible, the researchers conclude, was the availability of an efficient and inexpensive postal system, which allowed leaders on the Eastern Seaboard to communicate with members throughout the vast country, at the time interconnected only by rail, unpaved roads, and a few telegraph lines.[44]

After World War II Congress enacted what was called the G.I. Bill, a system of cash benefits that helped millions of returning veterans go to college and obtain vocational training. Suzanne Mettler studied how veterans who took advantage of this program were affected with respect to their participation in civic affairs, a phenomenon that she measured by quantifying their membership in civic organizations and active participation in politics, such as contributing to a campaign. Her conclusion is that civic involvement was indeed increased, and she offers two explanations. One is that the benefited vets felt they should "pay society back" for the assistance received. The other is that the program's universality and easy access enabled millions of underprivileged young men to enter the educated stratum of society that is accustomed to civic participation. Mettler joins Skocpol in urging that it is time to "bring the state back in" to studies of social capital formation.[45]

Christopher Simon examined the effects on civic participation that result from volunteer service in the federal government's AmeriCorps program, which was formed in 1993 by incorporating several existing community service programs, including Volunteers in Service to America (VISTA) and the National Civilian Community Corps. In order to assess the consequence of AmeriCorps service, Simon conducted pretest and posttest surveys of samples of program participants (that is, both prior to and following their enrollment) in four western states. He found that, despite the relatively short period of service (about one year), after the experience the volunteers were more active in community groups, expressed more confidence in civic institutions, and exhibited public-oriented values to a greater degree. This outcome was true regardless of gender or race.[46]

A final area of scholarly interest in the area of civic participation relates to the effects of employment in bureaucracy itself as a factor in encouraging such involvement. In chapter 5 we noted that public employees tend to surpass other citizens in belonging to groups, participating in politics, supporting democratic principles, and paying taxes on time. Gene Brewer, one of the contributors to the literature cited there, recently published a study on how public servants contribute to social capital, drawing on survey data from the University of Michigan's American National Election Study. Brewer concludes that public employees, compared to others in the society, score higher on indices reflecting a number of value clusters, including social trust, social altruism, equality, diversity, and humanitarian concern for others. Also, public servants report higher levels on several indicators of actual participation in civic groups. Brewer went one step further, conducting a multivariate statistical analysis that isolates the influence of variables associated with civic participation. He found that, independent of age, education, income, and the value clusters, the variable of being a public servant has a strong and significant predictive impact on civic participation. Brewer believes that his work takes the findings of Skocpol and others to a higher level.

> The present study emboldens and advances their finding by showing that public employees are catalysts for building social capital at the individual level. That is, in addition to their formal job roles, which often involve pursuing the common good and furthering the public interest, public servants also perform a variety of extra-role behaviors described here as civic engagement. These activities are crucial in forming and sustaining social capital in society at large.[47]

To summarize, in this chapter we have found that common perceptions of bureaucracy's bigness and badness are much overblown. Now, in addition, we recognize that this absence of bureaucratic badness is complemented by the presence of some unexpected goodness—not in doing bureaucracy's direct work but in more broadly enriching our democracy.

Chapter 7 Fads and Fundamentals of Bureaucracy

This book began with an anticipatory brief for the case for bureaucracy. Its final chapter opens with a summary recapitulation of that case and then proceeds to consideration of the many reform proposals that have been put forward for American public administration. The book ends with some parting observations on the fundamentals of bureaucracy.

The Case Recapitulated

The underlying theme of this book is that governmental administration in America, despite conventional opinion to the contrary, is relatively effective, reasonably efficient, and supportive of our democratic way of life. While waste, incompetence, and corruption will always exist in government—and in all organizational sectors, for that matter—in the United States these problems are far less common and significant than we commonly believe. In general, government agencies and government employees in America do their jobs surprisingly well in view of their reputation. This is true at the federal, state, and local levels. As a consequence, I seize the popular synonym for bad government, "bureaucracy," and redefine it as a general social asset for the society.

Bureaucracy's true nature is not best discovered in campaign rhetoric or in exposé-style television reporting. Many academic theories about the nature of bureaucracy are also misleading, and much of this book is devoted to refuting them with the ample empirical evidence that is available.

Gratuitous attacks on the institutions of government have seemed to subside since the mid-1990s, and for this we can be grateful. At the same time, it is important to remember that, all along, American citizens have been telling survey researchers that bureaucracy usually works. Broadly speaking, between two-thirds and three-fourths have reported their encounters with agencies as satisfactory. The American Customer Satisfaction Index, probably the most sophisticated measure of its kind, scores the federal government at 70 on a scale of 100, a level close to that attained by all consumer production in the economy.

In addition, several kinds of output and outcome statistics are available on bureaucratic performance. Overall, these demonstrate quality program performance and measurable success. The vast majority of mail arrives regularly on time, for example. Benefit checks do as well, and almost always in the right amount. The measured productivity of government on the basis of output per employee year has risen substantially in recent decades. Many indicators show recent upturns in policy success—for which bureaucracy deserves at least part of the credit—in the areas of environmental protection, public safety, and child and adult welfare.

Empirical research also dispels a number of specific myths about American bureaucracy. One of these is the notion that its "bureaucratic" structure as modeled by Max Weber leads inevitably to rigidity or other negative characteristics. Yet "twin" research projects that study two bureaucracies of identical organization and others that compare welfare rules and offices demonstrate wide variation in behavior and culture. The idea that bureaucracy, as essentially a middle-class institution, is discriminatory to the poor and racial minorities is also refuted. Bureaucrats tend to follow professional standards in providing urban services, and inequities in public infrastructure that result are usually based on such factors as the age and density of neighborhoods.

The common belief that the private sector is always more efficient than the public is seriously questioned by the available evidence. In studies that compare public and private provision of services such as refuse collection, public utilities, and transport, the verdict is mixed. Many studies confirm the orthodox view, but many do not. Hence, the automatic superiority of the private sector cannot be assumed. The same is true of the common assumption that private organizations are always more innovative than government agencies. Case studies exist to the contrary, and many awards have been given to bureaucrats for management and policy innovation.

The time-honored cry of "red tape" is still heard across the land, but in many instances it is the consequence of rules designed for one objective, such as fairness, interfering with other desirable goals such as efficiency or timeliness. Bureaucrats often find themselves in no-win situations, in which different groups demand opposite outcomes.

In the United States public administration faces special challenges of fragmentation and complexity in implementation. One relates to how the federal system is organized. Much of what bureaucracy tries to accomplish is carried out not internally but by other agencies and governments, via grants or mandates. This devolution process divorces responsibility and control. Another feature of U.S. administrative implementation is great reliance on the dispersal of public action to private organizations, particularly business firms under contract and nonprofit organizations receiving grants. Hence the chain of implementation is doubly extended, compounding complexity and reducing control. Because of this attenuated structure, and because of the intractability of many problems given bureaucracy to solve, policy progress must usually be measured in terms of headway, not goal attainment.

America employs approximately 21 million civilian bureaucrats, at all levels of government. Whereas some decades ago they were predominantly white males, today women and minorities populate their ranks heavily, and, increasingly, the upper civil service and leadership positions have strong female and minority representation as well. This demographically representative bureaucracy is expressive of a spectrum of policy and political viewpoints that mirrors the population at large, with a modest lean toward the spectrum's liberal end. Bureaucrats tend to be good citizens in that they participate in the political process and pay their taxes more regularly than do other Americans.

Contrary to the academic stereotype of a bureaucratic "personality," these 21 million individuals do not exhibit tendencies toward being inflexible, rule-bound, cautious, impersonal, haughty, fearful, deceptive, alienated, or secretive. To the contrary, these characteristics are often notable for their absence. With respect to motivational structure, the models of budget-maximizing bureaucrats and dueling principals and agents do not hold up under empirical examination, either. Comparisons with the private sector suggest that, for bureaucrats, the inherent importance of the mission, rather than personal gain, is the main motivator for action.

In the popular culture, bureaucracy's image is that of a huge, impersonal organization. Yet when one investigates the actual number of employees working in government offices, the common pattern is not massiveness but small-to-modest size. Another false image, often harbored by academic theorists, is that bureaucracy inevitably expands in size and, over time, deteriorates in quality. Both allegations are refuted by the evidence. Also, the frequently-cited notion that bureaucracies never "die" is shown to be false.

The political power of bureaucracy is often feared. Indeed, it is often argued that bureaucracy is too powerful to be safely compatible with democracy. A number of surveys and field studies conducted on this question have concluded, however, that bureaucrats respond with remarkable loyalty to policy guidance from elected officials and administrations, including those newly gaining power. Foot-dragging, leaks, and sabotage are relatively rare.

Bureaucracy's political clout is thus checked by a number of constitutional and normative forces, but it is not chained down so as to be ineffectual. In fact, it makes essential larger contributions to our democratic system, including fueling it with revenue and sustaining core missions over time that might otherwise be neglected. Bureaucracy's resilience and reliability make elections count by assuring that the winner's program will be enacted. Elected officials in power are backstopped by the bureaucrats in emergencies and reality-checked when they exaggerate facts. Often unwittingly, bureaucratic institutions strengthen democracy by bringing citizens into the social mainstream and into active citizenship.

The Reforms Reviewed

Reform! is the watchword for American public administration. Strategies for reform are on everyone's lips, books on reform are on everyone's shelves, consultants on reform are on every agency's doorstep, experts on reform speak at every conference, and authors on reform are quoted in every classroom. Bureaucracy, almost everyone assumes, is so obviously awful that one hardly needs to make the case for the need for it to be reformed. The only issue is how to do it.

In this book, however, you have heard my case not for reform but for bureaucracy. Hence you already realize that I do not share the enthusiasm of most of my public administration brethren on reform. This does not mean, however, that I believe bureaucracy is so good that it need not be changed or improved. Far from it. My view, in fact, is that many, many things can be done to improve our administrative institutions and practices. We must never be satisfied with administrative performance in this country or complacent about its future. The correct approach to take, however, is not to "re-form" bureaucracy into something entirely different, for that would mean loss of a precious social asset. A far better watchword, I suggest, is *continuous improvement.*

At the end of this chapter I offer some thoughts on how this alternative watchword may best guide us in the future. But first I want to turn the lectern over to the reformers, to report what they have said and done. Along the way (as you might suspect by now), I will make some comments and provide comments of others on the implications of the reforms, to help you react to their "case."

The number of proposed reforms is legion. Many acronyms have been deployed, among them MBO, OD, PPBS, QC, TQM, and ZBB. Also, "re" words abound—Eugene McGregor counts thirteen: Realignment, Rebuilding, Reconfiguration, Redesigning, Reengineering, Reforming, Reinventing, Remaking, Renewing, Reorganizing, Restructuring, Rethinking, and Retrenchment. The labels are so numerous that scholars surveying the subject of governmental reform find it useful not to list them all but to create broad categories instead. Guy Peters, for example, discusses four types of emerging vision: the Market Model, Participative Government, Flexible Government, and Deregulated Government. Paul Light describes four "tides of reform": Scientific Management, the War on Waste, the Watchful Eye, and Liberation Management. These classifications are not scientific taxonomies, of course, but descriptive rubrics that serve various purposes. I shall add one more set of categories, to serve my own purposes. They are the Consolidate-Control Perspective, the Downsize-Outsource Perspective, and the Business Model. We look at each in turn.[1]

The Consolidate-Control Perspective

This approach to reform was deeply ingrained in the field's thinking in its early years. In the Progressive era, a principal theme was to enhance the power of the chief executive. This official, whether elected as in the case of president and governor, or appointed as with a city manager, was seen as needing full power to control and direct the bureaucracy in order to assure that administration is efficient, orderly, and coordinated. The executive branch needs to be *managed,* the thinking went, not only for efficiency but also for democratic responsiveness. The chief executive was regarded as *the* principal channel through which policies and programs are to be shaped in accord with electoral and statutory guidance.

It was from this intellectual heritage that many of the early reforms sprang, including the city manager system itself, the executive budget concept, centralized personnel administration, and the notion of a general management staff serving the chief executive. These ideas were at the core of such seminal documents as the reports of the Taft Commission in 1912 and the Brownlow Commission in 1937.

Another key theme of this perspective is administrative reorganization—to consolidate scattered agencies and departments so as to simplify executive control and force coordination. While urged in the Brownlow report and the two Hoover Commission reports of 1949 and 1955, the most dramatic such reorganization actually to occur was creation of the Department of Defense in 1949, at the urging of President Harry Truman. Later, President Richard Nixon, who felt particularly threatened by the specter of a disloyal bureaucracy, proposed massing much of the federal establishment into four super-departments, but this idea never got off the ground.

The Consolidate-Control vision in its purest form, then, is one of an integrated executive branch, pyramidal in shape and controlled by a single chief executive at the top. In today's world, this image may seem a little old-fashioned, for, on its face, it is incompatible with divided government, networked policymaking, bottom-up influence, and collaborative governance. Yet at the same time, many chief executives continue to emphasize top-down, centralized management. Central staff controls show no sign of abating in the context of the American presidency, as reflected in the fact that for years now the Executive Office of the President (EOP) has employed well over 3,000 people.

Far from old hat, the consolidation theme has reemerged with a vengeance in the aftermath of the terrorist attacks of 11 September 2001. The executive branch was at the center of the nation's response, and the moral and political leadership of the president was inevitably strengthened. An Office of Homeland Security was formed in the EOP as a coordination point for the numerous domestic facets of the antiterrorist effort. Later, a Department of Homeland Security was created, incorporating all or parts of twenty-two federal agencies and forming a bureaucratic structure of at least 170,000 employees, which makes it the biggest cabinet agency in the government aside from Defense and Veterans' Affairs.

The stimulus, of course, for this unprecedented act of consolidation was that a dangerous national and global emergency had come into being. In the months following September 11th there was near-unanimity of opinion that, under the circumstances, everything possible must be done to step up law enforcement, improve intelligence, control borders, protect water and food supplies, and safeguard the transportation infrastructure. In short, America's natural distaste for bureaucracy did not interfere with mobilizing it when the chips were down.

At the same time, the transfer of some bureaucracies and the splitting up of others raised questions about the disruptive nature of reorganization, at least in the short run. Programs shifted to a new departmental milieu temporarily lose ground with respect to momentum, power base, and culture. Thus it was no doubt wise not to include the FBI and CIA in Homeland Security. Another issue is whether the bureaucracies that are broken up by dividing their responsibilities between the old and new organizational frameworks will run the risk of seeing their excluded functions downplayed, such as search-and-rescue by the Coast Guard and natural disaster assistance by the Federal Emergency Management Agency (FEMA).

Also the new department was given broad discretion in designing its personnel system outside normal civil service rules. Similar autonomy has been sought by the Defense Department, which, if adopted, would mean that the existing civil service system would be reduced to less than half its current coverage. The reason given for the change is a need for greater departmental discretion in hiring, firing, evaluations, and transfers.[2]

The breadth of executive authority related to national security raises deeper questions as well. President George W. Bush has declared a "war on terrorism." Yet it is not a formal declaration of war as envisioned in the Constitution, for the enemy is not a foreign state, also this is a conflict that can continue indefinitely, as long as the threat is declared to be present. In addition, in antiterrorist law enforcement a new emphasis is being placed on prevention rather than punishment. By means of the Patriot Act, Congress has given the Justice Department broad wiretapping, interception, and data-collection powers, checked only by a secret Foreign Intelligence Surveillance Court. As time goes by, incidents may easily arise whereby the president and Congress disagree fundamentally on the use of these "wartime" powers.

My colleague John Rohr propounds a constitutional theory of public administration that could come into play here. He regards bureaucracy as a subordinate institution under the Constitution—subordinate not to the presidency alone but to all three branches of government. When conflict emerges among the separated powers, Rohr believes that bureaucrats can most faithfully carry out their constitutional oath by performing as a balance wheel among the competing branches. In so doing, they exercise thoughtful discretion in deciding which constitutional master they favor under the circumstances or, alternatively, how they might promote a consensus. In the years ahead, one may easily anticipate instances of major legislative-executive disagreement in administering the Patriot Act and the Homeland Security Department. If the bureaucracy does function in Rohr's balance-wheel manner in such instances, we will have yet another political contribution by bureaucracy to add to the previous chapter's matrix.[3]

The Downsize-Outsource Perspective

This is reform's second category. Layoffs, or reductions-in-force, are used in the private sector when demand for the product or service declines—a painful but perfectly logical step. Downsizing in the public sector, however, occurs not in response to declining market demand but in reaction to either budget shortfalls or substantive decisions against the mission. Since in most program areas the public's need for services is relatively stable or growing, public-sector downsizing often causes one of two results, or both: overworking the employees who remain, or reducing the quality or timeliness of services to the public. Examples are overcrowded public school classrooms, fewer investigations of wife-battering and child abuse, and skipped inspections of trucks, coal mines, or restaurants. Such outcomes hurt not only affected citizens but also agency morale, compounding the adverse effects.

Vice President Al Gore's National Performance Review (NPR, later called National Partnership for Reinventing Government) had as an initial objective the elimination of 252,000 federal employees, a number later increased to 272,900. These figures were not derived from specific reinventing government plans, however; critics saw them as arbitrary goals set purely for political purposes. Although by some counts federal employment during the Clinton years dropped by more than 300,000, the final record shows that between 1993 and 2000 the number of nontemporary civilian employees in the Executive Branch declined by 193,000, or 6.5 percent.[4]

A major target of Gore's downsizing efforts was what is loosely referred to as middle management. The notion of carving out the center of the hierarchy is in accord with fashionable restructuring doctrine in business, where too many layers of management are seen as standing between executives at the top and the people who do the work down below. The goal is a "flat" organization, which is thought to be more flexible, responsive, and innovative. Although the NPR set out to eliminate 140,000 middle managers, in actuality their numbers probably increased.[5]

This is probably fortunate. James Colvard, a long-time naval executive, points out that mid-level managers are crucial to an organization because of their connecting function. They translate the visions of top management to actions by line employees and, in the reverse direction, explain to the front office the real-world problems being encountered on the front line. With respect to local government, Douglas Morgan and his coauthors argue that middle managers perform the indispensable functions of facilitating interjurisdictional cooperation, finding common ground across fragmented implementation structures, developing relationships among stakeholders, and providing sensitive antennae to unmet community needs.[6]

Outsourcing is another approach to reform, in that it is conceived as substituting efficient business firms for inefficient bureaucracies. It is seen as one path to "privatization," a goal of vague and varying meanings. Outside the

United States, this term often refers to the sale of government enterprises to private owners, but comparatively little of this happens in America, since we have so little "socialism" to start with.

In this country, the principal means of privatization has been not *selling off* government but *buying by* government. Contracting out, not sale of whole programs, has been the dominant tool; as noted in chapter 4, contracting out by American government goes back hundreds of years. Understandably, government's huge outsourcing potential has drawn the attention of reformers. The Reagan administration's main reform effort, known as the Grace Commission, sought to increase substantially what is contracted out, thereby hopefully saving billions of dollars. It proposed, for example, to contract out the military commissary system, Coast Guard search-and-rescue operations, patient care in small military hospitals, and municipal wastewater treatment. Gore's overall reinventing government movement did not take on this kind of outsourcing agenda, but it succeeded in streamlining the cumbersome procurement regulations that had produced the famous $640 toilet seat and fifteen pages of specifications for chocolate chip cookies. The NPR changes included experimenting with performance-based contracting and amending the procurement regulations so as to encourage sensible discretion on the part of acquisition teams. This was the single most constructive governmentwide change resulting from the NPR. It undoubtedly saved the taxpayers much money, but how much would be impossible to calculate.[7]

In 1998 Congress passed the Federal Activities Inventory Reform Act (FAIR), which required agencies to list all jobs that are not "inherently governmental" in nature. The idea was that everything not on the list would then be fair game for outsourcing. When the George W. Bush administration arrived on the scene, the activities listed embraced some 850,000 jobs. In 2001, prior to September 11th, the Office of Management and Budget ordered that 40,000 of these jobs be put up for competitive bidding and announced that the eventual bidding-out goal would be 425,000 positions, a fourth of federal workers. In 2002 another step was taken in this direction when the Commercial Activities Panel, a congressionally-mandated body of government officials, outside experts, union members, and contractors, recommended changes in the system of A-76 public-private competitive bidding described in chapter 4. The plan was to supplement cost considerations with a "best value" approach that also weighs technical expertise, past performance, potential for innovation, and ability to recruit and retain workers.[8] Late in 2003, the administration's competitive outsourcing program was substantially cut back, limiting it to 103,412 positions. One reason for the new goal was congressional resistance to the millions of dollars in costs associated with competitive bidding.

Hence the policy of contracting out seems to be slated for both wider use and better handling in American public administration. This is so despite the absence of empirical research that supports the presumption of innately better performance by the private sector than by the public sector, as discussed earlier (see pp. 48–54). Nonetheless, the step is attractive from a political standpoint, for it allows elected officials to claim that government has been "cut back" in terms of employment. The unpleasant truth is that in most instances no money whatever is saved by outsourcing a task that has been performed in-house. Ross Prizzia recently summarized the results of dozens of empirical studies conducted around the world on privatization, defined both as sale of public enterprises and contracting out. He reports that far from constituting a panacea for government's problems, privatization may actually cost more in the long term, as well as doing more harm than good to human, social, and ecological dimensions of communities.[9]

A more serious issue relates to erosion of government capabilities. If a vital mission of public health or safety is contracted out to the extent that the bureaucracy no longer possesses competence in it, the public loses a back-up option in case of contractor failure. Also, the agency is then in no position to monitor contracts adequately and is placed in a weak bargaining position upon contract renewal. Unfortunately, outsourcing agencies have on occasion become little more than contract-management shops, sometimes called "virtual" bureaucracies. At one time the EPA Superfund, facing a situation that combined an esoteric field that no one inside the agency understood and a congressional cap on in-house spending, had to depend on contractors not only for all technical operations but also for its own internal management. Contractor personnel drafted regulations and memos, recorded decisions and filed reports, trained other contractor personnel, evaluated their performance, responded to congressional inquiries, and wrote annual reports.[10]

An even more fundamental question is what is "inherently governmental," the key phrase in the FAIR statute. That law defines it as matters "so intimately related to the public interest as to require performance by Federal Government employees." The definition is then elaborated as the exercise of judgment and discretion in the application of government authority and the execution of U.S. laws so as to: (1) legally bind the government; (2) protect the country by military or diplomatic action; (3) conduct judicial proceedings; (4) engage in contract management; (5) significantly affect the life, liberty, or property of persons; (6) appoint or direct officers of the United States; and (7) control government property or funds. Explicitly not included are gathering information, giving advice to officials, and performing ministerial and internal duties such as building security, housekeeping, and the operation and maintenance of facilities.[11]

Specifying as inherently governmental control of any functions that "significantly affect the life, liberty, or property of private persons" could be interpreted as covering some activities that are currently privatized. An example is conducting background investigations on prospective federal employees. At one time this function was carried out by the security and investigations unit of the Office of Personnel Management, but in 1996 it was transferred to the U.S. Investigations Service (USIS), a newly-created private corporation owned by the 700 civil servants who had previously comprised the unit and were now retained as its employees. These shareholders operate from the unit's former physical quarters, and in so doing they have access to government computer databases that are closed to the public. Supporters of USIS see it as a creative response to OPM's much-diminished role during the 1990s, while critics regard it as performing an inherently governmental function that should be carried out by government employees working directly under federal statutes pertaining to security and privacy.[12]

Prison management is another area that may cross the inherently governmental boundary. All federal penitentiaries are operated by the Bureau of Prisons, although some U.S. detention centers, such as those designated for immigrants, are contracted out. Several state correctional systems, however, include privatized prisons. At the local level, some jails and juvenile detention homes are contractor-run, as are many community halfway houses and drug rehabilitation centers. A number of private companies, the biggest of which is Corrections Corporation of America, specialize in the prison business. Empirical studies show that privately managed prisons operate at somewhat lower costs than government-run facilities, although the savings are not substantial or universal.

Criticism of the practice centers on the fact that inmates are a captive population that is concentrated into small, intimate spaces that are removed from external scrutiny. Wardens and guards have total control over the lives of prisoners by means of coercive, deadly force, as well as an internally administered discipline system. A portion of the cost savings derives from the hiring of low-salaried guards, which could mean less professionalism than one would expect from career state employees. At a deeper level, physical imprisonment is an ultimate exercise of state sovereignty over the individual; hence, the details of administering incarceration offer a good measure of how the society balances out competing values of state authority and fundamental human dignity.[13]

One wonders if the screening of airport baggage is an inherently governmental matter, especially following the terrorist attacks. Certainly, "the life, liberty, or property of private persons" are significantly affected. In any case, following initial hesitation by President Bush and strong opposition from House Republicans, on 19 November 2001 the Transportation Security Agency was created, the largest new bureaucracy organized since World War II. Its main mission is to hire, train, and manage a force of 28,000 airport baggage screeners and airport security managers. In order to cover all 429 U.S. airports, the agency employs 63,000 men and women—more than six cabinet departments. Initially housed under the Department of Transportation, it has since been transferred to Homeland Security. This act of "federalization" in an era of privatization stands as quite a contradiction to the norm.[14]

Yet the overall tendency toward contracting out is in no danger of becoming outmoded. It is common at all levels of government, and it serves the interests of business, so the idea has instinctive appeal to conservatives. Often individual bureaucracies with rising workloads and frozen hires have no choice but to contract out, even if it costs more. The issue, then, is not whether to contract out but when. Donald Kettl says outsourcing works best "where markets are lively, where information is abundant, where decisions are not irretrievable, and where externalities are limited." Steven Kelman poses the issue in terms of the "make-or-buy" choice that industry managers see themselves making.[15] His position is that the degree to which the following conditions prevail determines whether it is better to buy, not make:

- The more precisely a task or result can be specified in advance
- The more performance can be evaluated after the fact
- The more competition there is among potential providers
- The less the activity is core to the agency's mission
- The more the government faces surges and ebbs in demand for the product or service
- The more private contractors have an easier time hiring people with skills the government needs
- The more there are economies of scale in production

To stimulate your thinking, let me rewrite Kelman's conditions but reverse the terms of the warrant, to stipulate when making would be better than buying:

- When no one has ever really faced the problem before
- When measures of success are not quantifiable or are unclear until after the fact
- When only one available contractor (or perhaps none) has had experience with the subject
- When the agency has had decades of professional experience doing the work
- When the needed expertise must be available in case of emergency
- When the work is such that staff motivation comes from dedication to the mission, not money
- When the work to be done takes place under isolated, harsh, or dangerous conditions

Question: How often, do you suppose, would the first set of conditions apply versus the second?

The Business Model

The Business Model is my third category for discussing administrative reforms in the United States. Unlike the Consolidate-Control Perspective, this approach implies loose rather than tight control. Unlike the Downsize-Outsource Perspective, its central message is to go beyond outsourcing government's work to business. Instead, it seeks to make the government itself more like business.

The idea is not new. In his founding charter for the study of public administration, Woodrow Wilson said that "the field of administration is a field of business." The Progressive idea of the city manager was a conscious effort to bring the efficiencies of business to local government. Frederick Taylor's Scientific Management and Edwards Deming's Total Quality Management were introduced to public administration from the private sector in order to replicate the successes that were said to occur there. The public corporation, popular during the New Deal and world wars as a means of giving government the flexibility of business, lives on today in the U.S. Postal Service and in numerous similar but smaller entities.

Beginning in the 1980s, the ideal of making government more businesslike acquired even greater traction. The Grace Commission instructed its investigative task forces, composed mainly of business executives, to ask how the agencies being studied could be made into good candidates for corporate takeover.[16] Vice President Gore's National Performance Review, while it relied on federal bureaucrats rather than business executives for ideas, proposed reinventing government in ways that emulate corporate practices in many ways. The Government Performance and Results Act, passed independently by Congress at the time the NPR got underway, embodies a parallel outlook. Conceptually, the Business Model is articulated in academic circles by a school of thought known as the New Public Management. Linguistically, public administration mimics corporate rhetoric; agencies formulate "business plans," organize "regional business centers," and hire "chief financial officers." Surveying the government reform scene in general, Steven Hays and Richard Kearney conclude that most public management reform engages in "adulation of the business model," with strategies "forged within a business ethic."[17]

Embedded in the Business Model are four core concepts: market creation, entrepreneurial conduct, performance measurement, and customer orientation.

Market creation. The first concept seeks to import into bureaucracy as many market-like features as possible. One way to do this is to create competition within government itself. David Osborne and Ted Gaebler, whose 1993 book *Reinventing Government* became the bible of the NPR, argue that if government's service providers compete against one another they will keep their costs down, respond quicker to changing demands, and strive harder for excellence. Perhaps more than any other reform, they say, introducing competition "will unlock the bureaucratic gridlock that hamstrings so many public agencies." Nonetheless, the reinventers counsel caution: while work teams can compete against each other, they say, individual employees should not. Also, the policy-making and regulation realms should be exempt, which includes an awful lot of government.[18]

Different kinds of internal government market are possible. For several decades local governments have created quasi-markets among themselves by entering into interjurisdictional contracts for services such as police protection, ambulance coverage, and snow removal. Contemporary reformers propose a more radical version of this idea: the creation of businesslike, semi-autonomous enterprises within government that regularly sell goods and services on a cost-reimbursable basis to other departments and governments. The business term for this practice is franchising. The Government Management Reform Act of 1994 endorsed this idea by encouraging what are called Cooperative Administrative Support Units (CASU). The Department of the Interior's CASU, called the National Business Center, offers the following "business lines": financial management, payroll and personnel, aircraft services, procurement and electronic commerce, web development, quarters management, drug testing, career development, on-line training, information technology, telecommunications, facilities acquisition, and property management.[19]

In addition to creating internal markets, the Business Model endorses exposing bureaucracy to external private markets in various ways. We have already encountered this in connection with the A-76 process, whereby government facilities compete with private vendors in a quality-managed bidding process. The same process takes place in local government. A well-known example occurred when the public works department of the City of Phoenix competed unsuccessfully against private garbage haulers four times but, after enhancing its own capacity, finally took back the mission.[20]

Finally, those endorsing the Business Model are sometimes attracted to incorporating market principles into public policy. In the field of education, voucher programs and charter schools have long been held out as ways to bypass supposedly inferior public schools. The results have been mixed, however; student discipline is often greater but accountability for expenditure of public funds often less. Moreover, a study of standardized test scores in ten states covering the years 1999–2001 showed lower scores by students in charter schools than in public schools. In another policy realm, foreign unrest and terrorism, the Pentagon's Defense Advanced Research Projects Agency launched a short-lived "future's market" intended to predict assassinations and military intervention in the Middle East—"traders" would buy and sell "futures contracts" depending on what they thought would happen. After senators called the idea a "federal betting parlor on atrocities" and "unbelievably stupid," it was quickly abandoned.[21]

Application of the market concept to governance has been challenged on political theory grounds. Linda deLeon and Robert Denhardt contend that market processes are essentially anarchic, in that they involve no common community ideals, only privately beneficial deals. Moreover, the language used to communicate—essentially prices—is, they say, impoverished in terms of nuanced understanding or emotional connection. The equilibria achieved by the market via rational, self-interested choice under conditions of scarcity and competition are no substitute, deLeon and Denhardt believe, for the stakeholder consensus or definitions of the public interest arrived at by processes of political deliberation, collaboration, and negotiation. In fairness to them, the reinventers do not suggest that public managers communicate only as buyers and sellers, nor for that matter do they reject collective action in the community's interests. But they do, as deLeon and Denhardt point out, ask that public bureaucracy adopt not only the techniques of business but its values as well.[22]

Entrepreneurial conduct. The second core principle of the Business Model is encouragement of entrepreneurial conduct on the part of managers. The term *entrepreneur* was coined two hundred years ago by the French economist J. B. Say, who used it to mean an economic actor who shifts resources from low-yield activities to high. Contemporary applications of the word include spotting opportunities for innovation unnoticed by others, introducing change in the organization to take advantage of new technologies or market shifts, leveraging resources, capitalizing on unmet needs, and taking calculated risks versus playing a conservative game.[23]

Some commentators interpret the New Public Management as assuming that entrepreneurial management is a generic function that can be transferred in portable fashion among organizations and across the private-public boundary. Essential to the entrepreneur's success in any domain is discretion to achieve results, sometimes referred to as "free to manage" room. The entrepreneurial manager is regarded as fully in charge of the organization and ranked well above other managers and technical professionals. In order to recruit and retain individuals with the background needed, it is assumed that such leaders will be paid steep salaries and offered handsome bonuses.[24]

Institutional arrangements conducive to entrepreneurship are increasingly common in American public administration. One is the franchising technique discussed earlier. Another is the "performance-based organization" (PBO), a concept developed by Gore's NPR. The idea envisions hiring as head of the PBO a Chief Operating Officer (COO) who is compensated above government standards, plus bonus rights of up to 50 percent. The COO is held personally accountable for achieving goals with respect to straightening out a problem-plagued bureaucracy through bold innovation. The latitude given includes exemption from numerous regulations and freedom to handpick a management team.[25]

Although Gore wanted to create eight PBOs, Congress consented to only two, the Patent and Trademark Office in the Commerce Department and the Office of Student Financial Assistance Programs in Education. The Patent Office, where inventors were complaining it took too long to secure patents, was converted to a wholly fee-financed operation. The Student Financial Assistance organization, a $60 billion student loan and grants program that was experiencing information management problems, hired as its first COO a member of Gore's NPR staff, who, among other things, upgraded the organization's IT system to allow borrowers to access their accounts online.[26]

At the state and local levels of government, entrepreneurial arrangements include a number of ways to augment public funds creatively, although not always without controversy. In *Reinventing Government* Osborne and Gaebler tell how the State of Michigan allowed its pension fund to invest 5 percent of the fund's assets in venture-capital initiatives. The fund's investments lost more money than state pensioners could tolerate, however, and the practice was quietly dropped.[27]

Gaebler served for a time as city manager of Visalia, California. During his tenure he launched many entrepreneurial projects, all enthusiastically described in *Reinventing Government.* Gaebler's successor in Visalia pursued a similar course, and one of his projects was a partnership with a developer to construct a hotel on leased city land in exchange for part of the profits. The developer could not secure a construction loan, so the city guaranteed a bank loan and itself advanced a $3 million credit. But before the hotel was finished, the developer left town, leaving the city in the lurch with an empty shell of a building and liabilities of $20 million. A writer who visited Visalia in 1994 startled the reinvention community by contributing to *Governing* magazine an article entitled "Entrepreneurial Government: The Morning After." In it, the city of Visalia was described as not only deeply stung by the hotel debacle but fatigued in general from years of entrepreneurial projects developed by its city administration.[28]

Writing on the subject of the personality traits of entrepreneurs, Linda deLeon says that five virtues and five vices seem necessary, but she argues that the vices are really virtues in disguise. The vice of egotism, for example, facilitates needed maverick behavior. Selfishness reinforces personal will and drive. Waywardness is required for bending and breaking rules. Domination permits imposition of a personal vision on all employees. Opportunism permits the entrepreneur to seize chance straws in the wind that may pay off.[29] Now there's a fine public servant for you!

Indeed, Robert Behn, the New Public Management scholar, recognizes that it may be difficult for a public executive to possess at the same time the arrogant, flashy style that makes for successful entrepreneurship and the more modest and appealing demeanor that sits well with the press and the public. Let's hope he is right. One might also hope that government executives who adopt the business style will set aside such Enron-style practices as looting the corporation, deceiving stockholders, and inventing fraudulent accounting practices.[30]

Performance measurements. The third keystone of the Business Model is performance measurement. Its essential idea is to develop explicit indicators of program accomplishment in order to assess how the organization is performing. This is seen as introducing to the organization a degree of accountability that safely permits freedom from detailed supervision. In other words, it creates "free to manage" room.

It is assumed that the measures should be quantitative if possible. They should also be derived from specific goals set in advance, in accord with a broad plan. Actions (outputs) may be measured, but it is preferable to assess results, such as impacts on society (outcomes). The whole idea is to make it possible to identify where the organization is falling down, thus permitting targeted correction. Performance measurement thus integrates good management, better accountability, and improved work. In the words of Patrick

Murphy and John Carnevale, it "encapsulates sound management and accountability in aligning the operation of an organization with the realization of a defined set of outcomes or end states."[31]

Based as it is on ideals of rationality, objectivity, and accountability, the concept is innately appealing. It is presented in business schools as an article of faith, and for a long time its doctrines have been seeping into the public sector, as in performance budgeting, management by objectives, and performance evaluation of employees. The standardized-test movement in the public schools is yet another manifestation. Christopher Hood terms performance measurement a "thermostatic" control over bureaucracy because of its properties of arms-length steering, transparent targets, and negative feedback. Robert Behn sees it is a way of introducing innovation through the setting of goals, in contrast to spontaneous, "garbage-can" decision making. Behn also lauds performance measurement as a way to augment managerial discretion to the point where "charter agencies"—organizations that he envisions as highly autonomous and highly accountable at the same time—can evolve.[32]

Performance measurement is practiced to some degree by most state governments, by over half of the nation's municipalities, and by about a third of county governments. In many jurisdictions the capacity or will for complete deployment of the system is lacking, however. Reported shortcomings include insufficient indicators, lack of timely data, too few analysts, inadequate information technology, and lack of support at the top. Patria Julnes argues that performance measurement should not be judged a success or failure depending on how it actually drives decisions, however. In telephone interviews he conducted with administrators familiar with its actual practice in government, he found that the principal uses are to justify budget requests, to fulfill political needs for transparency, and to inform debate among bureaucrats and officials on progress toward goals.[33]

In the national government, performance measurement is widespread, a dual consequence of Gore's National Performance Review and the Government Performance and Results Act of 1993. GPRA called for an extensive strategic planning process in which each agency articulates mission statements, sets goals and objectives, outlines strategies for meeting them, and indicates measures of satisfactory achievement. The law requires that agencies consult with Congress on the drafting of the plans; later they are to submit reports to Congress on how well programs have performed against the goals.

Beryl Radin studied how the GPRA process has worked out. Several factors operated against its success, she believes, including complexities of the budget process, pressures to cut the budget, rivalries between Congress and the presidency, partisan deadlock, and the devolved nature of American public administration. Another reality is that federal managers are already required to deal with several other governmentwide reporting duties and accountability requirements, spawned by previous reform efforts. Radin counts ten such requirements imposed over the past fifteen years.[34]

She also points out that in many program areas the results of program intervention are beyond the control of managers, which makes predetermined, quantitatively measured goals an exercise in futility. This is especially true when program outcomes depend on uncontrollable variables such as the weather, crime rates, or the conduct of foreign nations. In prevention programs, performance measurement is almost impossible since there is no way of counting what did not happen. Radin concludes that because of these problems, combined with GPRA's lack of fit with existing institutional constraints and the fragmented governance system, the statute's main consequence has been to breed cynicism and contention rather than to achieve the kind of major changes anticipated. She urges a "period of benign neglect" for application of the law and recommends concentration instead on piecemeal, agency-specific reforms rather than sweeping governmentwide approaches.[35]

Hyong Yi, a practicing administrator in the District of Columbia government, comes to a similar conclusion, explaining that all too many management fads inspired by practices in the private sector have come and gone in government. Each one has been oversold as *the* answer to all organizational problems. Managers eager to find the Holy Grail have embraced each fad enthusiastically, only to be disappointed. Yi believes that after a decade of experimentation, GPRA has reached this point. This does not mean, he adds, that each new technique, including GPRA, does not address some particular shortcoming and thus add value. "We have to realize," he says, "that the road to improving governmental performance is not a sprint, but a never-ending marathon over many different types of terrain that will require a multitude of tools to achieve."[36]

Customer service. The final component of the Business Model of administrative reform is customer service. For many years corporate managers have received the admonition that "excellence" happens when they focus on not just what they want, but on what their customers want. A principal initiative of the Clinton administration in this realm, arising directly from the NPR, was Executive Order 12862, issued 11 September 1993. It required all agencies that provide "significant services directly to the public" to identify and survey their customers and then post customer-service standards. The results of the surveys were to be held against goals set in these standards. A year later the president issued a report listing more than 1,500 customer-service standards representing pledges from more than one hundred agencies. On the day the report was released, cabinet members and other high officials provided photo ops for the press as they personally served members of the public around Washington, D.C. Clinton pronounced, "There has been a renaissance in quality and customer service in corporate America. There's no reason these same principles cannot apply . . . in our government."[37]

In analyzing the customer-service aspect of the reinventing government effort, Kettl comments that some spectacular early successes did occur, such as a team approach to claim processing at the Veterans Administration and one-stop career service centers at the Department of Labor. But, he cautions, while the customer-service concept has potential for better exercise of discretion on the firing line, it would be a mistake to think that customer preferences should determine government action. Different citizens want different things from government, and their wants may conflict. "The road that, in a big snowstorm, needs to be plowed first is always in front of one's own home," he dryly comments. Also, many government programs do not render service to the public at all but enforce the law (for example the IRS), and those targeted for enforcement will never be happy customers.[38]

Others raise philosophical objections to the customer-service concept. George Frederickson points out that citizens are owners of the government, not its customers. James Carroll believes that the idea converts the government from a protector of constitutional rights to an instrument of service consumption. DeLeon and Denhardt contend that it promotes the ethos of self-interest at the expense of concern for the public interest, as well as the solitary pursuit of individual preference instead of engagement in democratic discourse. The debate goes on.[39]

Overall, how has the Business Model worked as a new mode of doing the public's work? It is difficult to say—enthusiasts and skeptics equally abound. In one attempt at a systematic appraisal, George Boyne analyzed the results of sixty-five empirical studies of improvement in public service performance. He concluded that the adoption of new laws, market principles, and organizational shifts such as decentralization seem less important than providing sufficient resources to agencies and giving employees morale-enhancing leadership.[40]

If one asks the bureaucrats themselves, here too the answers will vary. Yet those without experience in government may be surprised by how philosophically public servants accepted the changes. At the same time, they resented their wholesale importation from the business world. Two self-styled "twenty-five-year bureaucrats" of the federal government, when invited to reflect on the changes they had seen, agreed that many good things had been attempted even though not all had reached maturity. And they made a point of saying that they did not arrogantly reject the ideas at the time.

> Actually, we take them all seriously and hope we have absorbed their best aspects. These include the principle of being systematic, quantifying and specifying goals and objectives, hanging in there, being open to good ideas from all sources, and keeping our eye on the customer.
>
> Someday perhaps, the outsiders will ask us instead of telling us how things should be done. Most of the government programs we are involved in are a lot more complicated than those of private-sector enterprises.[41]

Bureaucracy's Fundamentals as Metaphor

Regardless of whether reformations of America's bureaucracy will stick, its fundamentals are lasting and profound. As such, they are best expressed not as formulas or models, but as metaphors that catch the imagination. I offer two, one for each of a duality of fundamental features I find in American bureaucracy.

The first fundamental is that a good bureaucracy is indispensable to a free society, a democratic polity, and a capitalist economy. The freedom to wander the streets at night, for example, depends on competent law enforcement. The ability to vote a government out of office without disruption requires a reliable administrative apparatus. A prosperous business community demands good schools, highways, health departments, post offices, and water and sewer systems.

To convey this truism we can liken bureaucracy to the trunk of a tree. This stout post supports the tree's overhead crown of leaves, fruits, and flowers. The crown can be said to represent society's civil, political, and economic life. Distinctly less flashy than the crown, the trunk below allows the more visible part of the tree to absorb solar energy, reproduce, and provide food and shade. The trunk anchors the tree in the ground of law and representative government, and its cambium transports to the crown the nutrients and water of public institutional capacity. The trunk's flexible strength of civilian and military resources allows the crown to survive turbulence from the external environment, while its annual growth rings of renewal and innovation make possible an increasingly prolific crown as the years go by.

The second fundamental characteristic of bureaucracy is that, in view of its indispensability, it must be properly tended. It is too valuable to the society to ignore or fail to maintain. It is also too precious to be undermined by thoughtless manipulation or frivolous experimentation. As a complex social institution rooted in the past and embodying the minds, skills, and hopes of living human beings, it must be nurtured with care. The responsibility for such nurture lies with the field of public administration and its practitioners and professors.

Frederickson offers a metaphor for public administration's responsibility in this regard. It is gardening. Gardening is in part a science, in that verified knowledge has been accumulated about soils and genetics. Yet the gardener does not proceed according to instructions received from the extension service alone but from personal observation and experience. Moreover, the gardener's aesthetic sense will apply to laying out the plants, making administrative gardening also an art. Flexibility over the timing of change is necessary, in that seeds ordered in the winter will grow according to each spring's rains and each summer's heat. As a gardener rather than a farmer, the administrator's cultivation of organizational change is not carried out on a mass, field-size scope but by the individual plant, treating each institutional situation according to its own properties.[42]

I want to conclude this book by using these two metaphors to provide a normative backdrop for some concrete recommendations about the future of American bureaucracy and public administration. These recommendations center on two themes: bureaucratic change and antibureaucratic cynicism.

With respect to change, I urge that we respect the tree trunk's indispensability and adopt the gardener's individualized approach to action. We should not espouse drastic, destroy-and-replace measures to girdle or saw off the tree's trunk. Instead we should take care to follow individualized gardening approaches to continuous improvement, aiming to enhance in value the existing assets of particular institutions. This strategy would be in keeping with Radin's advice to deemphasize governmentwide approaches to administrative reform and concentrate on agency-specific actions, as well as with Hyong Yi's counsel to conceive of administrative reform as a never-ending process that draws on the advantages of many separate tools.

Thus, beyond creative and empathetic leadership, a spirit of good will, and a commitment to the public weal, I offer no universal "how to do it" instructions on administrative improvement. The twenty-five-year bureaucrats know more than the rest of us about what strengths, weaknesses, and opportunities for productive change exist. At the same time, however, some adaptable mechanisms for developing situation-specific ideas for continuous improvement have been successfully employed across the country, and it would seem wise to consider them for fuller application.

One is the *demonstration project.* To me, the most valuable aspect of Al Gore's National Performance Review was the establishment of 325 "reinvention laboratories" in the federal bureaucracy. These consisted of individual agencies or offices, each of which was selected to try out a new idea of some type in projects that were in large part developed and directed by the bureaucrats themselves. Some labs installed standard NPR concepts such as performance measurement and customer service; others explored tailored, program-specific possibilities, for example, a particular system of record-keeping, a new data-collection technique, or an attempt at negotiated rulemaking. Could not this approach to change be profitably used throughout American bureaucracy, at all levels, indefinitely into the future?[43]

Another potentially useful mechanism is the *organizational report card.* For some years external scorekeepers have publicly rated various service providers, such as colleges, airlines, hospitals, and nursing homes. Also, various independent publications and research institutes have issued report cards for individual programs and projects. An example is the Chesapeake Bay Foundation's annual reports on the ecological health of the body of water that is its focus. An alternative would be to adapt the community scorecard concept used in some U.S. cities. An agency could be individually assessed in a cooperative manner by representatives of several stakeholders, such as its leaders, employees, clients, and relevant interest and community groups. Representatives of each type of stakeholder would collectively develop tailored performance indicators for the institution, in such realms as service quality, appropriate technology, customer results, financial results, and staff development. Periodically, the representatives would then jointly score the agency on each dimension and release a report to the press. This approach avoids the inflexibility of imposed, standardized assessment criteria and lays the basis for ongoing dialogue on how to improve the institution's work.[44]

A third possible tool is *external accreditation*. This process is applied to colleges and universities, police and fire departments, and health care providers across the nation. The accrediting bodies in these instances are professional associations that are independent of governmental authority yet maintain good ties with it. Potentially they offer both expertise in the pertinent field and an appropriate form of informed independence. While some accreditation bodies apply overly structured and restrictive standards, it is possible to adopt a philosophy that welcomes responsible creativity. Indeed, this is how the National Association of Schools of Public Affairs and Administration monitors the country's M.P.A. programs. Such accreditation might also be useful for state penitentiaries, juvenile detention homes, municipal jails, sheriff's departments, crime labs, mine safety stations, county health departments, and state mental hospitals.

Turning to cynicism toward bureaucracy, the opening line of this book admits that making the case for bureaucracy seems a ridiculous idea, acknowledging from the start the natural mistrust people have toward bureaucracy. Yet even though understandable, such cynicism hurts bureaucracy, for it helps to create a self-fulfilling prophecy. Among other things, it discourages smart, idealistic young people from considering government work as a career. Cynicism also encourages current public servants to move to the private sector or to retire early. On the broader level of the public image of government, antibureaucratic contempt feeds the media's appetite to be ready to construe any public problem in terms of failure on the part of tax-financed institutions.

Other self-fulfilling effects occur at the micro level of citizen-bureaucrat interaction. Cynical citizens are more than prepared to interpret each obstacle, delay, or adverse decision by an administrator as clear confirmation of their worst suspicions about incompetence and/or malfeasance in the halls of government. Those suspecting stupidity are then ready to enter the doors of those halls with a belligerent attitude that then triggers responses from bureaucrats that can be interpreted in turn as officious and haughty. The escalating tensions thus set off only snowball further, until these incidents become the raw material for perpetuated stories of bureaucratic intransigence. Society's tree trunk is too valuable to allow such damage to be sustained without trying to do something about it.

But what *can* be done to stem the tide of antibureaucracy cynicism? Actually, much is being done now. Public administration associations and supporters have for years been conducting outreach campaigns in favor of the public service. One of the most important is Public Service Recognition

Week, held each May since 1985. Sponsored by the Public Employees Roundtable, a coalition of groups, this event features multiple activities directed to portraying public service in a favorable light. Rallies are organized, speakers brought in, and media coverage arranged. This is excellent work and well worth amplifying. Another constructive outreach activity involves public service award programs, sponsored by the American Society for Public Administration as well as other organizations.

These activities and ones like them are excellent, and they should be continued. However, they contain a flaw comparable to that found in governmentwide reform movements: they constitute mass-production agriculture and not individualized gardening. They skim at the surface of the antibureaucracy image, failing to penetrate below a public relations level. For the most part, attention is paid only by those already predisposed toward government, such as public employee groups and students and teachers of public administration. The media campaigns preach to the choir, so to speak.

What is also needed is conscious and concerted gardening in the realm of public perceptions of bureaucracy. Ways must be found to penetrate more deeply into the public psyche and to affect the mind-set of citizens who not only don't sing in the choir but would actively resist the idea of doing so. What is needed, I suggest, is something similar to what works best in improving bureaucracy—moving beyond standardized approaches and individually cultivating each plant. This strategy might be characterized as *inreach*, as opposed to outreach.

My suggestion is to ask the most creative minds in each bureaucracy or type of bureaucracy to think of ways in which members of the public could become *personally engaged* with the work of individual administrative institutions. In this way citizens could see the inside of bureaucracies and thus understand the quality of people who labor there, as well as the obstacles and no-win situations they face. Citizens could meet bureaucrats firsthand and learn that they are normal human beings, who don't wear green eyeshades and are not automatons or despots. They would find out how rare are outright solutions to policy problems, on which only incremental headway is usually possible. They would be amazed to discover the meager resources that bureaucrats are given to fulfill so many expectations. They would realize how public and media cynicism generates anxiety inside government and motivates bureaucrats to look for more private vocations.

So how do we get citizens inside bureaucracy? It will depend on the bureaucracy and what it does. If it is a police department, citizens can be enrolled in a citizen police academy. If it is an emergency service unit, they can be recruited as voluntary EMS workers. A public health department can invite volunteers to assist with inoculation drives. A county welfare department can ask ex-clients to help newcomers fill out applications or file appeals. The local weather service can be assisted by call-in weather watchers around the area. The National Park Service can appoint resident campground hosts, and the IRS can recruit retired accountants as tax-preparation advisers (as both do now). Public libraries may invite citizens to conduct surveys to evaluate their book acquisitions. Community social service organizations and mental health programs can ask citizens to sit on governing boards. Parks and recreation departments, planning departments, and historical preservation programs can mobilize panels of citizen advisers. National forests can sponsor stakeholder forums to chart out a mix of resource-use strategies. Municipalities can engage in collaborative visioning processes in which a cross-section of residents participate. Urban neighborhoods can join crime-watch programs. State highway departments can assign sections of roadway to civic groups for the purpose of picking up litter. Airport authorities may elect to create civil air patrol chapters, and sheriff departments may decide to ask school students to operate a bicycle registration program.

The list could go on and on. The point is that there are *many* ways to involve citizens in the work of bureaucracy. These ways are best identified from the perspective of the specific needs of *individual* agencies, programs, and jurisdictions. Citizen engagement thus emerges not just in the abstract categories of volunteering, co-production, power sharing, advice, collaboration, or education, but in concrete manifestations of all of these, in different mixtures and degrees. The point is that citizens themselves are invited to enter individual bureaucracies and to join individual bureaucrats in doing the work of the people. This is public administration gardening at its best. This is the way to protect the tree trunk of bureaucracy from damage and to permit its growth rings of renewal to multiply.

Notes

1. Bureaucracy Despised, Disparaged, and Defended

1. *Washington Post*, 3 October 1995.
2. *Roanoke Times*, 12 October 2003.
3. Donald Lambro, *The Federal Rathole* (New Rochelle, N.Y.: Arlington House, 1975) and *Fat City: How Washington Wastes Your Taxes* (South Bend, Ind.: Regnery/Gateway, 1980); J. Peter Grace, *Burning Money: The Waste of Your Tax Dollars* (New York: Macmillan, 1984); Jack Anderson and John Kidner, *Alice in Blunderland* (Washington, D.C.: Acropolis Books, 1983); Martin L. Gross, *The Government Racket: Washington Waste from A to Z* (New York: Bantam Books, 1992); Byron L. Johnson and Robert Ewegen, *B.S.: The Bureaucratic Syndrome* (Croton-on-Hudson, N.Y.: North River Press, 1982); George Roche, *America by the Throat: The Stranglehold of Federal Bureaucracy* (Old Greenwich, Conn.: Devin-Adair, 1983); and William J. Geekie, *Why Government Fails or What's Really Wrong With the Bureaucracy* (Roslyn Heights, N.Y.: Libra Publishers, 1976).
4. Beverly A. Cigler and Heidi L. Neiswender, "'Bureaucracy' in the Introductory American Government Textbook," *Public Administration Review* 51 (September/October 1991): 442–450.
5. H. H. Gerth and C. Wright Mills, eds., *From Max Weber: Essays in Sociology* (New York: Oxford University Press, 1946), 196–204. Weber lived from 1864 to 1920, and his work on bureaucracy was written around the time of World War I.
6. See my exchange with friend Ralph Hummel in "The Case for Public Servants" and "The Case against Deduced Pathology," *The Bureaucrat* 17 (summer 1988): 24–28.
7. John C. Beach et al., "State Administration and the Founding Fathers during the Critical Period," *Administration and Society* 28, no. 4 (February 1997): 511–530. This article was the product of a doctoral seminar I taught in the fall of 1993.
8. Brian J. Gaines, "Where's the Rally? Approval and Trust of the President, Cabinet, Congress, and Government since September 11," *PS: Political Science & Politics* 35, no. 3 (September 2002): 535.
9. "Changing Images of Government in TV Entertainment," *Public Voices* 6, nos. 2–3 (2003): 70–72; and Gaines, "Where's the Rally?" and *Washington Post*, 31 May 2002, 11 September 2002.
10. Robert D. Behn, *Rethinking Democratic Accountability* (Washington, D.C.: Brookings Institution, 2001), 23, 119.
11. Gerald E. Caiden, "Administrative Reform—American Style," *Public Administration Review* 54, no. 2 (March/April 1994): 123.
12. Irving Kristol, *Two Cheers for Capitalism* (New York: Basic Books, 1978); Milton and Rose Friedman, *Free to Choose: A Personal Statement* (New York: Avon, 1980); and George Gilder, *Wealth and Power* (New York: Basic Books, 1981).
13. William A. Niskanen, *Bureaucracy and Public Economics* (Aldershot, Hants, U.K.: Edward Elgar, 1994) [a reprint of *Bureaucracy and Representative Government*, 1971]; Niskanan, *Bureaucracy: Servant or Master?* (London: Institute of Economic Affairs, 1973); Gordon Tullock, *Private Wants, Public Means* (New York: Basic Books, 1970); James Buchanan et al., *The Economics of Politics* (London: Institute of Economic Affairs, 1978); Anthony Downs, *Inside Bureaucracy* (Boston:

Little, Brown, 1967); and John Baden and Richard L. Stroup, eds., *Bureaucracy vs. Environment: The Environmental Costs of Bureaucratic Governance* (Ann Arbor: University of Michigan Press, 1981).

14. Robert K. Merton, "Bureaucratic Structure and Personality," *Social Forces* 17 (1940): 560–568; Victor A. Thompson, *Modern Organization* (New York: Knopf, 1961); Michel Crozier, *The Bureaucratic Phenomenon* (Chicago: University of Chicago Press, 1964); Gordon Tullock, *The Politics of Bureaucracy* (Washington, D.C.: Public Affairs Press, 1965); Downs, *Inside Bureaucracy;* Guy Benveniste, *Bureaucracy,* 2d ed. (San Francisco: Boyd and Fraser, 1983); and Christopher Hodgkinson, *Towards a Philosophy of Administration* (Oxford, England: Basil Blackwell, 1978).
15. Richard Chackerian and Gilbert Abcarian, *Bureaucratic Power in Society* (Chicago: Nelson-Hall, 1983); Henry Jacoby, *Bureaucratization of the World* (Berkeley: University of California Press, 1973); Eugene H. Czajkoski and Laurin A. Wollan Jr., "Bureaucracy and Crime," *International Journal of Public Administration* 5 (1983): 195–216; and David C. Korton and Felipe B. Alfonso, eds., *Bureaucracy and the Poor: Closing the Gap* (West Hartford, Conn.: Kumarian Press, 1983).
16. Gerth and Mills, *From Max Weber,* 228–229, 232–233.
17. Karl A. Wittfogel, *Oriental Despotism* (New Haven: Yale University Press, 1957); Ludwig Von Mises, *Bureaucracy* (New Haven: Yale University Press, 1944); Eric Strauss, *The Ruling Servants* (New York: Praeger, 1961); Wolfgang Kraus, *The Return of the Individual: Rescue Attempts in a Bureaucratic Age,* trans. John Russell (Berne, Switzerland: Peter Lang, 1985), 161; and Michael Ledeen, "Common Sense 1992," *American Spectator* 25 (June 1992): 23–26 [quoted in Vernon Van Dyke, *Ideology and Political Choice: The Search for Freedom, Justice, and Virtue* (Chatham, N.J.: Chatham House, 1995), 158].
18. Robert Michels, *Political Parties* (Glencoe, Ill.: Free Press, 1949); Philip Selznick, *TVA and the Grass Roots* (New York: Harper & Row, 1966); Bengt Abrahamsson, *Bureaucracy of Participation* (Beverly Hills, Calif.: Sage, 1977); and Francis E. Rourke, ed., *Bureaucratic Power in National Politics* (Boston: Little, Brown, 1978).
19. Eugene Lewis, *American Politics in a Bureaucratic Age: Citizens, Constituents, Clients and Victims* (Cambridge, Mass.: Winthrop, 1977); John L. Cooper, *The Anti-Gravity Force: A Study of the Negative Impact of Public Bureaucracy on Society* (Dubuque, Iowa: Kendall Hunt, 1981), 24; and Ronald M. Glassman, William H. Swatos Jr., and Paul L. Rosen, eds., *Bureaucracy against Democracy and Socialism* (New York: Greenwood Press, 1987), 7. Other relevant sources are cited in the notes to chapter 6.
20. The Marx quote is from Frank Fischer and Carmen Sirianni, eds., *Critical Studies in Organization and Bureaucracy* (Philadelphia: Temple University Press, 1984), 40–41. See also Andras Hegedus, *Socialism and Bureaucracy* (London: Allison and Busby, 1976); Eugene Kamenka and Martin Krygier, *Bureaucracy: The Career of a Concept* (London: Edward Arnold, 1979); and B.C. Smith, *Bureaucracy and Political Power* (Sussex, England: Wheatsheaf, 1988), chap. 5.
21. Downs, *Inside Bureaucracy;* Niskanen, *Bureaucracy: Servant or Master?;* Frances Fox Piven and Richard A. Cloward, *Regulating the Poor* (New York: Pantheon, 1971); James O'Connor, *The Fiscal Crisis of the State* (New York: St. Martin's, 1973); and Edward S. Greenberg, *Capitalism and the American Political Ideal* (Armonk, N.Y.: M.E. Sharpe, 1985).

22. Warren Bennis, *Beyond Bureaucracy* (New York: McGraw-Hill, 1973); and Lynton K. Caldwell, "Biology and Bureaucracy: The Coming Confrontation," *Public Administration Review* 40 (January/February 1980): 1–12.
23. Frederick C. Thayer, *An End to Hierarchy and Competition: Administration in the Post-Affluent World,* 2d ed. (New York: Franklin Watts, 1981); David Schuman, *The Ideology of Form* (Lexington, Mass.: D.C. Heath, 1978); Joseph Bensman and Bernard Rosenberg, "The Meaning of Work in Bureaucratic Society," in *Identity and Anxiety,* ed. Maurice R. Stein, Arthur J. Vidich, and David M. White (Glencoe, Ill.: Free Press, 1960); Kathy Ferguson, *The Feminist Case against Bureaucracy* (Philadelphia: Temple University Press, 1984); and Cooper, *Anti-Gravity Force,* 54.
24. Michael P. Smith, "Self-Fulfillment in a Bureaucratic Society," *Public Administration Review* 29 (January/February 1969): 25–32; Ralph P. Hummel, *The Bureaucratic Experience,* 3d ed. (New York: St. Martin's, 1987); Michael A. Diamond, "Bureaucracy as Externalized Self-System," *Administration & Society* 16 (August 1984): 195–214; and Glassman et al., *Bureaucracy against Democracy and Socialism,* chaps. 4 and 7.
25. Strauss, *Ruling Servants;* Hummel, *Bureaucratic Experience;* Jeffrey M. Prottas, *People-Processing: The Street-Level Bureaucrat in Public Service Bureaucracies* (Lexington, Mass.: D.C. Heath, 1979); and Heiner Flohr, "Bureaucracy and Its Clients: Exploring a Biosocial Perspective," in *Biology and Bureaucracy: Public Administration and Public Policy from the Perspective of Evolutionary, Genetic and Neurobiological Theory,* ed. Elliott White and Joseph Losco (Lanham, Md.: University Press of America, 1986), 80–81, 88.
26. Merton, "Bureaucratic Structure and Personality"; Piven and Cloward, *Regulating the Poor;* Glenn Jacobs, "The Reification of the Notion of Subculture in Public Welfare," *Social Casework* 49 (November 1968): 527–534; Orion F. White Jr., "The Dialectical Organization: An Alternative to Bureaucracy," *Public Administration Review* 29 (January/February, 1969): 32–42; Hummel, *Bureaucratic Experience;* Norma Williams, Gideon Sjøberg, and Andree F. Sjøberg, "The Bureaucratic Personality: A Second Look," in *Bureaucracy as a Social Problem,* ed. W. Boyd Littrell, Gideon Sjøberg, and Louis A. Zurcher (Greenwich, Conn.: JAI Press, 1983), 178–179; and Yeheskel Hasenfeld and Daniel Steinmetz, "Client-Official Encounters in Social Service Agencies," in *The Public Encounter: Where State and Citizen Meet,* ed. Charles T. Goodsell (Bloomington: Indiana University Press, 1981), chap. 5.
27. Gideon Sjøberg, Richard A. Brymer, and Buford Farris, "Bureaucracy and the Lower Class," *Sociology and Social Research* 50 (April 1966): 325–337.
28. Michael Lipsky, *Street-Level Bureaucracy* (New York: Russell Sage Foundation, 1980); Michael K. Brown, *Working the Street: Police Discretion and the Dilemmas of Reform* (New York: Russell Sage Foundation, 1981); Mitchell F. Rice, "Inequality, Discrimination and Service Delivery," *International Journal of Public Administration* 1, no. 4 (1979): 409–433; and Jeffrey M. Prottas, "The Cost of Free Services," *Public Administration Review* 41 (September/October 1981): 526–534.
29. Robert B. Denhardt, "Toward a Critical Theory of Public Organization," *Public Administration Review* 41 (November/December 1981): 628–635; idem, *In the Shadow of Organizations* (Lawrence: Regents Press of Kansas, 1981); Gareth Morgan, "Paradigms, Metaphors, and Puzzle Solving in Organization Theory," *Administrative Science Quarterly* 25 (December 1980): 605–622; Gibson Burrell

and Gareth Morgan, *Sociological Paradigms and Organizational Analysis* (London: Heinemann, 1979); and Ferguson, *Feminist Case against Bureaucracy.*

30. Guy B. Adams and Danny L. Balfour, *Unmasking Administrative Evil* (Thousand Oaks, Calif.: Sage, 1998). For a spirited discussion of this work, see *Public Administration Review* 60 (September/October 2000): 464–482; and Gerson Moreno-Riano, "The Etiology of Administrative Evil: Eric Voegelin and the Unconsciousness of Modernity," *American Review of Public Administration* 31, no. 3 (September 2001): 296–312.
31. Ithiel de Sola Pool, "The Language of Politics: General Trends in Content," in *Propaganda and Communication in World History,* ed. Harold D. Lasswell (Honolulu: University Press of Hawaii, 1980), 180; Charles Perrow, *Complex Organizations* (Glenview, Ill.: Scott, Foresman, 1972), 32–35, 52–58; Christopher C. Hood, *The Limits of Administration* (London: Wiley, 1976), 205; and Stephen Miller, "Bureaucrat Baiting," *American Scholar* 47 (spring 1978): 205, 212.
32. Charles and William Beard, "The Case for Bureaucracy," *Scribner's Magazine* 93 (April 1933): 209–214 [reprinted in *Public Administration Review* 46 (March/April 1986): 107–112]. In the same issue of *PAR*, see my article, "Charles A. Beard, Prophet for Public Administration," 105–107.
33. Harlan Cleveland, "The Case *for* Bureaucracy," *New York Times Magazine*, 27 October 1963, 19, 113–114. In a letter, Cleveland told me that he had italicized the preposition so that the magazine's editor would not assume the word intended was *against.*
34. Werner J. Dannhauser, "Reflections on Statesmanship and Bureaucracy," in *Bureaucrats, Policy Analysts, Statesmen: Who Leads?* ed. Robert A. Goldwin (Washington, D.C.: American Enterprise Institute, 1980), 132; Herbert Kaufman, "Fear of Bureaucracy: A Raging Pandemic," *Public Administration Review* 41 (January/February 1981): 1–9 [see also his twenty-year update, "Major Players: Bureaucracies in American Government," *PAR* 61 (January/February 2001): 18–42]; Zahid Shariff, "Contemporary Challenges to Public Administration," *Social Science Quarterly* 62 (September 1981): 555–568, at 564; and H. Brinton Milward and Hal G. Rainey, "Don't Blame the Bureaucracy!" *Journal of Public Policy* 3 (October 1983): 149–168.
35. Dean Yarwood, "Stop Bashing the Bureaucracy," *Public Administration Review* 56 (November/December 1996): 611–613; William D. Richardson, *Democracy, Bureaucracy, and Character: Founding Thought* (Lawrence: University Press of Kansas, 1997), 3; and Henry Mintzberg, "Managing Government, Governing Management," *Harvard Business Review* (May/June 1996): 83.
36. Bernard Rosen, "Effective Continuity of U.S. Government Operations in Jeopardy," *Public Administration Review* 44 (September/October 1983): 383–392; Bruce Adams, "The Frustrations of Government Service," *Public Administration Review* 44 (January/February 1984): 5–13; Larry M. Lane and James F. Wolf, *The Human Resource Crisis in the Public Sector* (New York: Quorum, 1990), 1; and "Report to the President: The Crisis in Human Capital," Senate Subcommittee on Oversight of Government Management, Restructuring, and the District of Columbia, 106th Cong., 2d sess., December 2000.
37. George W. Downs and Patrick D. Larkey, *The Search for Government Efficiency: From Hubris to Helplessness* (Philadelphia: Temple University Press, 1986); Mark Holzer and Kathe Callahan, *Government at Work: Best Practices and Model*

Programs (Thousand Oaks, Calif.: Sage, 1998), ix; Kenneth J. Meier and John Bohte, "Not With a Bang, But a Whimper: Explaining Organizational Failures," *Administration and Society* 35, no. 1 (March 2003): 104–121; Steven Kelman, *Making Public Policy: A Hopeful View of American Government* (New York: Basic Books, 1987); Christopher K. Leman, "The Forgotten Fundamental: Successes and Excesses of Direct Government," in *Beyond Privatization: The Tools of Government Action,* ed. Lester M. Salamon (Washington, D.C.: Urban Institute Press, 1989), 53–92; and Lewis C. Mainzer, *Political Bureaucracy* (Glenview, Ill.: Scott, Foresman, 1973), 151.

38. André Blais and Stéphane Dion, eds., *The Budget-Maximizing Bureaucrat: Appraisals and Evidence* (Pittsburgh: University of Pittsburgh Press, 1991); Patrick Dunleavy, *Democracy, Bureaucracy and Public Choice: Economic Explanations in Political Science* (Englewood Cliffs, N.J.: Prentice Hall, 1991), chap. 7; and Hugh Stretton and Lionel Orchard, *Public Goods, Public Enterprise, Public Choice: Theoretical Foundations of the Contemporary Attack on Government* (New York: St. Martin's, 1994), 78–79.

39. David Beetham, *Bureaucracy* (Minneapolis: University of Minnesota Press, 1987); Eva Etzioni-Halévy, *Bureaucracy and Democracy: A Political Dilemma* (London: Routledge and Kegan Paul, 1983); and B. Dan Wood and Richard W. Waterman, *Bureaucratic Dynamics: The Role of Bureaucracy in a Democracy* (Boulder, Colo.: Westview, 1994).

40. Max Nieman, *Defending Government: Why Big Government Works* (Upper Saddle River, N.J.: Prentice Hall, 2000); Barry Bozeman, *Bureaucracy and Red Tape* (Upper Saddle River, N.J.: Prentice Hall, 2000), 1; Gary Wills, *A Necessary Evil: A History of American Distrust of Government* (New York: Simon and Schuster, 1999); H.T. Wilson, *Bureaucratic Representation: Civil Servants and the Future of Capitalist Democracies* (Leiden: Brill, 2001); Gyorgy Gajduschek, "Bureaucracy: Is It Efficient? Is It Not? Is That the Question?" *Administration and Society* 34, no. 6 (January 2003): 700–723; Larry M. Preston, *Freedom and the Organizational Republic* (Berlin: Walter de Gruyter, 1992); and Paul du Gay, *In Praise of Bureaucracy: Weber, Organization, Ethics* (London: Sage, 2000). For Friedrich's "core of modern government" idea, see his *Constitutional Government and Democracy: Theory and Practice in Europe and America,* rev. ed. (Boston: Ginn and Company, 1950), chap. 2.

41. John E. Schwarz, *America's Hidden Success: A Reassessment of Twenty Years of Public Policy* (New York: Norton, 1983); Paul E. Peterson, Barry G. Rabe, and Kenneth K. Wong, *When Federalism Works* (Washington, D.C.: Brookings Institution, 1986); and Merton C. Bernstein and Joan B. Bernstein, *Social Security: The System That Works* (New York: Basic Books, 1988).

42. Benjamin I. Page and James R. Simmons, *What Government Can Do: Dealing with Poverty and Inequality* (Chicago: University of Chicago Press, 2000); Jonathan Crane, ed., *Social Programs That Work* (New York: Russell Sage Foundation, 1998), 197; Derek Bok, "Measuring the Performance of Government," in *Why People Don't Trust Government,* ed. Joseph S. Nye Jr., Philip D. Zelikow, and David C. King (Cambridge, Mass.: Harvard University Press, 1997), 66–68.

43. Theodore W. Taylor, ed., *Federal Public Policy: Personal Accounts of Ten Senior Civil Service Executives* (Mt. Airy, Md.: Lemond, 1984); Howard Rosen, *Servants of the People: The Uncertain Future of the Federal Civil Service* (Salt Lake City:

Olympus, 1985), 7–8; and Jameson W. Doig and Erwin C. Hargrove, eds. *Leadership and Innovation: A Biographical Perspective on Entrepreneurs in Government* (Baltimore: Johns Hopkins University Press, 1987) [see also the abridged 1990 edition].

44. Christopher Bellavita, "The Public Administrator as Hero," *Administration & Society* 23 (August 1991): 155–185; Terry L. Cooper and N. Dale Wright, eds., *Exemplary Public Administrators* (Beverly Hills, Calif.: Sage, 1992); Norma M. Riccucci, *Unsung Heroes: Federal Execucrats Making a Difference* (Washington, D.C.: Georgetown University Press, 1995); and Robin M. Bittick, "Disposable Public Servants: Looking at Post-War Ethical Evaluations of Personnel Fighting the War against Terrorism," *Public Administration Times*, June 2002, 6.
45. Gary L. Wamsley, Robert N. Bacher, Charles T. Goodsell, Philip S. Kronenberg, John A. Rohr, Camilla M. Stivers, Orion F. White, and James F. Wolf, *Refounding Public Administration* (Beverly Hills, Calif.: Sage, 1990); and Gary L. Wamsley and James F. Wolf, eds., *Refounding Democratic Public Administration: Modern Paradoxes, Postmodern Challenges* (Thousand Oaks, Calif.: Sage, 1996). One of our most attentive critics is Robert T. Golembiewski, who discusses at length his views of *The Case for Bureaucracy* and *Refounding Public Administration* in chaps. 3 and 4, respectively, of *Practical Public Management* (New York: Marcel Dekker, 1995).

2. What Citizens Experience from Bureaucracy

1. Leonard D. White, *The Prestige Value of Public Employment in Chicago* (Chicago: University of Chicago Press, 1929), 145–147.
2. Montgomery Van Wart, "The First Step in the Reinvention Process: Assessment," *Public Administration Review* 55, no. 5 (September/October 1995): 433.
3. Susan M. Willis-Walton and Alan E. Bayer, *Quality of Life in Virginia: 2003* (Blacksburg: Center for Survey Research, Virginia Polytechnic Institute and State University, 2003), D9–D10.
4. Thomas I. Miller and Michelle A. Miller, "Standards of Excellence: U.S. Residents' Evaluations of Local Government Services," *Public Administration Review* 51, no. 6 (November/December 1991): 503–515, 507.
5. Theodore H. Poister and Gary T. Henry, "Citizen Ratings of Public and Private Service Quality: A Comparative Perspective," *Public Administration Review* 54, no. 2 (March/April 1994): 158.
6. John T. Tierney, *The U.S. Postal Service: Status and Prospects of a Public Enterprise* (Dover, Mass.: Auburn House, 1988), 5–6; and "Postal Service Really Delivers, Most in Poll Say," Associated Press, 23 January 1999.
7. CSM data obtained by e-mail from Christopher Lind, U.S. Postal Service, 6 February 2001.
8. *Washington Post*, 13 April 2000.
9. Mary-Jo Hall, "The American Customer Satisfaction Index," *Public Manager* 31, no. 1 (spring 2002): 23–26, 30. See also the web site of the University of Michigan Business School, www.theacsi.org.
10. Willis-Walton and Bayer, *Quality of Life in Virginia*, A3.
11. Stephen L. Percy, "In Defense of Citizen Evaluations as Performance Measures," *Urban Affairs Quarterly* 22 (September 1986): 66–83. I am grateful to Professor Percy for bringing his research to my attention. For other literature on this

debate, see Brian Stipak, "Using Clients to Evaluate Programs," *Computers, Environment and Urban Systems* 5 (1980): 137–154; idem, "Citizen Satisfaction with Urban Services: Potential Misuse as a Performance Indicator," *Public Administration Review* 39, no. 1 (January/February 1979): 46–52; Barbara A. Gutek, "Strategies for Studying Client Satisfaction," *Journal of Social Issues* 34 (1978): 44–56; Jeffrey L. Brudney and Robert E. England, "Urban Policy Making and Subjective Service Evaluation: Are They Compatible?" *Public Administration Review* 42, no. 2 (March/April 1982): 127–135; Karin Brown and Philip B. Coulter, "Subjective and Objective Measures of Police Service Delivery," *Public Administration Review* 43, no. 1 (January/February 1983): 50–58; and Roger B. Parks, "Linking Objective and Subjective Measures of Performance," *Public Administration Review* 44, no. 2 (March/April 1984): 118–127.

12. Blanche D. Blank et al., "A Comparative Study of an Urban Bureaucracy," *Urban Affairs Quarterly* 4 (March 1969): 344.
13. U.S. Postal Service, *Annual Report*, 2000: 24, 47, 66, 68, 70; 1998: 5, 35, 46.
14. U.S. Postal Service, *Annual Report*, 1998: 2.
15. U.S. Postal Service, *The Household Diary Study*, March 1992, IV–113 and IV–115.
16. U.S. Postal Service, "Window Clerk Transaction Studies," 1980; and U.S. General Accounting Office, *Postal Service: Postage Charges in Two Geographic Areas Were Accurate Most of the Time,* Report GGD-86-127 (September 1986).
17. Dalbar Financial Services, Inc., *World-Class Benchmarks* (April 1995). I appreciate receiving a copy of this report from Gordon M. Sherman.
18. *Washington Post*, 27 September 2003, A4; Office of Management and Budget, "Informing Regulatory Decisions: 2003 Report to Congress on the Costs and Benefits of Federal Regulations and Unfunded Mandates on State, Local, and Tribal Entities," September 2003, available at www.whitehouse.gov/omb/inforeg/regpol-reports_congress.html.
19. U.S. Department of Agriculture, Food and Nutrition Service, *Food Stamp Program Quality Control Annual Report*, FY 1999 (December 2000), iii.
20. U.S. Department of Labor, Employment and Training Administration, *UI Performs: CY 1999 Annual Report* (August 2000), 7, 20, 37, 38.
21. Donald Fisk and Darlene Forte, "The Federal Productivity Measure Program: Final Results," *Monthly Labor Review* 120 (May 1997): 19–28.
22. U.S. Department of Labor, Bureau of Labor Statistics, *Measuring State and Local Government Labor Productivity: Examples from Eleven Services*, Bulletin 2495 (June 1998): 43, 49, 87.
23. On environmental protection, see *Washington Post*, 6 May 1998 and 19 October 2001; *Roanoke Times*, 16 April 1995, 10 January 2001, 1 July 2003; and www.epa.gov/tri/tridata/tri01/index.htm. On public safety, see *Washington Post*, 24 July 2001, 13 August 2001, 15 August 2001; and *Roanoke Times*, 30 December 1997, 23 October 2001, 9 September 2002, 17 December 2002, 25 August 2003, 18 September 2003. On health and welfare, see *Washington Post*, 1 February 2002, 27 September 2003; and *Roanoke Times*, 9 September 2000, 6 June 2001, 26 September 2001, 13 September 2002, 25 September 2002. On child well-being, see *Washington Post*, 19 July 2001; and *Roanoke Times*, 20 December 2001, 12 July 2002, 27 September 2002.
24. One of the few scholars to study systematically the actual effects of government programs on the amelioration of policy problems is Evan J. Ringquist. Applying

statistical regression and path analysis to EPA air-quality data, he found that states with stronger air-quality programs experience greater reductions in nitrogen dioxide and sulfur dioxide. He concludes that effective regulation at the state (and federal) level is the most important causal variable related to this outcome; hence, "regulation does matter." See his "Does Regulation Matter? Evaluating the Effects of State Air Pollution Control Programs," *Journal of Politics* 55 (November 1993): 1022–1045. Also note "Is 'Effective Regulation' Always Oxymoronic? The States and Ambient Air Quality," *Social Science Quarterly* 76 (March 1995): 69–87.

3. More Bureaucracy Myths to Delete

1. James D. Thompson, "Authority and Power in 'Identical' Organizations," *American Journal of Sociology* 62 (November 1956): 290–301.
2. James L. Price, "Use of New Knowledge in Organizations," *Human Organization* 23 (fall 1964): 224–234.
3. William E. Turcotte, "Control Systems, Performance, and Satisfaction in Two State Agencies," *Administrative Science Quarterly* 19 (March 1974): 60–73.
4. Tana Pesso, "Local Welfare Offices: Managing the Intake Process," *Public Policy* 26 (spring 1978): 305–330.
5. Michael Lipsky, *Street-Level Bureaucracy* (New York: Russell Sage Foundation, 1980), 89, 95; Jeffrey M. Prottas, *People-Processing: The Street-Level Bureaucrat in Public Service Bureaucracies* (Lexington, Mass.: D.C. Heath, 1979), 24; idem, "The Cost of Free Services," *Public Administration Review* 41, no. 5 (September/October 1981): 526–534; Frances Fox Piven and Richard A. Cloward, *Regulating the Poor* (New York: Pantheon, 1971), 149, 165; and Barry Schwartz, *Queuing and Waiting* (Chicago: University of Chicago Press, 1975).
6. Charles T. Goodsell, "Welfare Waiting Rooms," *Urban Life* 12 (January 1984): 467–477.
7. Charles T. Goodsell, Raymond E. Austin, Karen L. Hedblom, and Clarence C. Rose, "Bureaucracy Expresses Itself: How State Documents Address the Public," *Social Science Quarterly* 62 (September 1981): 576–591.
8. Paul R. Dimond, *A Dilemma of Local Government: Discrimination in the Provision of Public Services* (Lexington, Mass.: D.C. Heath, 1978); Robert K. Yin and Douglas Yates, *Street-Level Governments* (Lexington, Mass.: D.C. Heath, 1975); Gideon Sjøberg, Richard A. Brymer, and Buford Farris, "Bureaucracy and the Lower Class," *Sociology and Social Research* 50 (April 1966): 325–337; Saad Z. Nagi, "Gate-Keeping Decisions in Service Organizations: When Validity Fails," *Human Organization* 33 (spring 1974): 47–58; Richard A. Cloward and Frances Fox Piven, "The Professional Bureaucracies: Benefit Systems as Influence Systems," in *Blacks and Bureaucracy,* ed. Virginia B. Ermer and John H. Strange (New York: Crowell, 1972), 206–222; and Julius A. Roth, "Some Contingencies of the Moral Evaluation and Control of Clientele: The Case of the Hospital Emergency Service," *American Journal of Sociology* 77 (March 1972): 839–856.
9. Frank Levy, Arnold J. Meltsner, and Aaron Wildavsky, *Urban Outcomes: Schools, Streets, and Libraries* (Berkeley: University of California Press, 1974), chap. 2; and Kenneth R. Mladenka, "Responsive Performance by Public Officials," in *The Public Encounter: Where State and Citizen Meet,* ed. Charles T. Goodsell (Bloomington: Indiana University Press, 1981), chap. 8.

10. George E. Antunes and John Plumlee, "The Distribution of an Urban Public Service: Ethnicity, Socioeconomic Status, and Bureaucracy as Determinants of the Quality of Neighborhood Streets," *Urban Affairs Quarterly* 12 (March 1977): 313–332.
11. Philip B. Coulter, "Measuring Inequity of Service Delivery: A Case Study of Tuscaloosa, Alabama," paper presented at the annual meeting of the Southwestern Political Science Association, Dallas, 1981, 16–19; and Philip B. Coulter, "Inferring the Distributional Effects of Bureaucratic Decision Rules," *Policy Studies Journal* 12 (December 1983): 347–355.
12. Robert L. Lineberry, *Equality and Urban Policy: The Distribution of Municipal Public Services* (Beverly Hills, Calif.: Sage, 1977).
13. Kenneth R. Mladenka and Kim Quaile Hill, "The Distribution of Benefits in an Urban Environment: Parks and Libraries in Houston," *Urban Affairs Quarterly* 13 (September 1977): 78–81; and Levy et al., *Urban Outcomes.*
14. Kenneth R. Mladenka, "The Urban Bureaucracy and the Chicago Political Machine: Who Gets What and the Limits to Political Control," *American Political Science Review* 74 (December 1980): 992–993; and Bryan D. Jones, *Service Delivery in the City: Citizen Demand and Bureaucratic Rules* (New York: Longman, 1980), 116–117, 132–135.
15. Levy et al., *Urban Outcomes,* chap. 1.
16. David L. Cingranelli, "Race, Politics and Elites: Testing Alternative Models of Municipal Service Distribution," *American Journal of Political Science* 25 (November 1981): 664–692.
17. Naomi Kroeger, "Bureaucracy, Social Exchange, and Benefits Received in a Public Assistance Agency," *Social Problems* 23 (December 1975): 189; and Schwartz, *Queuing and Waiting,* 122.
18. Julia Beckett, "The 'Government Should Run Like a Business' Mantra," *American Review of Public Administration* 30 (June 2000): 185–204.
19. Robert M. Spann, "Public versus Private Provision of Governmental Services," in *Public Management: Public and Private Perspectives,* ed. James L. Perry and K. L. Kraemer (Palo Alto, Calif.: Mayfield, 1983), 346 [originally published in *Budgets and Bureaucrats: The Sources of Government Growth,* ed. Thomas E. Borcherding (Durham, N.C.: Duke University Press, 1977)]; Robert Millward, "The Comparative Performance of Public and Private Ownership," in *The Mixed Economy,* ed. Lord Roll of Ipsden (London: Macmillan, 1982), 58–93; Thomas E. Borcherding, Werner W. Pommerehne, and Friedrich Schneider, *Comparing the Efficiency of Private and Public Production: The Evidence from Five Countries* (Zurich: Institute for Empirical Research in Economics, University of Zurich, 1982) [results summarized in Charles Wolf Jr., *Markets or Governments: Choosing between Imperfect Alternatives* (Cambridge, Mass.: MIT Press, 1988), 137, 192–199]; David Parker, "Is the Private Sector More Efficient? A Study in the Public v. Private Debate," *Public Administration Bulletin,* August 1985, 1–23; and J. Norman Baldwin with Quinton A. Farley, "Comparing the Public and Private Sectors in the United States: A Review of the Empirical Research," in *Handbook of Comparative and Development Public Administration,* ed. Ali Farazmand (New York: Marcel Dekker, 1990), 35.
20. E. S. Savas, *Privatization and Public-Private Partnerships* (New York: Chatham House, 2000), 16–64.

21. Ibid., 161.
22. Graeme A. Hodge, *Privatization: An International Review of Performance* (Boulder, Colo.: Westview, 2000), 155; William J. Pier, Robert B. Vernon, and John H. Wicks, "An Empirical Comparison of Government and Private Production Efficiency," *National Tax Journal* 27 (December 1974): 653–656; W. Hirsch, "Cost Functions of Government Service: Refuse Collection," *Review of Economics and Statistics* 47 (February 1965), 85–93; "Customers Rate Refuse Service," *Waste Age* 12 (November 1981): 82, 85, 86, 88; and Julia Marlowe, "Private versus Public Provision of Refuse Removal Service: Measure of Citizen Satisfaction," *Urban Affairs Quarterly* 20 (March 1985): 355–363.
23. Ronald Teeples and David Glyer, "Cost of Water Delivery Systems: Specification and Ownership Effects," *Review of Economics and Statistics* 69 (August 1987): 399–408; W. Mark Crain and Asghar Zardkoohi, "A Test of the Property-Rights Theory of the Firm: Water Utilities in the United States," *Journal of Law and Economics* 21 (October 1978): 395–408; and Thomas H. Bruggink, "Public versus Regulated Private Enterprise in the Municipal Water Industry: A Comparison of Operating Costs," *Quarterly Review of Economics and Business* 22 (spring 1982): 111–125.
24. Sam Peltzman, "Pricing in Public and Private Enterprises: Electric Utilities in the United States," *Journal of Law and Economics* 14 (April 1971): 124, 143; Louis De Alessi, "An Economic Analysis of Government Ownership and Regulation: Theory and the Evidence from the Electric Power Industry," *Public Choice* 19 (1974): 1–42; and Scott E. Atkinson and Robert Halvorsen, "The Relative Efficiency of Public and Private Firms in a Regulated Environment: The Case of U.S. Electric Utilities," *Journal of Public Economics* 29 (1986): 281–294.
25. Roger S. Ahlbrandt Jr., "Efficiency in the Provision of Fire Services," *Public Choice, (*fall 1973): 1–15; Randy L.Ross, *Government and the Private Sector: Who Should Do What?* (New York: Crane Russak, 1988), 62–63; and Michael Krashinsky, "The Cost of Day Care in Public Programs," *National Tax Journal* 31 (December 1978): 363–372.
26. Barbara J. Stevens, "Comparing Public- and Private-Sector Productive Efficiency: An Analysis of Eight Activities," *National Productivity Review* 3 (autumn 1984): 395–406.
27. James L. Perry, "Organizational Form and Transit Performance: A Research Review and Empirical Analysis," report prepared for Urban Mass Transportation Administration, September 1984, 14–18, 25; and James L. Perry and Timlynn T. Babitsky, "Comparative Performance in Urban Bus Transit: Assessing Privatization Strategies," *Public Administration Review* 46 (January/February 1986): 57–66.
28. David G. Davies, "The Efficiency of Public versus Private Firms: The Case of Australia's Two Airlines," *Journal of Law and Economics* 14 (April 1971): 149–165; P. J. Forsyth and R. D. Hocking, "Property Rights and Efficiency in a Regulated Environment: The Case of Australian Airlines," *Economic Record* 56 (June 1980): 182–185; and Douglas W. Caves and Laurits R. Christensen, "The Relative Efficiency of Public and Private Firms in a Competitive Environment: The Case of Canadian Railroads," *Journal of Political Economy* 88 (October 1980): 958–976.
29. Cotton M. Lindsay, "A Theory of Government Enterprise," *Journal of Political Economy* 84 (October 1976): 1070, 1073; Lawrence G. Hrebiniak and Joseph A.

Alutto, "A Comparative Organizational Study of Performance and Size Correlates in Inpatient Psychiatric Departments," *Administrative Science Quarterly* 18 (September 1973): 373; and George W. Wilson and Joseph M. Jadlow, "Competition, Profit Incentives, and Technical Efficiency in the Provision of Nuclear Medicine Services," *Bell Journal of Economics* 13 (autumn 1982): 472–482.

30. David Osborne and Peter Plastrik, *Banishing Bureaucracy: The Five Strategies for Reinventing Government* (Reading, Mass.: Addison-Wesley, 1997), 258–259.
31. Richard T. LaPiere, *Social Change* (New York: McGraw-Hill, 1965), 408–413.
32. Gerald E. Caiden, "What Really Is Public Maladministration?" *Public Administration Review* 51 (November/December 1991): 491–492.
33. J. David Roessner, "Incentives to Innovate in Public and Private Organizations," *Administration & Society* 9 (November 1997): 359.
34. Peter M. Blau, *The Dynamics of Bureaucracy* (Chicago: University of Chicago Press, 1963), 246–247.
35. Louis K. Bragaw, *Managing a Federal Agency: The Hidden Stimulus* (Baltimore: Johns Hopkins University Press, 1980).
36. Mark Schneider and Paul Teske, *Public Entrepreneurs: Agents for Change in American Government* (Princeton: Princeton University Press, 1995), 88–89, 94–99, 148.
37. Bruce Rocheleau and Liangfu Wu, "Public versus Private Information Systems: Do They Differ in Important Ways? A Review and Empirical Test," *American Review of Public Administration* 32, no. 4 (December 2002): 379–397.
38. "Innovations in American Government: Creative Solutions to Public Concerns," brochure of Ford Foundation and Kennedy School of Government program, in partnership with The Council for Excellence in Government, 2000, circulated by *Governing* magazine; and *Washington Post*, 5 April 2001.
39. Sandford Borins, "Loose Cannons and Rule Breakers, or Enterprising Leaders? Some Evidence about Innovative Public Managers," *Public Administration Review* 60 (November/December 2000): 500; and idem, *Innovating with Integrity: How Local Heroes Are Transforming American Government* (Washington, D.C.: Georgetown University Press, 1998), 38.
40. Borins, *Innovating with Integrity*, 39–40, 47, 49, 51; and idem, "Loose Cannons and Rule Breakers," 504.
41. John D. Donahue, ed., *Making Washington Work: Tales of Innovation in the Federal Sector* (Washington, D.C.: Brookings Institution, 1999), 14.
42. Christopher K. Leman, "Direct Government," in *The Tools of Government: A Guide to the New Governance*, ed. Lester M. Salamon (Oxford: Oxford University Press, 2002), 71.

4. Ask the Impossible of Bureaucracy? Easy!

1. James Q. Wilson, *Bureaucracy: What Government Agencies Do and Why They Do It* (New York: Basic Books, 1989), 158.
2. *Washington Post*, 13–14 March 2002.
3. *Washington Post*, 27 March 2000, 24 July 2002.
4. David L. Dillman, "The Paradox of Discretion and the Case of Elian Gonzalez," *Public Organization Review: A Global Journal* 2, no. 2 (June 2002): 165–185; and *Miami Herald*, 23 April 2000.

5. Alvin W. Gouldner, "Red Tape as a Social Problem," in *Reader in Bureaucracy*, ed. Robert K. Merton et al. (New York: Free Press, 1952), 418. For an attempt to treat red tape as an empirically measurable concept, see Sanjay K. Pandey and Patrick G. Scott, "Red Tape: A Review and Assessment of Concepts and Measures," *Journal of Public Administration Research and Theory* 12, no. 4 (October 2002): 553–580.
6. Paul H. Appleby, *Big Democracy* (New York: Knopf, 1945), 64.
7. *Roanoke Times*, 15 November 1993.
8. Herbert Kaufman, *Red Tape* (Washington, D.C.: Brookings Institution, 1977), 7–13ff.
9. Michael Hill, *The State, Administration and the Individual* (Totowa, N.J.: Rowman & Littlefield, 1976), 79.
10. Barry Bozeman, *Bureaucracy and Red Tape* (Upper Saddle River, N.J.: Prentice Hall, 2000).
11. Christopher C. Hood, *The Limits of Administration* (London: Wiley, 1976), 6; Lewis A. Gunn, "Why Is Implementation So Difficult?" *Management Services in Government* 33 (1978): 169–176 [quoted in Wayne Parsons, *Public Policy: An Introduction to the Theory and Practice of Policy Analysis* (Aldershot, U.K.: Edward Elgar, 1995), 466]; and Malcolm L. Goggin, Ann O'M. Bowman, James P. Lester, and Laurence J. O'Toole Jr., *Implementation Theory and Practice: Toward a Third Generation* (HarperCollins, 1990), 182.
12. Jeffrey L. Pressman and Aaron Wildavsky, *Implementation: How Great Expectations in Washington Are Dashed in Oakland; Or, Why It's Amazing That Federal Programs Work At All—This Being a Saga of the Economic Development Administration as Told by Two Sympathetic Observers Who Seek to Build Morals on a Foundation of Ruined Hopes* (Berkeley: University of California Press, 1st ed., 1973; 3d ed., 1984).
13. H. T. Colebatch, *Policy* (Minneapolis: University of Minnesota Press, 1998), 38.
14. The term *public action*—by which he means the joining together of multiple actors into a network for the purpose of achieving public goals—originates with Dutch scholar Peter Bogason. See his *Public Policy and Local Governance: Institutions in Postmodern Society* (Cheltenham, U.K.: Edward Elgar, 2000).
15. Thad E. Hall and Laurence J. O'Toole Jr., "Structures for Policy Implementation: An Analysis of National Legislation, 1965–1966 and 1993–1994," *Administration & Society* 31 (January 2000): 667–686.
16. *Statistical Abstract of the United States: 2002*, 264.
17. David R. Beam and Timothy J. Conlan, "Grants," in *The Tools of Government: A Guide to the New Governance*, ed. Lester M. Salamon (Oxford: Oxford University Press, 2002), 345–348.
18. Daniel W. Williams, "Reinventing the Proverbs of Government," *Public Administration Review* 60, no. 6 (November/December 2000): 529.
19. Catherine Lovell and Charles Tobin, "The Mandate Issue," *Public Administration Review* 41 (May/June 1981): 318–331.
20. Beam and Conlan, "Grants," 352.
21. Robert Agranoff and Michael McGuire, "American Federalism and the Search for Models of Management," *Public Administration Review* 61, no. 6 (November/December 2001): 671–681. See also Robert P. Stoker, *Reluctant Partners: Implementing Federal Policy* (Pittsburgh: University of Pittsburgh Press, 1991).

22. Paul C. Light, *The True Size of Government* (Washington: Brookings Institution, 1999), 38.
23. On this point, see Carl R. Templin, "Defense Contracting Buyer-Seller Relationships: Theoretical Approaches," *Acquisition Review Quarterly* 1 (spring 1994): 117.
24. Steven J. Kelman, "Contracting," in Salamon, *Tools of Government*, 287–288.
25. *Washington Post*, 19 May 2003, A2; 27 August 2003, A13.
26. Graeme A. Hodge, *Privatization: An International Review of Performance* (Boulder, Colo.: Westview, 2000), 155; Donald F. Kettl, *Sharing Power: Public Governance and Private Markets* (Washington, D.C.: Brookings Institution, 1993), 160–162; Jeffrey D. Greene, "Does Privatization Make A Difference? The Impact of Private Contracting on Municipal Efficiency," *International Journal of Public Administration* 17 (1994): 1299–1325; and George A. Boyne, "Bureaucratic Theory Meets Reality: Public Choice and Service Contracting in U.S. Local Government," *Public Administration Review* 58, no. 6 (November/December 1998).
27. Kettl, *Sharing Power*, chap. 3; and *Washington Post*, 30 January 2002.
28. Wallace O. Keene, "ICE-MAN and the Aftermath," *Public Manager* 28 (winter 1999–2000): 34–36, 41; and *Washington Post*, 22 May 1997.
29. Hodge, *Privatization*, 142–144; and Kettl, *Sharing Power*, 4–5, 164.
30. David M. Van Slyke, "The Mythology of Privatization in Contracting for Social Services," *Public Administration Review* 63, no. 3 (May/June 2003): 296–315, at 303; and *Washington Post*, 14 July 2003.
31. *Washington Post*, 28 August 2003, A1. *Roanoke Times*, 26 October 2003.
32. Kettl, *Sharing Power*, chap. 9.
33. Patricia Fredericksen and Rosanne London, "Disconnect in the Hollow State: The Pivotal Role of Organizational Capacity in Community-Based Development Organizations, *Public Administration Review* 60, no. 3 (May/June 2000): 230–239.
34. Michelle Murphy, "So Alike, Yet So Different: A Comparative Analysis of Two Community Development Organizations," M.P.A. final paper, Center for Public Administration and Policy, Virginia Tech University, April 2002.
35. Sheila Suess Kennedy and Wolfgang Bielefeld, "Government Shekels without Government Shackles? The Administrative Challenges of Charitable Choice," *Public Administration Review* 62, no.1 (January/February 2002): 4–11, quote at 4.
36. Richard K. Ghere, "Probing the Strategic Intricacies of Public-Private Partnership: The Patent as a Comparative Reference," *Public Administration Review* 61 (July/August 2001): 441–451. Also, idem, "Ethical Futures and Public-Private Partnerships: Peering Far Down the Track," *Public Organization Review: A Global Journal* 1, no. 3 (September 2001): 303–319; and Roger Wettenhall, "The Rhetoric and Reality of Public-Private Partnerships," *Public Organization Review* 3, no. 1 (March 2003): 77–107.
37. On State Rural Development Councils, see Agranoff and McGuire, "American Federalism and the Search for Models of Management," 677. On Tillamook County, see John Kamensky, "Getting Results When No One Is In Charge," *Public Manager* 31, no.1 (spring 2002): 22. On the National Quality Forum, see www.qualityforum.org.
38. Jerry Mitchell, "Business Improvement Districts and the Management of Innovation," *American Review of Public Administration* 31, no. 2 (June 2001): 201–217.

39. Erik Ferguson, Catherine Ross, and Michael Meyer, "Transportation Management Associations," *Transportation Quarterly* 47, no. 2 (April 1993): 207–219. I hereby thank Professor Goktug Morcol of Kennesaw State University for bringing the BIDs and TMAs to my attention.
40. *Roanoke Times*, 4 May 2003.

5. Looking Closer at Those Bureaucrats

1. John D. Weaver, *The Great Experiment* (Boston: Little, Brown, 1965), 273.
2. Norton E. Long, "Bureaucracy and Constitutionalism," *American Political Science Review* 46 (September 1952): 814.
3. Kenneth J. Meier, "Representative Bureaucracy: An Empirical Analysis," *American Political Science Review* 69 (June 1975): 531, 532, 537, 538.
4. *Statistical Abstract of the United States: 2002*, 321, 369, 400.
5. James C. Garand, Catherine T. Parkhurst, and Rusanne Jourdan Seoud, "Bureaucrats, Policy Attitudes, and Political Behavior: Extension of the Bureau Voting Model of Government Growth," *Journal of Public Administration Research and Theory* 1 (April 1991): 177–212.
6. Gregory B. Lewis, "In Search of the Machiavellian Milquetoasts: Comparing Attitudes of Bureaucrats and Ordinary People," *Public Administration Review* 50 (March/April 1990): 220–227.
7. *Washington Post*, 19 March 1990.
8. Robert P. Watson, "Politics and Public Administration: A Political Profile of Local Bureaucrats in Alabama," *Administration and Society* 29 (May 1997): 189–200.
9. Stanley Rothman and S. Robert Lichter, "How Liberal Are Bureaucrats?" *Regulation* 7 (November/December 1983): 16–22.
10. Gene A. Brewer and Sally Coleman Selden, "The Promise of Active Citizenship: Does Participation Increase Trust in Government?" paper delivered to the annual meeting of the American Political Science Association, Boston, September 1998.
11. William Blair and James C. Garand, "Are Bureaucrats Different? Democratic Values, Political Tolerance, and Support for the Political System among Government Employees and Other Citizens, 1982–1992," paper delivered to the annual meeting of the American Political Science Association, Chicago, September 1995. Data on IRS filings from *Washington Post*, 19 March 1996 and 24 March 2002.
12. Data on race from Don Hellriegel and Larry Short, "Equal Employment Opportunity in the Federal Government: A Comparative Analysis," *Public Administration Review* 32 (November/December 1972): 854. Data on sex from Mary E. Guy, "Three Steps Forward, Two Steps Backward: The Status of Women's Integration into Public Management," *Public Administration Review* 53, no. 4 (July/August 1993): 287.
13. U.S. Office of Personnel Management, *Federal Civilian Workforce Statistics: Demographic Profile of the Federal Workforce As of September 30, 2000* (May 2001), table 1-1. (Postal employees are not included.) Percentages of the resident population and state-local figures are from *Statistical Abstract of the United States: 2001*, 13, 295.
14. Office of Personnel Management, *Federal Civilian Workforce Statistics*, tables 1.2, 1.4, 1.5, and 1.7.
15. *Washington Post,* 8 July 1998, 28 July 1994.

16. *Statistical Abstract of the United States: 2001,* 297; and Angela M. Bullard and Deil S. Wright, "Circumventing the Glass Ceiling: Women Executives in American State Governments," *Public Administration Review* 53, no. 3 (May/June 1993): 191.
17. Vernon Greene, Sally Selden, and Gene Brewer, "Measuring Power and Presence: Bureaucratic Representation in the American States," *Journal of Public Administration Research and Theory* 11 (July 2001): 379–402.
18. *Statistical Abstract of the United States: 2002,* 385; and Nelson C. Dometrius and Lee Sigelman, "Assessing Progress toward Affirmative Action Goals in State and Local Government: A New Benchmark," *Public Administration Review* 44, no. 3 (May/June 1984): 244.
19. *Washington Post,* 18 January 1993.
20. Peter Eisinger, "Local Civil Service Employment and Black Socioeconomic Mobility," *Social Science Quarterly* 67 (March 1986): 169–175.
21. Sally Coleman Selden, *The Promise of Representative Bureaucracy: Diversity and Responsiveness in a Government Agency* (Armonk, N.Y.: M.E. Sharpe, 1997).
22. Sylvester Murray, Larry D. Terry, Charles A. Washington, and Lawrence F. Keller, "The Role Demands and Dilemmas of Minority Public Administrators: The Herbert Thesis Revisited," *Public Administration Review* 54, no. 5 (September/October 1994): 409–417.
23. Robert Merton, "Bureaucratic Structure and Personality," *Social Forces* 17 (1940): 560–568.
24. Anthony Downs, *Inside Bureaucracy* (Boston: Little, Brown, 1967), 96–100.
25. Charles Peters, "Can Anything Be Done about the Federal Bureaucracy?" *Washington Post Magazine,* 1 October 1978, 14.
26. Guy Benveniste, *Bureaucracy,* 2d ed. (San Francisco: Boyd and Fraser, 1983), esp. chap. 4.
27. Joseph Bensman and Bernard Rosenberg, "The Meaning of Work in Bureaucratic Society," in *Identity and Anxiety: Survival of the Person in Mass Society,* ed. Maurice R. Stein, Arthur J. Vidich, and David M. White (Glencoe, Ill.: Free Press, 1960), 181–197.
28. Frederick C. Thayer, *An End to Hierarchy and Competition: Administration in the Post-Affluent World,* 2d ed. (New York: Franklin Watts, 1981), A1–A6, 46–52.
29. Ralph P. Hummel, *The Bureaucratic Experience: A Critique of Life in the Modern Organization,* 4th ed. (New York: St. Martin's, 1994), 3.
30. Ibid., chap. 1.
31. Melvin L. Kohn, "Bureaucratic Man: A Portrait and an Interpretation," *American Sociological Review* 36 (June 1971): 461–474.
32. Another study, supporting Kohn's findings, showed that senior managers working in larger, more bureaucratized British companies tended to be more flexible and risk-prone individuals. Tony Ellis and John Child, "Placing Stereotypes of the Manager into Perspective," *Journal of Management Studies* 10 (October 1973): 235–255.
33. Charles Bonjean and Michael Grimes, "Bureaucracy and Alienation: A Dimensional Approach," *Social Forces* 48 (March 1970): 365–373.
34. Gerald H. Moeller and W. W. Charters, "Relation of Bureaucratization to Sense of Power among Teachers," *Administrative Science Quarterly* 10 (March 1966): 444–465.

35. Dennis W. Organ and Charles N. Greene, "The Effects of Formalization on Professional Involvement: A Compensatory Process Approach," *Administrative Science Quarterly* 26 (June 1981): 237–251. For a parallel argument, see Larry M. Preston, "Freedom and Bureaucracy," *American Journal of Political Science* 31 (November 1987): 773–795.
36. John Clayton Thomas and Victoria Johnson, "The Urban Public Hospital as Street-Level Bureaucracy: The Employee Perspective," *Public Personnel Management* 20 (fall 1991): 271–284.
37. Clarence Stone and Robert Stoker, "Deprofessionalism and Dissatisfaction in Urban Service Agencies," paper presented to the annual meeting of the Midwest Political Science Association, Chicago, 1979, 47–48. Data supplied by Professor Stone.
38. David Nachmias, "Are Federal Bureaucrats Conservative? A Modest Test of a Popular Image," *Social Science Quarterly* 65 (December 1984): 1080–1087.
39. John L. Foster, "Bureaucratic Rigidity Revisited," *Social Science Quarterly* 71 (June 1990): 223–238.
40. Fred Reed, "Military Minds," *Washington Post*, 2 October 1979.
41. See note 13 of chapter 1 above.
42. Julie Dolan, "The Budget-Minimizing Bureaucrat? Empirical Evidence from the Senior Executive Service," *Public Administration Review* 62, no. 1 (January/February 2002): 45, 46.
43. Ibid., 46, 47.
44. André Blais, Donald E. Blake, and Stéphane Dion, "The Voting Behavior of Bureaucrats," in *The Budget-Maximizing Bureaucrat: Appraisal and Evidence*, ed. Blais and Dion (Pittsburgh: University of Pittsburgh Press, 1991), 205–230; and idem, *Governments, Parties, and Public Sector Employees: Canada, United States, Britain, and France* (Pittsburgh: University of Pittsburgh Press, 1997).
45. André Blais and Stéphane Dion, "Conclusions: Are Bureaucrats Budget Maximizers?" in *Budget-Maximizing Bureaucrat*, 355–361.
46. Patrick Dunleavy, *Democracy, Bureaucracy and Public Choice: Economic Explanations in Political Science* (Englewood Cliffs: Prentice Hall, 1991), 247.
47. John Brehm and Scott Gates, *Working, Shirking and Sabotage: Bureaucratic Response to a Democratic Public* (Ann Arbor: University of Michigan Press, 1997), 89, 108.
48. Ibid., 114, 115.
49. Ibid., 202. The "principled agent" conclusion was also arrived at by John D. DiIulio Jr., with respect to employees of the U.S. Bureau of Prisons. See his "Principled Agents: The Cultural Bases of Behavior in a Federal Government Bureaucracy," *Journal of Public Administration Research and Theory* 4, no. 3 (July 1994): 277–318.
50. Hal G. Rainey and Barry Bozeman, "Comparing Public and Private Organizations: Empirical Research and the Power of the A Priori," *Journal of Public Administration Research and Theory* 10, no. 2 (April 2000): 459–462.
51. David J. Houston, "Public-Service Motivation: A Multivariate Test," *Journal of Public Administration Research and Theory* 10, no. 4 (October 2000): 713–727; Dennis Wittmer, "Serving the People or Serving for Pay: Reward Preferences among Government, Hybrid Sector, and Business Managers," *Public Productivity and Management Review* 14 (summer 1991): 369–383.
52. For another source where the lesser-known are discussed in greater detail, see Norma M. Riccucci, *Unsung Heroes: Federal Execucrats Making a Difference* (Washington, D.C.: Georgetown University Press, 1995).

53. *Washington Post*, 7 December 1999.
54. *Washington Post*, 24 May 1999.
55. *Washington Post*, 13 June 2002.
56. *Washington Post*, 20 September 1999.
57. *Washington Post*, 14 September 1999.
58. *Roanoke Times*, 24 February 2003.
59. *Roanoke Times*, 25 January 1998.
60. Provided by Matthew Lesko of Information USA, Inc., in Kensington, Maryland. In 1990 Mr. Lesko conducted a $5,000 contest for the best story sent in by a citizen on "How a Government Bureaucrat Helped You." After the *Wall Street Journal* ran a negative story on the contest, in which it was predicted there could be no entries, over 1,000 were submitted. Barbara Mann's letter was no. 47 and Jennifer Grogan's no. 72.
61. *Detroit Free Press*, 27 January 1997.
62. "A Living Shrine to My Heroes," speech by Charles Tolchin at groundbreaking of the Mark O. Hatfield Clinical Research Center, National Institutes of Health, November 1997; and "Charlie Tolchin, 34, Dies; AOL Ad Executive Battled Cystic Fibrosis," *Washington Post*, 8 August 2003, B6.
63. *Roanoke Times*, 1 April 2001.
64. *Washington Post*, 30 December 1995.

6. Bureaucratic Bigness and Badness Reconsidered

1. Saul Pett, "The Bureaucracy," *Roanoke Times*, 14 June 1981, A1, A16–17.
2. *Statistical Abstract of the United States: 2002*, 296, 329, 367.
3. U.S. Dept. of Commerce, Bureau of the Census, *Historical Statistics of the United States: Colonial Times to 1957* (Washington, D.C.: Government Printing Office, 1960), 709; and Marshall W. Meyer, *Limits to Bureaucratic Growth* (New York: Walter de Gruyter, 1985), 36. The percentages for 1980, 1990, and 2000 are, respectively, 16.3, 15.5, and 15.4 (calculated from *Statistical Abstract of the United States: 2002*, 296, 367).
4. U.S. Census, *Compendium of Public Employment*, 1997, table 13, heading for Public Welfare (local numbers only); and U.S. Office of Personnel Management, *Biennial Report of Employment by Geographic Area*, 1998, table 5, heading for Social Security Administration (data do not cover Baltimore County, Los Angeles, or New York City).
5. See *The Case for Bureaucracy*, 3d ed. (Chatham, N.J.: Chatham House, 1994), 135–138. The federal employment analysis, except for postal data obtained directly from the U.S. Postal Service, was derived by secondary analysis for all departments and agencies enumerated on a county-city basis in the Office of Personnel Management's *Biennial Report of Employment by Geographic Area*, 1990, table 5. Local government figures were derived from the Census Bureau's *Compendium of Public Employment* for 1987, table 24.
6. U.S. Office of Personnel Management, *Biennial Report of Employment by Geographic Area, 1998*, 48, 52, 85, 152; and *Statistical Abstract of the United States: 2002*, 301–302.
7. C. Northcote Parkinson, *Parkinson's Law and Other Studies in Administration* (Boston: Houghton Mifflin, 1957), 12.

8. Anthony Downs, *Inside Bureaucracy* (Boston: Little, Brown, 1967), 16–17, 140–143, 158–160.
9. Ibid., 5–23.
10. Marver H. Bernstein, *Regulating Business by Independent Commission* (Princeton, N.J.: Princeton University Press, 1955), 74–95. The term *capture* was not used by Bernstein but introduced later by others to refer to his idea.
11. Williamson's position is discussed by William Orzechowski in "Economic Models of Bureaucracy: Survey, Extensions, and Evidence," in *Budgets and Bureaucrats: The Sources of Government Growth*, ed. Thomas E. Borcherding (Durham, N.C.: Duke University Press, 1977), 232–236. For Tullock's views, see *The Politics of Bureaucracy* (Washington, D.C.: Public Affairs Press, 1965).
12. Vincent Ostrom, *The Intellectual Crisis in American Public Administration* (University: University of Alabama Press, 1973).
13. *Statistical Abstract of the United States: 1976*, 249, 250; *1992*, 330; *2001*, 319.
14. *Statistical Abstract of the United States: 1990*, 302; *1996*, 322; *2002*, 298–299. The data are full-time equivalents performing the functions of Public Welfare and Highways (state only).
15. *Statistical Abstract of the United States: 1976*, 530, 531; *2001*, 698.
16. James A. Christenson and Carolyn E. Sachs, "The Impact of Government Size and Number of Administrative Units on the Quality of Public Services," *Administrative Science Quarterly* 25 (March 1980): 96, 99–100.
17. Research Triangle Institute, Center for Population and Urban-Rural Studies; and North Carolina Department of Natural Resources and Community Development, Division of Community Assistance, "Comparative Performance Measures for Municipal Services," December 1978.
18. D. S. Pugh, D. J. Hickson, C. R. Hinings, and C. Turner, "The Context of Organization Structures," *Administrative Science Quarterly* 14 (March 1969): 91–114.
19. Howard E. McCurdy, "Organizational Decline: NASA and the Life Cycle of Bureaus," *Public Administration Review* 51, no. 4 (July/August 1991): 308–315.
20. Kenneth J. Meier and John Plumlee, "Regulatory Administration and Organizational Rigidity," *Western Political Quarterly* 31 (March 1978): 80–95.
21. Robert M. Stein and Kenneth N. Bickers, *Perpetuating the Pork Barrel: Policy Subsystems and American Democracy* (New York: Cambridge University Press, 1995), 140; and *Washington Post*, 21 October 2002.
22. Herbert Kaufman, *Are Government Organizations Immortal?* (Washington, D.C.: Brookings Institution, 1976), 23–24, 34–35, 46, 53, 60–61, 68–69. For Kaufman's later thoughts on this subject, see his *Time, Chance, and Organizations: Natural Selection in a Perilous Environment*, 2d ed. (Chatham, N.J.: Chatham House, 1991).
23. Woodrow Wilson, "The Study of Administration," *Political Science Quarterly* 2 (June 1887): 197–222; and Norton E. Long, "Power and Administration," *Public Administration Review* 9 (autumn 1949): 257.
24. Joel D. Aberbach and Bert A. Rockman, *In the Web of Politics: Three Decades of the U.S. Federal Executive* (Washington, D.C.: Brookings Institution, 2000), 114.
25. Cornell G. Hooten, *Executive Governance: Presidential Administrations and Policy Change in the Bureaucracy* (Armonk, N.Y.: M.E. Sharpe, 1992).

26. Irene S. Rubin, *Shrinking the Federal Government: The Effect of Cutbacks on Five Federal Agencies* (New York: Longman, 1985), 196.
27. Marissa Martino Golden, *What Motivates Bureaucrats? Politics and Administration during the Reagan Years* (New York: Columbia University Press, 2000). On the Hirschman typology, see Albert Hirschman, *Exit, Voice and Loyalty: Responses to Decline in Firms, Organizations, and States* (Cambridge, Mass.: Harvard University Press, 1970).
28. Golden, *What Motivates Bureaucrats?* 154.
29. B. Dan Wood and Richard W. Waterman, *Bureaucratic Dynamics: The Role of Bureaucracy in a Democracy* (Boulder, Colo.: Westview, 1994), chap. 3.
30. Ibid., 150.
31. Brian J. Cook, *Bureaucracy and Self-Government: Reconsidering the Role of Public Administration in American Politics* (Baltimore: Johns Hopkins University Press, 1996), chap. 1.
32. Ibid., chap. 6. A related point made by H.T. Wilson in his *Bureaucratic Representation: Civil Servants and the Future of Capitalist Democracies* (Leiden: Brill, 2001) is that bureaucracy provides an essential linkage between elected officials and the public by mediating among special interests in favor of general interests.
33. Goodsell, *Case for Bureaucracy*, 3d ed., 158–159.
34. Cook, *Bureaucracy and Self-Government*, 151.
35. Ibid., 151–152.
36. *Statistical Abstract of the United States: 2001*, 278, 284, 313.
37. *Washington Post*, 19 May 1999, 11 October 2002, 19 March 2003.
38. *Roanoke Times*, 24 July 2003, 5 October 2003.
39. Paul C. Light, "Government's Greatest Achievements of the Past Half Century," Reform Watch Brief No. 2 (Washington, D.C.: Brookings Institution, 2000).
40. See Charles T. Goodsell, *Administration of a Revolution: Executive Reform in Puerto Rico under Governor Tugwell, 1941–1946* (Cambridge, Mass.: Harvard University Press, 1965).
41. Steven Cohen, William Eimicke, and Jessica Horan, "Catastrophe and the Public Service: A Case Study of the Government Response to the Destruction of the World Trade Center," *Public Administration Review* 62 (September 2002): 24–32.
42. *New York Times*, 1 February 2003; and *Washington Post*, 13 February 2003.
43. *Statistical Abstract of the United States: 2002*, 138–139.
44. Theda Skocpol, Marshall Ganz, and Ziad Munson, "A Nation of Organizers: The Institutional Origins of Civic Volunteerism in the United States," *American Political Science Review* 94, no. 3 (September 2000): 527–546, 541.
45. Suzanne Mettler, "Bringing the State Back into Civic Engagement: Policy Feedback Effects of the G.I. Bill for World War II Veterans," *American Political Science Review* 96, no. 2 (June 2002): 351-365.
46. Christopher A. Simon, "Testing for Bias in the Impact of AmeriCorps Service on Volunteer Participants: Evidence of Success in Achieving a Neutrality Program Objective," *Public Administration Review* 62, no. 6 (November/October 2002): 670–678.
47. Gene A. Brewer, "Building Social Capital: Civic Attitudes and Behavior of Public Servants," *Journal of Public Administration Research and Theory* 13, no. 1 (January 2003): 5–25, quote at 20.

7. Fads and Fundamentals of Bureaucracy

1. Eugene B. McGregor Jr., "Making Sense of Change," in *Advancing Public Management: New Developments in Theory, Methods, and Practice*, ed. Jeffrey L. Brudney, Laurence J. O'Toole Jr., and Hal G. Rainey (Washington, D.C.: Georgetown University Press, 2000), 127–128; B. Guy Peters, *The Future of Governing: Four Emerging Models* (Lawrence: University Press of Kansas, 1996); and Paul C. Light, *The Tides of Reform: Making Government Work, 1945–1955* (New Haven: Yale University Press, 1997).
2. On contemplated Defense Department changes, see *Washington Post*, 23, 29, and 30 August 2003.
3. John A. Rohr, *Public Service, Ethics, and Constitutional Practice* (Lawrence: University Press of Kansas, 1998), chap. 11.
4. *Statistical Abstract of the United States: 2001*, 320.
5. Donald F. Kettl, *The Global Public Management Revolution: A Report on the Transformation of Governance* (Washington, D.C.: Brookings Institution, 2000), 22.
6. James E. Colvard, "In Defense of Middle Management," *Government Executive*, May 1994, 57–58; Douglas Morgan, Kelly G. Bacon, Ron Bunch, Charles D. Cameron, and Robert Deis, "What Middle Managers Do in Local Government: Stewardship of the Public Trust and the Limits of Reinventing Government," *Public Administration Review* 56, no. 4 (July/August 1996): 359–366.
7. Charles T. Goodsell, "The Grace Commission: Seeking Efficiency for the Whole People?" *Public Administration Review* 44, no. 3 (May/June 1984): 196–204, at 200; and Steven J. Kelman, "Contracting," in *The Tools of Government: A Guide to the New Governance*, ed. Lester M. Salamon (New York: Oxford University Press, 2002), 313. Kelman was personally responsible for spearheading these reforms. Donald Kettl summarizes the overall impact of NPR in *Global Public Management Revolution*, 19–25.
8. *Washington Post*, 8 June 2001, 1 May 2002, 19 April 2003; and Denise Lindsey Wells, "Competitive Sourcing: The Controversial Initiative?" *Public Manager* 31, no. 3 (fall 2002): 9–12.
9. Ross Prizzia, "An International Perspective of Privatization: The Need to Balance Economic and Social Performance," *American Review of Public Administration* 33, no. 3 (September 2003), 316–332.
10. *Washington Post*, 4 October 2003; and Donald F. Kettl, *Sharing Power: Public Governance and Private Markets* (Washington, D.C.: Brookings Institution, 1993), chap. 5.
11. Federal Activities Inventory Reform Act of 1998, Public Law 105-270, 105th Cong., 112 Stat. 2382. Provisions not in quotes are paraphrased.
12. Ronald C. Moe, "The Emerging Federal Quasi Government: Issues of Management and Accountability," *Public Administration Review* 61, no. 3 (May/June 2001): 290–312, at 304–305.
13. David Shichor, *Punishment for Profit: Private Prisons/Public Concerns* (Thousand Oaks, Calif.: Sage, 1995), 256.
14. *Washington Post*, 20 November 2001, 17 January 2002, 25 April 2002, 10 July 2002, 22 July 2002.
15. Kettl, *Sharing Power*, 39; and Kelman, "Contracting," 305–308.

16. Goodsell, "Grace Commission," 198.
17. Steven W. Hays and Richard C. Kearney, "Riding the Crest of a Wave: The National Performance Review and Public Management Reform," *International Journal of Public Administration* 20, no. 1 (1997): 34.
18. David Osborne and Ted Gaebler, *Reinventing Government: How the Entrepreneurial Spirit Is Transforming the Public Sector* (New York: Penguin Books, 1993), 79–80.
19. Arie Halachmi, "Franchising in Government: Can a Principal-Agent Perspective Be the First Step toward the Development of a Theory?" in *Entrepreneurial Management and Public Policy*, ed. Van R. Johnston (Huntington, N.Y.: Nova Science Publishers, 2000). Information on the National Business Center is from *People, Land and Water* (the Department of the Interior's in-house newspaper), August 2002, 19. See also Anne Laurent, *Entrepreneurial Government: Bureaucrats as Businesspeople* (Arlington, Va.: PricewatershouseCoopers Endowment for The Business of Government, May 2000).
20. Osborne and Gaebler, *Reinventing Government*, 76–78.
21. *Washington Post*, 19 June 2003, A13, and 23, September 2003; and *Roanoke Times*, 29–30 July 2003.
22. Linda deLeon and Robert B. Denhardt, "The Political Theory of Reinvention," *Public Administration Review* 60, no. 2 (March/April 2000): 90–91.
23. Linda deLeon, "Ethics and Entrepreneurship," in Johnston, *Entrepreneurial Management and Public Policy*, 222–223. British scholars Charles Edwards, Geoff Jones, Alan Lawton, and Nick Llewellyn believe that entrepreneurship, perceived as a desirable trait for government managers, is restricted primarily to the U.K., U.S., and Australia, but not found elsewhere. See their "Public Entrepreneurship: Rhetoric, Reality, and Context," *International Journal of Public Administration* 25, no. 12 (2002): 1541–1554.
24. Joe Wallis and Brian Dollery, "Wolf's Model: Government Failure and Public Sector Reform in Advanced Industrial Democracies," *Review of Policy Research* 19, no. 1 (spring 2002): 183, 186, 197.
25. *Washington Post*, 17 September 1997.
26. James R. Thompson, "The Clinton Reforms and the Administrative Ascendancy of Congress," *American Review of Public Administration* 31, no. 3 (September 2001): 252–255; *Washington Post*, 2 December 1998; and www.ed.gov/offices/OSFAP/.
27. Osborne and Gaebler, *Reinventing Government*, 295; and Peter Kobrak, "The Social Responsibilities of a Public Entrepreneur," *Administration & Society* 28, no. 2 (August 1996): 212.
28. Ibid., 212; and Rob Gurwitt, "Entrepreneurial Government: The Morning After," *Governing*, May 1994, 34–40.
29. DeLeon, "Ethics and Entrepreneurship," 224–227.
30. Robert D. Behn, "The New Public Management Paradigm and the Search for Democratic Accountability," *International Public Management Journal* 1, no. 2 (1999). 150–151.
31. Patrick J. Murphy and John Carnevale, "The Challenge of Developing Cross-Agency Measures: A Case Study of the Office of National Drug Control Policy," in *Managing for Results 2002*, ed. Mark A. Abramson and John M. Kamensky (Lanham, Md.: Rowman & Littlefield, 2001), 57.

32. Christopher Hood, "Control, Bargains, and Cheating: The Politics of Public-Service Reform," *Journal of Public Administration Research and Theory* 12, no. 3 (July 2002): 309–332; and Robert D. Behn, "Do Goals Help Create Innovative Organizations?" in *Public Management Reform and Innovation: Research, Theory, and Application*, ed. H. George Frederickson and Jocelyn M. Johnston (Tuscaloosa: University of Alabama Press, 1999), 70–88. See also Behn, *Rethinking Democratic Accountability* (Washington, D.C.: Brookings Institution, 2001).
33. Evan Berman and XiaoHu Wang, "Performance Measurement in U.S. Counties: Capacity for Reform," *Public Administration Review* 60, no. 5 (September/October 2000): 409–420; and Patria de Lancer Julnes, "The Question of Whether Performance Measurement Works: Good News for Real Managers," *Public Administration Times*, July 2002, 6.
34. Beryl A. Radin, "The Government Performance and Results Act (GPRA): Hydra-Headed Monster or Flexible Management Tool?" *Public Administration Review* 58, no. 4 (July/August 1998): 307–316.
35. Beryl A. Radin, "The Government Performance and Results Act and the Tradition of Federal Management Reform: Square Pegs in Round Holes?" *Journal of Public Administration Research and Theory* 10, no. 1 (January 2000): 111–135, quote at 134.
36. Hyong Yi, "The Myth of Public Performance Management," *Public Manager* 31, no. 2 (summer 2002): 57–58.
37. *Washington Post*, 21 September 1994.
38. Donald F. Kettl, *Reinventing Government? Appraising the National Performance Review* (Washington, D.C.: Brookings Institution, 1994), 33–40.
39. H. George Frederickson, "Painting Bull's Eyes around Bullet Holes," *Governing*, October 1992, 13; James D. Carroll, "The Rhetoric of Reform and Political Reality in the National Performance Review," *Public Administration Review* 55, no. 3 (May/June 1995): 309; and DeLeon and Denhardt, "Political Theory of Reinvention," 93–95.
40. George A. Boyne, "Sources of Public Service Improvement: A Critical Review and Research Agenda," *Journal of Public Administration Research and Theory* 13, no. 3 (July 2003): 367–394.
41. June Gibbs Brown and George Grob, "The 25-Year Bureaucrat," *Public Manager* 25, no. 1 (spring 1996): 13–16, at 15.
42. H. George Frederickson, "Public Administration and Gardening," *Public Administration Times*, February 2002, 10. My use of the metaphor takes some liberties with his; Frederickson credits Peter Szanton with originating the analogy.
43. See James R. Thompson and Patricia W. Ingraham, "The Reinvention Game," *Public Administration Review* 56, no. 3 (May/June 1996): 291–298; and James R. Thompson, "The Reinvention Laboratories: Strategic Change by Indirection," *American Review of Public Administration* 30, no. 1 (March 2000): 46–68.
44. William T. Gormley Jr. and David L. Weimer, *Organizational Report Cards* (Cambridge, Mass.: Harvard University Press, 1999); Tony Bovaird, Elke Loeffler, and Jeremy Martin, "From Corporate Governance to Local Governance: Stakeholder-Driven Community Score-Cards for UK Local Agencies?" *International Journal of Public Administration* 26, nos. 8–9 (2003): 1037–1060.

Selected Books

Aberbach, Joel D., and Bert A. Rockman. *In the Web of Politics: Three Decades of the U.S. Federal Executive.* Washington, D.C.: Brookings Institution, 2000.

Abrahamsson, Bengt. *Bureaucracy or Participation.* Beverly Hills, Calif.: Sage, 1977.

Adams, Guy B., and Danny L. Balfour. *Unmasking Administrative Evil.* Thousand Oaks, Calif.: Sage, 1998.

Appleby, Paul H. *Big Democracy.* New York: Knopf, 1945.

Barzelay, Michael. *Breaking through Bureaucracy.* Berkeley: University of California Press, 1992.

Beetham, David. *Bureaucracy.* Minneapolis: University of Minnesota Press, 1987.

Behn, Robert D. *Rethinking Democratic Accountability.* Washington: Brookings Institution Press, 2001.

Bennis, Warren. *Beyond Bureaucracy.* New York: McGraw-Hill, 1973.

Benveniste, Guy. *Bureaucracy.* 2d ed. San Francisco: Boyd and Fraser, 1983.

Bernstein, Marver H. *Regulating Business by Independent Commission.* Princeton, N.J.: Princeton University Press, 1955.

Bernstein, Merton C., and Joan B. Bernstein. *Social Security: The System That Works.* New York: Basic Books, 1988.

Berry, William D., and David Lowery. *Understanding United States Government Growth: An Empirical Analysis of the Postwar Era.* New York: Praeger, 1987.

Blais, André, and Stéphane Dion, eds. *The Budget-Maximizing Bureaucrat: Appraisals and Evidence.* Pittsburgh: University of Pittsburgh Press, 1991.

Blau, Peter M. *The Dynamics of Bureaucracy.* Chicago: University of Chicago Press, 1963.

Bogason, Peter. *Public Policy and Local Governance: Institutions in Postmodern Society.* Cheltenham, U.K.: Edward Elgar, 2000.

Bok, Derek. *The Trouble with Government.* Cambridge, Mass.: Harvard University Press, 2001.

Borcherding, Thomas E., ed. *Budgets and Bureaucrats: The Sources of Government Growth.* Durham, N.C.: Duke University Press, 1977.

Borins, Sanford. *Innovating with Integrity: How Local Heroes Are Transforming American Government.* Washington, D.C.: Georgetown University Press, 1998.

Box, Richard C. *Citizen Governance: Leading American Communities into the 21st Century.* Thousand Oaks, Calif.: Sage, 1998.

Bozeman, Barry. *Bureaucracy and Red Tape.* Upper Saddle River, N.J.: Prentice Hall, 2000.

Bragnaw, Louis K. *Managing a Federal Agency: The Hidden Stimulus.* Baltimore: Johns Hopkins University Press, 1980.

Brehm, John, and Scott Gates. *Working, Shirking, and Sabotage: Bureaucratic Response to a Democratic Public.* Ann Arbor: University of Michigan Press, 1997.

Breton, Albert, and Ronald Wintrobe. *The Logic of Bureaucratic Conduct: An Economic Analysis of Competition, Exchange, and Efficiency in Private and Public Organizations.* Cambridge, England: Cambridge University Press, 1982.

Campbell Public Affairs Institute. *Governance & Public Security.* Syracuse, N.Y.: Maxwell School of Citizenship and Public Affairs, Syracuse University, 2002.

Chackerian, Richard, and Gilbert Abcarian. *Bureaucratic Power in Society.* Chicago: Nelson-Hall, 1983.

Cook, Brian J. *Bureaucracy and Self-Government: Reconsidering the Role of Public Administration in American Politics.* Baltimore: Johns Hopkins University Press, 1996.

Cooper, John L. *The Anti-Gravity Force: A Study of the Negative Impact of Public Bureaucracy on Society.* Dubuque, Iowa: Kendall Hunt, 1981.

Cooper, Terry L., and N. Dale Wright, eds. *Exemplary Public Administrators.* San Francisco: Jossey Bass, 1992.

Crane, Jonathan, ed. *Social Programs That Work.* New York: Russell Sage Foundation, 1998.

Denhardt, Robert B. *In the Shadow of Organizations.* Lawrence: Regents Press of Kansas, 1981.

Derthick, Martha. *Agency under Stress: The Social Security Administration in American Government.* Washington, D.C.: Brookings Institution, 1990.

Doig, Jameson W., and Erwin C. Hargove, eds. *Leadership and Innovation: A Biographical Perspective on Entrepreneurs in Government.* Baltimore: Johns Hopkins University Press, 1987.

Donahue, John D., ed. *Making Washington Work: Tales of Innovation in the Federal Sector.* Washington, D.C.: Brookings Institution, 1999.

Downs, Anthony. *Inside Bureaucracy.* Boston: Little, Brown, 1967.

Downs, George W., and Patrick D. Larkey. *The Search for Government Efficiency: From Hubris to Helplessness.* Philadelphia: Temple University Press, 1986.

Du Gay, Paul. *In Praise of Bureaucracy: Weber, Organization, Ethics.* London: Sage, 2000.

Dunleavy, Patrick. *Democracy, Bureaucracy and Public Choice: Economic Explanations in Political Science.* Englewood Cliffs, N.J.: Prentice Hall, 1991.

Dvorin, Eugene P., and Robert H. Simmons. *From Amoral to Humane Bureaucracy.* San Francisco: Canfield Press, 1972.

Elling, Richard C. *Public Management in the States.* Westport, Conn.: Praeger, 1992.

Ermer, Virginia B., and John H. Strange, eds. *Blacks and Bureaucracy.* New York: Crowell, 1972.

Etzioni-Halévy, Eva. *Bureaucracy and Democracy: A Political Dilemma.* London: Routledge and Kegan Paul, 1983.

Ferguson, Kathy E. *The Feminist Case against Bureaucracy.* Philadelphia: Temple University Press, 1984.

Frederickson, H. George. *New Public Administration.* University: University of Alabama Press, 1980.

———. *The Spirit of Public Administration.* San Francisco: Jossey-Bass, 1997.

Glassman, Ronald M., William H. Swatos Jr., and Paul L. Rosen, eds. *Bureaucracy against Democracy and Socialism.* Westport, Conn.: Greenwood, 1987.

Golden, Marissa Martino. *What Motivates Bureaucrats? Politics and Administration during the Reagan Years.* New York: Columbia University Press, 2000.

Goodsell, Charles T. *Administration of a Revolution: Executive Reform in Puerto Rico under Governor Tugwell, 1941–1946*. Cambridge, Mass.: Harvard University Press, 1965.

———, ed. *The Public Encounter: Where State and Citizen Meet*. Bloomington: Indiana University Press, 1981.

Gore, Al. *From Red Tape to Results: Creating A Government that Works Better and Costs Less*. Washington, D.C.: National Performance Review, 1993.

Gormley, William T., Jr. *Taming the Bureaucracy: Muscles, Prayers, and Other Strategies*. Princeton, N.J.: Princeton University Press, 1989.

Gormley, William T., Jr. and David L. Weimer. *Organizational Report Cards*. Cambridge, Mass.: Harvard University Press, 1999.

Gruber, Judith. *Controlling Bureaucracies: Dilemmas in American Governance*. Berkeley: University of California Press, 1987.

Hargrove, Erwin, and John C. Glidewell, eds. *Impossible Jobs in Public Management*. Lawrence: University Press of Kansas, 1990.

Hegedus, Andras. *Socialism and Bureaucracy*. London: Allison and Busby, 1976.

Hill, Larry B., ed. *The State of Public Bureaucracy*. Armonk, N.Y.: M.E. Sharpe, 1992.

Hill, Michael. *The State, Administration, and the Individual*. Totowa, N.J.: Rowman and Littlefield, 1976.

Hodge, Graeme A. *Privatization: An International Review of Performance*. Boulder, Colo.: Westview, 2000.

Hood, Christopher C. *The Limits of Administration*. London: Wiley, 1976.

Hooten, Cornell G. *Executive Governance: Presidential Administrations and Policy Change in the Bureaucracy*. Armonk, N.Y.: M.E. Sharpe, 1997.

Hummel, Ralph P. *The Bureaucratic Experience*. 3d ed. New York: St. Martin's, 1987.

Hyneman, Charles S. *Bureaucracy in a Democracy*. New York: Harper, 1950.

Ingraham, Patricia W., and Donald F. Kettl, eds. *Agenda for Excellence: Public Service in America*. Chatham, N.J.: Chatham House, 1992.

Jacoby, Henry. *The Bureaucratization of the World*. Berkeley: University of California Press, 1973.

Johnson, Cathy Marie. *The Dynamics of Conflict between Bureaucrats and Legislators*. Armonk, N.Y.: M.E. Sharpe, 1992.

Jones, Bryan D. *Service Delivery in the City: Citizen Demand and Bureaucratic Rules*. New York: Longman, 1980.

Kamenka, Eugene, and Martin Krygier. *Bureaucracy: The Career of a Concept*. London: Edward Arnold, 1979.

Katz, Daniel, Barbara A. Gutek, Robert L. Kahn, and Eugenia Barton. *Bureaucratic Encounters*. Ann Arbor: Institute for Social Research, University of Michigan, 1975.

Kaufman, Herbert. *Are Government Organizations Immortal?* Washington, D.C.: Brookings Institution, 1976.

———. *Red Tape*. Washington, D.C.: Brookings Institution, 1977.

———. *The Administrative Behavior of Federal Bureau Chiefs*. Washington, D.C.: Brookings Institution, 1981.

———. *Time, Chance, and Organizations: Natural Selection in a Perilous Environment*. 2d ed. Chatham, N.J.: Chatham House, 1991.

Kelman, Steven. *Making Public Policy: A Hopeful View of American Government*. New York: Basic Books, 1987.

Kettl, Donald F. *Government by Proxy: [Mis?]Managing Federal Programs.* Washington, D.C.: CQ Press, 1988.

———. *Sharing Power: Public Governance and Private Markets.* Washington, D.C.: Brookings Institution, 1993.

———. *Reinventing Government?: Appraising the National Performance Review.* Washington, D.C.: Brookings Institution, 1994.

———. *The Global Public Management Revolution: A Report on the Transformation of Governance.* Washington, D.C.: Brookings Institution, 2000.

Khandwalla, Pradip N. *Revitalizing the State: A Menu of Options.* New Delhi: Sage, 1999.

Kilpatrick, Franklin P., Milton C. Cummings, and M. Kent Jennings. *The Image of the Federal Service.* Washington, D.C.: Brookings Institution, 1964.

King, Cheryl Simrell, and Camilla Stivers. *Government Is Us: Public Administration in an Anti-Government Era.* Thousand Oaks, Calif.: Sage, 1998.

Kraus, Wolfgang. *The Return of the Individual: Rescue Attempts in a Bureaucratic Age.* Berne, Switzerland: Peter Lang, 1985.

Lane, Larry M., and James F. Wolf. *The Human Resource Crisis in the Public Sector.* New York: Quorum, 1990.

Levitan, Sar A., and Robert Taggart. *The Promise of Greatness.* Cambridge, Mass.: Harvard University Press, 1976.

Levy, Frank, Arnold J. Meltsner, and Aaron Wildavsky. *Urban Outcomes: Schools, Streets, and Libraries.* Berkeley: University of California Press, 1974.

Lewis, Eugene. *American Politics in a Bureaucratic Age: Citizens, Constituents, Clients and Victims.* Cambridge, Mass.: Winthrop, 1977.

———. *Public Entrepreneurship: Toward a Theory of Bureaucratic Power.* Bloomington: Indiana University Press, 1980.

Light, Paul C. *Monitoring Government: Inspectors General and the Search for Accountability.* Washington, D.C.: Brookings Institution, 1993.

———. *The Tides of Reform: Making Government Work, 1945–1995.* New Haven: Yale University Press, 1997.

Lineberry, Robert L. *Equality and Urban Policy: The Distribution of Municipal Public Services.* Beverly Hills, Calif.: Sage, 1977.

Lipsky, Michael. *Street-Level Bureaucracy.* New York: Russell Sage Foundation, 1980.

Littrell, W. Boyd, Gideon Sjøberg, and Louis A. Zurcher, eds. *Bureaucracy as a Social Problem.* Greenwich, Conn.: JAI Press, 1983.

Mainzer, Lewis C. *Political Bureaucracy.* Glenview, Ill.: Scott, Foresman, 1973.

Meyer, Marshall W. *Change in Public Bureaucracies.* Cambridge, England: Cambridge University Press, 1979.

———. *Limits to Bureaucratic Growth.* New York: Walter de Gruyter, 1985.

Mouzelis, Nicos P. *Organization and Bureaucracy.* Chicago: Aldine, 1967.

Nachmias, David, and David H. Rosenbloom. *Bureaucratic Government USA.* New York: St. Martin's, 1980.

Neiman, Max. *Defending Government: Why Big Government Works.* Upper Saddle River, N.J.: Prentice Hall, 2000.

Niskanen, William A. *Bureaucracy and Representative Government.* Chicago: Aldine Atherton, 1971.

———. *Bureaucracy: Servant or Master?* London: Institute of Economic Affairs, 1973.

Osborne, David, and Ted Gaebler. *Reinventing Government: How the Entrepreneurial Spirit Is Transforming the Public Sector.* Reading, Mass.: Addison-Wesley, 1992.

Osborne, David, and Peter Plastrik. *Banishing Bureaucracy: The Five Strategies for Reinventing Government.* Reading, Mass.: Addison-Wesley, 1997.

Ostrom, Vincent. *The Intellectual Crisis in American Public Administration.* University: University of Alabama Press, 1973.

Page, Benjamin I., and James R. Simmons. *What Government Can Do: Dealing with Poverty and Inequality.* Chicago: University of Chicago Press, 2000.

Page, Edward C. *Political Authority and Bureaucratic Power: A Comparative Analysis.* Knoxville: University of Tennessee Press, 1985.

Parkinson, C. Northcote. *Parkinson's Law and Other Studies in Administration.* Boston: Houghton Mifflin, 1957.

Peirce, William S. *Bureaucratic Failure and Public Expenditure.* New York: Academic Press, 1981.

Perrow, Charles. *Complex Organizations: A Critical Essay.* Glenview, Ill.: Scott, Foresman, 1972.

Peterson, Paul E., Barry G. Rabe, and Kenneth K. Wong. *When Federalism Works.* Washington, D.C.: Brookings Institution, 1986.

Pommerehne, Werner W., and Friedrich Schneider. *Comparing the Efficiency of Private and Public Production: The Evidence from Five Countries.* Zurich: University of Zurich, 1982.

Pressman, Jeffrey L., and Aaron Wildavksy. *Implementation.* Berkeley: University of California Press, 1973.

Prottas, Jeffrey M. *People-Processing: The Street-Level Bureaucrat in Public Service Bureaucracies.* Lexington, Mass.: D.C. Heath, 1979.

Riccucci, Norma M. *Unsung Heroes: Federal Execucrats Making a Difference.* Washington, D.C.: Georgetown University Press, 1995.

Riley, Dennis D. *Controlling the Federal Bureaucracy.* Philadelphia: Temple University Press, 1987.

Rohr, John A. *To Run a Constitution: The Legitimacy of the Administrative State.* Lawrence: University Press of Kansas, 1986.

———. *Public Service, Ethics, and Constitutional Practice.* Lawrence: University Press of Kansas, 1998.

Rose, Richard. *Understanding Big Government: The Programme Approach.* London: Sage, 1984.

Rosen, Howard. *Servants of the People: The Uncertain Future of the Federal Civil Service.* Salt Lake City: Olympus, 1985.

Ross, Randy L. *Government and the Private Sector: Who Should Do What?* New York: Crane Russak, 1988.

Rubin, Irene S. *Shrinking the Federal Government: The Effects of Cutbacks on Five Federal Agencies.* New York: Longman, 1985.

Salamon, Lester M., ed. *Beyond Privatization: The Tools of Government Action.* Washington, D.C.: Urban Institute Press, 1989.

———, ed. *The Tools of Government: A Guide to the New Governance.* Oxford: Oxford University Press, 2002.

Savas, E. S. *Privatization: The Key to Better Government.* Chatham, N.J.: Chatham House, 1987.

______. *Privatization and Public-Private Partnerships.* New York: Chatham House, 2000.

Schneider, Mark, and Paul Teske. *Public Entrepreneurs: Agents for Change in American Government.* Princeton, N.J.: Princeton University Press, 1995.

Schwarz, John E. *America's Hidden Success: A Reassessment of Twenty Years of Public Policy.* New York: Norton, 1983.

Selden, Sally Coleman. *The Promise of Representative Bureaucracy: Diversity and Responsiveness in a Government Agency.* Armonk, N.Y.: M.E. Sharpe, 1997.

Shichor, David. *Punishment for Profit: Private Prisons/Public Concerns.* Thousand Oaks, Calif.: Sage, 1995.

Smith, B.C. *Bureaucracy and Political Power.* Sussex, England: Wheatsheaf, 1988.

Stein, Lana. *Holding Bureaucrats Accountable: Politicians and Professionals in St. Louis.* Tuscaloosa: University of Alabama Press, 1991.

Stoker, Robert P. *Reluctant Partners: Implementing Federal Policy.* Pittsburgh: University of Pittsburgh Press, 1991.

Strauss, Eric. *The Ruling Servants.* New York: Praeger, 1961.

Taylor, Theodore W., ed. *Federal Public Policy: Personal Accounts of Ten Senior Civil Service Executives.* Mt. Airy, Md.: Lemond, 1984.

Terry, Larry D. *Leadership of Public Bureaucracies: The Administrator as Conservator.* Thousand Oaks, Calif.: Sage, 1995.

Thayer, Frederick C. *An End to Hierarchy and Competition: Administration in the Post-Affluent World.* 2d ed. New York: Franklin Watts, 1981.

______. *Rebuilding America.* New York: Praeger, 1984.

Thompson, Victor A. *Modern Organization.* New York: Knopf, 1961.

______. *Without Sympathy or Enthusiasm.* University: University of Alabama Press, 1975.

______. *Bureaucracy and the Modern World.* Morristown, N.J.: General Learning Press, 1976.

Tolchin, Susan J., and Martin Tolchin. *Dismantling America: The Rush to Deregulate.* Boston: Houghton Mifflin, 1983.

Tullock, Gordon. *The Politics of Bureaucracy.* Washington, D.C.: Public Affairs Press, 1965.

Von Mises, Ludwig. *Bureaucracy.* New Haven: Yale University Press, 1944.

Waldo, Dwight, ed. *Public Administration in a Time of Turbulence.* Scranton, Pa.: Chandler, 1971.

Wamsley, Gary L., Robert N. Bacher, Charles T. Goodsell, Philip S. Kronenberg, Camilla M. Stivers, Orion F. White, and James F. Wolf. *Refounding Public Administration.* Beverly Hills, Calif.: Sage, 1990.

Wamsley, Gary L., and James F. Wolf, eds. *Refounding Democratic Public Administration: Modern Paradoxes, Postmodern Challenges.* Thousand Oaks, Calif.: Sage, 1996.

Weaver, John D. *The Great Experiment.* Boston: Little, Brown, 1965.

West, William F. *Controlling the Bureaucracy: Institutional Constraints in Theory and Practice.* Armonk, N.Y.: M.E. Sharpe, 1995.

White, Leonard D. *The Prestige Value of Public Employment in Chicago.* Chicago: University of Chicago Press, 1929.

Wickwar, Hardy. *Power and Service: A Cross-National Analysis of Public Administration.* Westport, Conn.: Greenwood Press, 1991.

Wildavsky, Aaron. *Speaking Truth to Power: The Art and Craft of Public Analysis.* Boston: Little, Brown, 1979.

Wilson, H.T. *Representative Bureaucracy: Civil Servants and the Future of Capitalist Democracies.* Leiden: Brill, 2001.

Wilson, James Q. *Bureaucracy: What Government Agencies Do and Why They Do It.* New York: Basic Books, 1989.

Wittfogel, Karl A. *Oriental Despotism.* New Haven: Yale University Press, 1957.

Wolf, Charles, Jr. *Markets or Governments: Choosing between Imperfect Alternatives.* Cambridge, Mass.: MIT Press, 1988.

Wood, B. Dan, and Richard W. Waterman. *Bureaucratic Dynamics: The Role of Bureaucracy in a Democracy.* Boulder, Colo.: Westview, 1994.

Yates, Douglas. *Street-Level Governments.* Lexington, Mass.: D.C. Heath, 1975.

———. *Bureaucratic Democracy: The Search for Democracy and Efficiency in American Government.* Cambridge, Mass.: Harvard University Press, 1982.

Index